GROWTH, POPULATION, AND INCOME DISTRIBUTION

Selected Essays

Also by Simon Kuznets

Economic Change
Economic Growth and Structure
Population, Capital, and Economic Growth

Growth, Population, and Income Distribution

Selected Essays

SIMON KUZNETS

W · W · NORTON & COMPANY

NEW YORK LONDON

Library of Congress Cataloging in Publication Data

Kuznets, Simon Smith, 1901–
    Growth, population, and income distribution.

    1. Economic development–Addresses, essays, lectures.
2. Population–Economic aspects–Addresses, essays,
lectures. 3. Underdeveloped areas–Addresses, essays,
lectures. 4. Fertility, Human–Addresses, essays,
lectures. 5. Income distribution–Addresses, essays,
lectures. I. Title.
HD82.K868   330.9′04   79–16550
ISBN 0–393–95061–1

1 2 3 4 5 6 7 8 9 0

Contents

Preface

The essays in this volume were written over the past ten years and appear here essentially in their original form. They bear upon interrelated topics, in that the economic growth of a nation is associated with distinctive patterns of growth and movement of its population, while the demographic aspects of a nation's growth are bound up with the changing distribution of income. The approach to the several topics is largely from an historical perspective, with short-term aspects of economic and demographic differentials considered only as they yield insights into long-term trends. The result of this emphasis on trends in economic and demographic processes is to suggest long chains of interrelations—between technological innovations providing new production and life opportunities, and social and institutional adjustments required to channel these opportunities into effective use for economic and social development.

I hope that this volume will make the essays more accessible and hence more useful. At the time of their original publication and circulation they profited greatly from the comments of friends and colleagues. I wish to thank the various publishers, as noted in the footnotes to each essay, for permission to reprint in this volume.

July, 1979   Simon Kuznets

GROWTH, POPULATION, AND INCOME DISTRIBUTION

Selected Essays

Two Centuries of Economic Growth: Reflections on U.S. Experience

Over most of the two past centuries, the country's growth was a movement from the small, largely agricultural, economy of thirteen divided colonies on the Atlantic shores, to a unified, industrialized, advanced economy of continental dimensions. The combination of a high rate of growth of population, peopling an expanding territory, with a rise in per capita product and productivity associated with a stream of technological innovations and rapid shifts in the structure of production, was of uniquely large impact in the United States; and while sharing much in common with the growth experience of other, currently developed, countries, displayed several distinctive features.

Reflecting on this process, one may raise four questions. First, how was the high rate of population growth attained? Second, how was the impressive rate of growth in per capita product sustained over most of the period, at least back to the early nineteenth century? Third, how, in the face of divisive sectional interests and differential impacts of rapid economic growth, was unity preserved and economic inequality affected? Fourth, how

Richard T. Ely Lecture 1976, reprinted from *American Economic Association Papers and Proceedings,* February 1977, pp. 1–14.

does one evaluate the drastic shifts that occurred since World War I in the international framework within which this country lived and grew? Such broad questions, and their implications, can be treated only briefly and incompletely; but, at least, they may help to organize the discussion.

I. The Growth of Population

In the mid-1770s, the population of the thirteen original colonies was 2.5 million. At that time, the population of Great Britain was 9 million; of France over 24 million; of Europe, excluding Russia, 128 million (all within the 1914 boundaries). By 1910, the population of the United States was 91.6 million (excluding, for comparability, the minor group of nonwhites other than Negroes) —over twice that of either Great Britain or France (each with about 40 million at that date). By mid-1975, the population of the United States was close to 214 million. The multiplication factor over the two centuries was over 85 for the *U.S.* population; for Europe, including or excluding European Russia, it was about 4; for the more rapidly growing among the European countries, not much more than 7. Nor was the contrast less striking in comparison with the population growth of Japan.

The contrast is, of course, the result of a long period of cumulation of the excess of annual or decennial rates of increase in the United States. Over the two centuries, the average rate of population growth *per year* was about 2¼ percent in the United States, and 0.9 percent in Great Britain. Taken over a decade or two, the cumulative difference would not be large; taken over two centuries, it cumulated to a contrast in multiples between over 85 and barely over 6.

A high population growth rate can be due to a high birth rate, or to a low death rate, or to a high net in-migration rate. In comparison with other developed countries, specifically those in Europe, the death rates, crude or refined, were not that much lower in this country as to contribute significantly to the much greater capacity of U.S. population to grow. The sources of the difference lay largely in the birth and in-migration rates. The birth rate in the United States in the early nineteenth century was estimated at close to 50 per thousand—high even by current standards in the less developed countries. While it dropped rapidly in the early decades of the last century and moved further downwards to the low levels of today, it tended to remain distinctly higher than in the older developed countries—as was also the case in the other young overseas countries like Canada, Australia, and New Zealand.

The other major source of growth was immigration. For the country's black population, immigration, or rather importation, was of significant proportions between 1770 and 1810, but negligible thereafter. For the far larger white population, immigration contributed little between the Revolution and the mid-1830s, but was an important factor over the eight decades prior to World War I and for a few years after the war. The magnitude of this immigration (on which we shall concentrate henceforth) can be illustrated by references to the millions of immigrants who came in and stayed. But one must also take account of the offspring of these immigrants in succeeding generations, a net addition if we assume that the birthrates of the original, nonimmigrant population would have declined just as much, if not more, without immigration. The assumption is reasonable, since we find substantial declines in native white birthrates in periods (before 1840) and later also in regions (South and rural non-South), that were relatively little affected by white immigration. A calculation, made by a Census expert (W. S. Rossiter) using the native white birthrates prevailing in the past, estimated the contribution of the original white stock (i.e., the one in this country at the time of the Revolution) to the 1920 population of the United States at 47.3 million out of a total white population of 94.8 million—the rest being immigrants and their descendants. This result, that half of the population was to be credited to immigrants and their descendants, would be roughly valid for total population, including the Negroes; and would also hold true of the more recent dates after 1920.

The persistence, over two centuries, of birthrates higher than those in the older developed countries of Europe and Japan, and the prevalence over some eight to nine decades of net immigration that contributed so much to population increase, may reasonably be associated with the "newness" of the United States. The "newness" meant the presence, and an awareness of the presence, of vast resources in unsettled land of a geographically expanding nation; a population that had detached itself from the European economic and institutional constraints on early marriage and on prolific child bearing; a willingness to welcome and encourage immigration, if, after a while, only within limits as to the cultural areas of origin. These features of the United States as a new country, the first among the overseas offshoots of Europe to achieve political sovereignty, are well known and hardly need documentation, even were it feasible here. But we might note aspects that seem relevant to understanding some distinctive characteristics of this country's growth.

The first comment relates to the long period over which obviously large reserves of land and resources remained and could continue to exercise effects on birth and immigration rates. The land area of the country within the continental United States (i.e., except Hawaii and Alaska), as it became fixed in the twentieth century, amounted, at the censuses of 1790 and 1800, to 0.82 million square miles, grew by the census of 1810 to 1.7 million miles (reflecting the Louisiana Purchase) and to 2.94 million, the present size, after the census of 1840. A more telling series relates to the area of *settled* land, land with a population density of at least two persons per square mile. From 1790 to 1890, this area, originally 0.24 million square miles, grew at an average of over 50 percent every twenty years, including a growth of 53 percent from 1870 to 1890. Even when the limit was reached at 1.9 million in 1890, the closing of the frontier did not mean the absence of room for expansion. A similar story of a long process of settlement of a wide, and for a long while expanding, territorial base is told by the dates of admission of new states into the Union: the last in the continental United States were admitted as late as 1907 and 1912—over a century and a quarter after the founding of the Republic. That native birth rates began declining so early is no reflection of a pressure of limits, but indicates a sensitivity to increasing affluence and to greater density in the *older* settled parts of the country; or, conversely, to the costs of internal migration toward the still abundant land.

Second, the desire to people the continent, to use the country's sovereignty to extend its area and to add to its population without interference from a metropolitan, colonial monarchy, was explicitly indicated in the Declaration of Independence—with its reference to the attempt on the part of the British monarch "to prevent the population of these States; for that purpose obstructing the Laws of Naturalization of foreigners; refusing to pass others to encourage their migration hither. . . ." And this declared willingness, subject later to some selective restrictions, to admit immigrants from a wide range of European countries and those in the Americas, persisted until shortly after World War I. Thus, for some three-quarters of the two-century span, the United States was a country of open immigration, the only one with so long a record and with a huge absorptive capacity combined with a high standard of living.

In considering the impact of immigration, one must keep in mind its selectivity. There was selectivity not only with respect to age and sex, which resulted in a high proportion of males in prime working ages; not only with respect to occupations and attachments within the country of origin, which made for high proportions of farmers and farm workers, common laborers and semi-skilled artisans; not only with respect to individual characteristics that favored the more adventurous and adaptable among the younger groups within the labor force; not only with respect to timing, which meant that, with the exception of the 1842 Irish famine, the impelling occasion was the entry of the sending country into modern economic growth, with its dislocating effects on rural population and that part of the urban population that might have been adversely affected by industrialization. There was also selectivity of immigration flows in their location, geographical and socio-structural, in the United States, the country of destination.

To begin with, few immigrants settled in the South, a census region largely identical with the slave-owning states and extending from Maryland and Delaware in the north to Florida in the south, and from the Atlantic coast states in the east to Texas and Oklahoma in the west. Already by 1860, when the foreign-born were close to 19 percent of all whites in the regions outside the South, the percentage in the South was below 6; an allowance for native-born of foreign or mixed parentage would raise the proportion of the foreign white stock to about 28 percent of the whites in the non-South and only 8½ percent in the South. This selectivity persisted, so that in 1910, when the foreign white stock proportion (close to 50 percent of all whites) was at its peak in the non-South, that proportion in the South was below 10 percent. Second, the immigrant flow tended toward the urban rather than rural areas, and to the bigger cities within the urban. Thus, already in 1850, the first year of data on the foreign-born, the proportion of foreign-born whites (and of free colored, a small component) to the corresponding total in the non-South was 14 percent; but it was 39 percent in the large cities, and 11 percent in the other city areas. By 1920, the foreign white stock accounted for 66 percent of total white population in cities of 500,000 and over; about 44 percent in cities of 25 to 500 thousand; 35 percent in the smaller cities; and only 20 percent of the rural population. Third, while this concentration in the urban areas and underrepresentation in the rural meant that the foreign stock, both foreign-born and the first generation of their descendants, were underrepresented in agriculture, there was selectivity even in the urban occupations, at least among the foreign-born. For obvious reasons they were concentrated in the laborers and operatives categories, and underrepresented among the white collar and professional pursuits.

Only a few tentative remarks can be made here on the impact of immigration on the country's economic growth. The direct economic effect was to add to the labor supply, particularly in the non-South, the addition representing human capital investment made in the country of origin; and to provide an inflow of labor to urban and related pursuits at costs presumably lower than those that would have been involved in attracting the native labor force to move from older pursuits in the countryside and smaller cities. The more indirect economic effects lay in making possible a more rapid growth to a larger scale, with whatever special economies and efficient production possibilities such more rapid growth and larger scale may have implied. The wider, less narrowly economic effects, lay in assisting to tilt the balance of power against the slave-holding South, white immigration representing an effective vote for the free labor, industrializing economy; in diversifying the cultural and historical sources of the American population, and affirming the role of the United States as the haven and long-term base of populations, dislocated, particularly in Europe—in the transition from the preindustrial to the industrial economy; and, in placing on the educational and cultural institutions of the country the task of assimilating the newcomers, and especially their children, into the community. In general, one may suggest that because of the availability of immigration, the U.S. economy and society were able to operate with a wider range of choice— at least in that part of the country to which the immigration flowed freely and in significant numbers.

The drastic reduction of immigration, combined with the continuing secular decline in the rate of natural increase, brought the period of an impressively high population growth to an end by the late 1920s. From 1790 to 1830, the rate was at 29.4 per thousand per year, with immigration negligible. From 1830 to 1885, the rate was 26.8 per thousand per year, and net immigration accounted for as much as 6.0 points, or almost a quarter. From 1885 to 1925, the rate was 18.1 per thousand per year, with immigration accounting for 4.8 points, or over a quarter. For 1925–1970, the rate was only 12.6 per thousand per year—still significantly higher than in most older developed countries—with immigration accounting for only 1.2 points, or less than a tenth.

The slowing down of population growth, and the drastic decline in the flow of economically oriented immigrant labor to the country, had a variety of consequences. Some of them are touched upon below. Here we can refer briefly to some effects of immigration restriction. Internally, it meant, once the worst of the depression of the 1930s was over, that the reduction in the inflow of immigrant labor opened up opportunities for more employment of native labor at similar skill levels, particularly of Negroes from the South. It is hardly an accident that while the proportion of all Negroes in the country residing in the South hovered at about 90 percent from 1770 to 1910, it began to decline with World War I, and by 1970 dropped to 53 percent, with substantial shares of Negro population appearing in the other regions, particularly the North. Conversely, the proportion of foreign-born in the total white population of the non-South, at a peak of about 21 percent in 1910, dropped to below 6 percent in 1970. Likewise, the cessation of mass immigration, flowing in the past largely to the middle-Atlantic shores, must have affected differentials in population growth among the various regions of the country. And, of course, immigration restriction signalled the end of the United States as an open country, as a haven for economically displaced workers and population from Europe and elsewhere.

II. Growth in Per Capita and Total Product

The high growth rate of population in the United States was combined with a substantial growth rate in per capita product. In shifting from numbers of people to the magnitude of the output that they turned out, we face the complexities of the economic and social coverage of net product (or gross of capital consumption only) and its valuation. One has to recognize that the magnitudes are affected by the price scales applied, the use of initial prices yielding higher growth rates than the use of terminal prices; that omission of some production in kind will impart an upward bias to growth rates; and so on. But we are concerned here with rough orders of magnitude, employing linked indexes of series in which quantities are weighted by changing price ratios.

In looking back to the 1770s, we find that the record to 1800 yields a rather uncertain result, with the period affected by revolution, war, the immediately following difficulties, and recovery. For 1800 to 1840 we have tentative estimates, which can be accepted as suggesting growth of about 1 percent per capita per year—a substantial rate of growth by the standards of the time. For the next forty-five years, from 1834–43 to 1879–88, the rate, based on totals inclusive of improvements in kind, and manufacturing value-added in agriculture, was between 1.3 and 1.5 percent per year. It then rose over the next two periods—from 1880–89 to 1920–29, and from 1920–29 to 1970—to between 1.6 and 1.8 percent per year. If, to secure a simple cumulative result, we assume that there was no growth in per capita product between 1770 and 1800, and cumulate over the remaining years from 1800 to 1970, we find that per capita product rose by a factor of somewhat over 11½ (over the two centuries). Before comparing it with the record for other developed countries, we should note that with the growth in population by a factor of over 85 and in per capita product of over 11½, the scale of the economy, as reflected in total product, must have grown by a factor close to 1,000. It is this latter figure that recapitulates the movement of the United States from a small, largely agrarian economy two hundred years ago, to the huge, industrialized economy of today.

In attempting comparison with other countries, we encounter difficulties in that the records for most other countries do not go back as far as for the United States; and, more important, that one should expect a higher growth rate in per capita product in a country that enters the phase of industrialization and modern economic growth later. We can compare the United States with Great Britain or United Kingdom for the stretch back to 1800 or to later initial dates; and overall, the growth rate in per capita product in the United States is distinctly higher, by perhaps a quarter. In comparisons with France (back to 1840) and Germany (back to 1850), we find the rates for the three countries fairly similar. Higher growth rates are found in the Scandinavian countries, particularly Sweden, the comparisons beginning in the 1860s; in Japan, the comparison beginning in the 1880s; and in Italy, the comparison beginning in the 1890s. But we know that in Italy and Japan the earlier periods in the nineteenth century were marked by low growth in per capita product; and the same may have been true of the Scandinavian countries prior to the 1860s, although we have no relevant evidence at hand. Hence, if the comparison between the United States and these several countries with higher growth rates in per capita product in the more recent (if still long) periods, were extended back to, say, 1800, the differences would most likely disappear, or be reversed. The suggestion, of more general relevance, is that a later entry into modern economic growth, assuming that the growth is then sustained, is associated with higher rates of increase in per capita product once growth begins; and extension to longer periods in the comparisons for countries that have attained an adequate level of development, reduces differences associated with the *timing* of the start. This *making-up* characteristic of modern economic growth is found also in other sequences (e.g., in connection with the differential impact of a war, or of other interruptions in the "normal" course of growth).

A study for 1970 (by Irving Kravis and others), based on detailed analysis of comparative prices, yields a per capita product for the United States that, in terms of international prices, exceeds that of the United Kingdom by a ratio of 100 to 60; of France and Germany by a ratio of 100 to 75; and is about equal to that of Sweden (with rough allowance made here for differences between exchange rate and international price conversions). Extrapolation of such ratios back by per capita growth rates in the United States and in other countries yields a relationship between the *initial* per capita products in the international prices of 1970, or in some hybrid set of prices if chain indexes of product adjusted by price indexes to different time bases were used. A direct comparison in the international prices of 1800, or 1840, or 1870, might look different. But the calculation still permits a judgment that the initial levels of per capita product in the United States were comparatively high, even before industrialization proceeded far. Indeed, it is doubtful that per capita product in this country in the early nineteenth century was much lower than that in Great Britain, the leading industrial country of the world at the time (the shortfall could hardly have been more than a fifth, if that); and it was clearly above the initial per capita product of the other European countries, which entered the process of industrialization in the 1840s or later. Thus, the United States, in the early nineteenth century (and the late eighteenth) was an agricultural country, but productive and rich. One of the sources of its quantitative dominance in the economic world of later and more recent decades was that the high growth rates of its population were combined with substantial growth rates of per capita product sustained over a long period *and* applied to an initial per capita income of a level that was already high.

One should have expected substantial growth in per capita product in this country, its major source being that associated with modern economic growth—i.e., technological advance, connected, in varying degrees of closeness, with the advance of science and useful knowledge. After all, the American revolution came at about the same time as the industrial revolution. Great Britain, the original mother country, was, through most of the nineteenth century, the leader in the industrial revolution; and the major technological breakthroughs connected with the textile and chemical industries, with the iron and steel industries, and the introduction of steam power, were easily accessible to and found prompt application in this country. Indeed, the United States, through most of the century, was noted for effective adaptation and modification of the advancing world technology to fit it better to the country's resource endowments; and then later, in the electric and internal combustion age, began to contribute more heavily to the initial inventions and innovations. In the still more recent period, beginning shortly after World War I—a period of some five decades marked by extraordinary advances in health, agriculture, the spread of internal combustion to air transport and of electricity to household services, the emergence and spread of the electronic and nuclear revolutions, and so on to space exploration—the United States played a far more active and leading role than it had in the technological revolutions of the century and a half that preceded World War I.

We are so used to sustained and substantial growth in per capita product that we tend to take it for granted—not realizing how exceptional growth of that magnitude is on the scale of human history; and how much it requires in the complicated process of invention, application, accumulation, and adjustment. If we find that, say, over a quarter of a century, per capita product rose by 50 percent, this means that usually with the same or smaller labor input per capita, the working population managed to produce that much more of final product—food, clothing, shelter etc., *and* whatever additional capital, material or human, was needed to produce it. Such a feat can be accomplished either because of a lucky gift of hitherto unused natural resources—hardly a sustainable source, except through advance of knowledge that creates resources out of hitherto useless components of nature; or because of greater learning, within the context of already available knowledge—again a quickly exhaustible source without creation of new knowledge that extends the limits within which learning can occur; or, and most importantly, because of new inventions, which, when applied, enlarge the productive capacity of human labor. And, indeed, when one looks behind the rather unrevealing economic aggregates, one finds a stream of technological changes representing the applications of new inventions and new knowledge—and contributing, when applied, to further learning, discovery, and invention. A glance at a single sector in the United States, say that of internal transport, reveals a sequence of canals and turnpikes, steamboats on internal waterways and steam railroads, electric railroads, internal combustion engine transport and highways, air transport—all of this in successive major breakthroughs, and cycles of emergence, learning, expansion, and eventually obsolescence.

Technological innovations, which constitute the major permissive source of modern economic growth, carry constraints of their own, even in a country like the United States that also enjoyed extensive expansion and access to additional natural resources. The innovations require, for effective application, specific responses from the society desirous of utilizing them. And these, in turn, mean adjustments in economic and social institutions, differential impacts on various groups within a society, and effects on even purely economic relations, e.g., the amounts of capital investment that have to be generated to embody the technological innovation, relative to the net product that it will yield. Thus, the domestic capital formation proportions that we find in the United States in the nineteenth century—at over 20 percent gross or close to 15 percent net—were substantially higher than the 10 to 12 percent gross in Great Britain or the Scandinavian countries at the time; and may be viewed as responses to the capital-demanding infra-structure of residential and related construction, railroads and other public utilities, in a continental country with a rapidly growing population. One may also note in the reproducible capital stock at the end of the century the high proportion of capital in transport, communication, housing and related construction—the capital investment in manufacturing and agriculture becoming proportionately greater only later. And the completion of capital-demanding infra-structure in the nineteenth century, and the marked slowing down in the growth of population and labor in the twentieth century, may perhaps explain the greater rate of growth of factor productivity in the recent decades—with a less capital-demanding technology.

But the effects of technological innovations were not only on capital formation and factor productivity. They were also on the organization of economic production or management units, in the pressure for the modern type of corporation; and they had a ramifying effect on industrial organization through the use of the discriminating power of monopoly. They affected conditions of work, with changes in labor force status, employment requirements, educational levels, and the active lifespan of the working population; and they affected conditions of life, through furthering urbanization and modifying patterns of consumption and other elements in the modes of living associated with rising economic standards. The various institutional adjustments, and shifts in conditions of work and life, required for effective channeling of the continuous stream of technological innovations, were neither easy, nor costless. The gap between the stock of knowledge and inventions as the necessary condition, and the institutional and social adjustments that would convert the former into a sufficient condition, is wide—as past history of the economically developed countries and the current history of the less developed amply show. That the United States achieved a sustained and fairly high rate of growth of per capita product over this long period is evidence of the country's capacity to modify its institutions and patterns of work and life, at rates sufficient to accommodate the technological potentials and in ways that preserved, except for the Civil War, a freely accepted social consensus.

The emphasis on the technological innovations, associated with a growing stock of knowledge, involves the implicit argument that conventional measures of factor productivity, even if expanded to include investment in human capital, are incomplete. This is so at least at present, when our understanding of the processes by which new knowledge and new inventions originate is so meager, and so long as the economic calculus is of limited application to a resource the returns from which are so wide-flung in space and time, and the identifiable costs of which are in such disproportion to returns when observable. One should also add that the feedback effects of the application of new inventions in mass production on the facilitation of additional knowledge and invention have not been studied sufficiently to provide an adequate body of data. Do we really understand, in economic terms, the succession of various sources of industrial power, and can we explain, e.g., the timing of the emergence of the electronic revolution in communication? Questions such as these are pertinent to the analysis of U.S. growth even in the nineteenth century, when the United States was a follower country applying largely European discoveries and inventions. They become of critical significance in the recent decades, when this country has attained sufficient leadership to become itself the major source of advance in new knowledge and invention.

III. Unity and Inequality

The political and social framework of a country sets the major conditions for economic growth, in formulating and monitoring rules of economic and social behavior; and changing them, when adjustments are required by new obstacles and opportunities brought by accumulated costs of the past, new knowledge, and new external circumstances. Since modern economic growth means a succession of differential impacts of innovations on different groups within a society, unified, effective decisions may be required to preserve consensus, minimize negative impacts, and maximize the positive contributions of growth. Indeed, a major function of modern sovereign government is to help channel social and political adjustments to economic growth, to modify old and create new institutional patterns that would facilitate growth while limiting its inequitable effects. Given the variety of, and likely conflicts among, the group interests affected, an overriding sovereign power is required that would represent the interests and values of the community.

The problem of maintaining flexible and creative unity despite divisiveness produced by modern economic growth was complicated, in the case of the United States, by several historical circumstances. To begin with, the nation was formed of thirteen colonies, which, by the time the new political entity began operating, had had well over a century of separate existence, and thus opportunity to develop different economic, political, and social characteristics. The distinction between the North and the South (more specifically the Northeast and the Southeast) was sharply marked, already in 1790—the year of the first census and within the country's first presidential term. In that year, of 1.97 million population in the North, only 3 percent were Negroes, and of these fewer than two-thirds were slaves; in the South, of a similar total population of 1.96 million, over 35 percent were Negroes and of these over 95 percent were slaves. One can also find data on the tonnage of trade of the various colonies in 1770, which clearly point to the dominance in the North of trade with the West Indies, and in the South of trade with Great Britain. The subsequent persistence of the original North-South cleavage, and its sharpening to a clash between incompatible bases of economic and social organization, led to a civil war almost a century after the American revolution. While the legal abolition of slavery marked, in one way, the end of this clash, the heritage persisted in the isolation of the South and the continued economic and social discrimination against the Negro—not to be effectively mitigated until the post-World War II decades.

Next, even setting aside the conflict with regard to slavery, a long period of political experimentation and innovation was required to weld the original, and increasing, number of states into an organization capable of formulating and enforcing unified decisions, and, indeed, of establishing the common interests that these decisions were intended to serve. At least three novel elements were involved, setting the conditions in which the evolution of a unified country had to take place. First, there was the basic decision to launch a new nation by agreement among former colonies that declared an end to their old allegiance to a single, outside, authority. This, in itself, represented a revolutionary novelty, a major innovation; and like all major innovations, it needed prolonged experimentation and adjustment before it could attain a realistically optimum level. The period of such adjustment would have been long even without additional complications of rapid geographic expansion, and, after an early date, of intensive industrialization and major technological advance. But, second, this new nation, with only emergent unifying powers and only gradually widening bases for common action, was in the process of rapid westward expansion, with special sets of problems created by the movement of people to the frontiers and the addition of new state units to the older commonwealth. The emergence, and conditions of admission, of these new units were of differing consequence to the several older parts of the country; and while such geographical expansion provided a strong sense of unity to the country, the specific changes had to be made without too much damage to the consensus. Third, and most relevant to economic growth, there was the process of industrialization and structural transformation, a flow of novel changes requiring new institutional and legal patterns, and affecting differently the several groups in the population. There was, consequently, need for some single authority—acting for the country and capable of evolving—to monitor and select the necessary institutional and legal adjustments, and try to provide the proper channels for economic advance while mitigating its adverse effects.

The results of U.S. economic growth are clearly seen in the high rates of growth of population and of per capita product; the process could also be viewed in a series of growth-setting decisions. These would begin with the commitment to political independence from outside, and political unity within; and would then involve the implementation of that independent and unifying power in a series of decisions—on the public domain, the treatment of debt, free labor and slavery, internal improvements, regulation of foreign trade, public education, and so on in a long list. It is not possible here, nor am I competent, to attempt such a list, in proper order and weight of decisions. One can only observe that the successive decades of the nineteenth and early twentieth centuries witnessed a series of secular or growth decisions, the long-term implications of which were largely perceived by the different groups aware of their interests but also cognizant of some common goals; that, if one can judge by the changing political organization, the trend has been toward a continuing widening in popular participation, at least in the election of representatives charged with exploring, and arriving at, the decisions; and that, finally, at least prior to World War I, there seemed to have been a persistent thread in these growth decisions. The thread was provided by a desire to people the continental span of the country, and to exploit the large-scale opportunities provided, on the one hand, by the stock of natural resources perceived as such in the light of knowledge existing at the time, and on the other, by the advance in modern technology which created new resources and widened markedly the range of productivity of human labor organized within an adequate social framework. Both extensive and intensive expansion was pursued, by a country open to immigration and unconcerned with external threats or, after the Civil War, with dangers to internal unity.

Extensive expansion ceased at some time in the early twentieth century, within a span of years extending from the closing of the frontier at the end of the nineteenth century, to the admission of the last state in the continental United States in 1912, to the effects of the 1914–18 war, to the sharp restriction of immigration in the mid-1920s. The period of five decades that followed was quite different; and even within it, there was a contrast between the first twenty-five years, from the mid-1920s to the end of the 1940s—with a major depression and a world war—and the last quarter of a century. It is only during the latter subperiod that a variety of adjustments occurred, adjustments to the cessation of mass immigration with its differential impact on regions and on communities of different size, and to major shifts in world conditions.

In turning now to economic inequality, changes in which are a potent source of unity and disunity, I find it difficult to deal broadly with this wide and complex aspect of the country's economic growth. My interest is largely in inequality generated by economic growth, and the difficulty is in finding data and analyses that would cover both the growth-induced income disparities and the offsets through mobility—all of this with proper cognizance also of changes in family and household structure generated by modern demographic trends. But it may be useful to call attention to special elements in our historical experience, which differed between the long sweep to World War I and the more recent period since the late 1920s.

In the earlier period, the existence of slavery over the first century after independence, and of effective legal and social discrimination in the South in later decades, introduce elements that render conventional economic measures unrevealing and inadequate. Whatever shortfalls there were in the calculated economic returns to the people bound in slavery, or to those with sharply restricted rights, they were a limited part of the story; and the major part was hardly susceptible of a purely economic calculation. Here was a case of economic, legal, and social deprivation that persisted over three quarters of the total long-time span, and allowed only limited relief through mobility—all of this applying to a substantial group within the country's population. In greatly reduced form, the observation may apply even to the majority of the white population in the South, relative to the white population in the other regions. The former were not afforded opportunities as great as those for the white population elsewhere, since the slave population and its custom-bound successors prior to World War I failed to provide the domestic markets, and thus the growing demand, that the local white population could satisfy and grow with. Nor were conditions in the South a good preparation for a would-be white migrant to regions outside the South, a fact that inhibited such migration.

Within the long period prior to the 1920s, in a subperiod beginning with the late 1830s, the income distribution among the population outside the South (almost all white) was complicated by the incidence of mass immigration. The latter, with the typically lower incomes of the foreign-born, meant an addition of weight to the lower tail of the income distribution—even though, to the immigrant himself, the income, even in his earlier years in the country, may have meant a marked advance over what he was earning in his country of origin. And, most likely, this income-inequality-widening effect of the entry of immigrants varied over time with variations in the relative inflow and the widening contrast between the income levels prevailing in the United States and those at which employment openings could be filled by the newcomers. But the same factor also made for higher mobility up the income ladder—in that with the passage of time and accumulation of experience, the income of the foreign-born would rise more rapidly than that of the native-born; and in that, as the data indicate, the incomes of the next generation, native-born of foreign parents, would show a rise over the incomes of their parents greater than between two successive generations of native-born of native parents.

With substantial mobility of labor in and out of the country in the decades before World War I, there was only limited pressure for sustained government intervention to supplement income during depressions by unemployment compensation or public works; or to provide for old-age pensions through governmental security plans. And with the hoped-for mobility up the economic ladder, at least for the white population, under conditions of peace and rapid growth, there was no great pressure for governmental policy to reduce income inequalities, except through assurance of equality of opportunity. The impression I have is that the income distribution in the United States, in the decades before World War I and for some years thereafter—until the great depression of the 1930s—was little modified by government intervention.

To what extent the situation changed after the mid-1920s and particularly since the early 1950s, is a matter for exploration by scholars more familiar with the trends in this recent period. I can only offer conjectures. As already indicated, there has been in the recent period a movement of Negroes away from the South and to other regions; and there has been a marked advance in removing limitations and discrimination, particularly after World War II. This should have led to a reduction of economic differentials, and, most important, to a weakening of restrictions on opportunities and on mobility. The marked reduction in the volume of net immigration and the shift in its composition away from dominance by labor of lower skills, should have reduced its contribution to the low tail of the income distribution among the white population in the non-South. At the same time, it should have reduced mobility over time within the income distribution. But there may well have been offsetting changes elsewhere.

Most impressive was the marked trend toward greater government intervention, to provide some offsets to the incidence of income deficiency occasioned by unemployment, illness, breakdown within the family, and old-age insecurity; and to extend equality of opportunity through enforcement of the rights of hitherto restricted minorities. The trend, emerging first during the depth of the depression of the 1930s, in response to critical levels of unemployment and economic deprivation, expanded much further after World War II. It was due partly to the stabilization of the U.S. population and labor force, following the reduction of immigration; and it was due partly to the slowly shifting views on the peace-type goals of economic and social life. But it was also due to the realization that with the incidence and dangers of wars affecting the country and threatening its population, the burdens imposed by discrimination, and by the purely competitive pressures of the unregulated private market, should not be tolerated. There was, apparently, a line of connection between changes in the international framework within which this country had to operate after World War I and the policies of the government (later involved in the massive programs connected with defense) bearing on equality of opportunities and on income distribution.

IV. Recent Changes in the International Framework

By the international framework within which a country lives and grows I mean the structure of the rest of the world, with which the given country engages either in peaceful exchange of goods, men, capital, and ideas, or in active, or potential, conflict involving the use of force. At a given time, this structure of the rest of the world would differ from country to country, depending on its size, location, economic and social characteristics, and the like; and it would change over time for a given country, as the latter and the rest of the world change, and as the means of contact among them also change.

One omission, among several, in our selective discussion so far is the neglect of the salient and changing aspects of the international framework within which this country has been operating since the early days of its political independence. This omission cannot be repaired here: doing so would require coverage of the peaceful flows of trade, migration, and capital; of the conditions of tension and conflict in the rest of the world, and between some of it and this country; and of the changing technology of international relations. Yet, because of its obvious major impact on the structure of economic growth of this country in recent decades, one should note briefly the marked change that occurred in the political and conflict aspects of the international framework as it may be perceived for this country.

World War I, coming after almost a century of relative peace (punctuated only by local wars), and followed within two decades by World War II, signified the beginning of a new period for the United States, as it did for many other nations. After withdrawal from European stresses and conflicts since the early nineteenth century, this country participated in both world conflicts; and modified its policies to suit the new conditions of growing world disarray. The very occurrence of "world" wars, i.e., ones characterized by prolonged and costly participation by a high proportion of the major developed countries of the world (together with some less developed partners), meant that, by the early twentieth century, the number of such large industrialized countries had grown sufficiently large to have generated numerous points of conflict. It also suggests that, despite the obvious mutual advantages of growing volumes of peaceful trade and capital flows, there were sufficiently large elements of international competition and friction in modern economic growth, under the auspices of increasingly nationalistic sovereign states, to make the occurrence of a war a high probability.

Several consequences of such major wars may be noted. First, and most direct, they accentuated the advance of war technology —which, however, in developed countries, is an integral part of the country's technological complex. Thus, the advance of technology since the late eighteenth century increased the capacity and productivity of long-distance transport and communication at least as much, if not more, than it did that of the production of commodities and other services. Modern technology bridged space gaps within and among countries that barred flows of goods and men for centuries; and it resulted, by the mid-twentieth century, in a world in which no part of mankind was really isolated from others (except, in some countries, by government fiat). But such revolutionary improvements in transport were just as important for delivery of war materiel and armies as they were for peace-type transport; and, indeed, the advance in the capacity of delivering war "goods" at long distance was clearly greater. Likewise, the increased technological power of mankind, i.e., the greater power to modify natural processes to satisfy human purposes, was perhaps as great, if not greater, when these purposes had to do with destruction in time of war than with construction for peaceful ends. Thus, the enormous advance in transport and communication resulted in economic and political interdependence among nations that was quite recent and new in the long history of human societies; and came after millenia of almost isolated existence, during which distinctive historical heritage was accumulated by different societies, little affected by, and indeed often unaware of, the rest of the world. But the removal of isolation meant also the removal of protection. For the United States, as for many other countries, protective (as well as inhibiting) distance from other powers shrank rapidly, particularly after World War II.

Second, participation in the prolonged and major conflicts meant, for the developed countries and their less economically developed partners, a strain that led often to political breakdowns and the emergence of new and deviant forms of political and social organization. In the less developed countries, like Russia and China, the heretofore gradually growing modern elements were weakened by World Wars I and II, sufficiently to give way to Communism. Among the developed countries of Europe, the First World War led to the dissolution of a multinational monarchy like Austria-Hungary, and the emergence of fascism in Italy, Germany, and some of the other European states—another case of the use of a hierarchically organized dictatorial party to force the growth of economic and political power of the country by ideologically claimed control over the population. Since these were new approaches, representing violent breaks with the past, explicit hostility to the past, and to other nations still associated with it and representing competing units, became a long-term policy at times taking particularly virulent forms. These outbreaks of deviant and self-proclaimed revolutionary regimes, emerging as engines of accelerated political and economic growth, introduced into the world, particularly after the 1920s, elements of cleavage and divisiveness that were absent, or only latent, before World War I.

Finally, one should note that the world wars came as a result of the culmination of antecedent and competitive expansion by the economically developed countries toward colonization of much of the rest of the world. A consequence of World War I was to demonstrate that the advantages of such colonization to the developed countries were limited. And this demonstration was greatly reinforced by the realization that the tutelage of the colonies by the metropolitan countries was self-terminating if there was to be sharing of modern values—a sharing inevitable in continued contact. The shift was finally completed in the course of World War II when distant colonies were lost so easily; and when it became evident that, with the advance of modern technology, the advantages of presumably secure natural resources in the colonies were limited, while the rights of the native inhabitants of the colonies to be the masters of their own political and hence, presumably, also economic, destinies, were paramount. The result was a remarkable spread of national sovereignty extending to large numbers of hitherto colonial areas, to some after World War I, but to others at a far greater rate after World War II.

It may seem paradoxical that precisely at the time when technological progress broke down the isolation in the world and made for increased economic interdependence, divisive boundaries of national sovereign statehood spread so widely; and that there occurred a striking decentralization of political power among a mushrooming number of new and small jurisdictions. But perhaps this is not paradox at all. If the world has become so much tighter, and countries are exposed to both benefits and dangers from so many possible outside sources, a national society that shares a strong feeling of community of kind, might desire to have the freedom of sovereign decision to be exercised in crucial choices. And this would be all the more so, when the government is in the hands of a monolithic minority party that might want to have the power and trappings of sovereignty to protect itself internally and to isolate the country from external influences, viewed as temptation or corrupting knowledge.

As the comments above suggest, the world wars were only a reflection of the underlying causes that brought about the major shifts in the international framework since the 1920s, and particularly rapidly since the early 1950s. They reflect the enormous technological contribution in the developed countries, which was accessible to, and adopted by much of the rest of the world, but in a selective way; and they also reflect the strains and stresses that economic growth was creating in both developed and developing countries and that led to nationalistic and aggressive policies—with whatever ideological claims were evolved to justify the latter. Even without overt wars, the combination of advances in technological power, for good and bad, with its differential spread to, and impact on, countries at different stages of development, and with the shrinking of distance in the world, would have resulted in much greater international tension than existed in the earlier periods of greater distance and isolation.

Whatever the causes, and comments above provide only tentative suggestions, the changes in the international framework in the recent decades—the increased divisiveness, more intensified ideologically powered hostility, and the greater danger of war-induced devastation—involve heavy costs to this country, as well as to many others. These costs should be noted not only in terms of large military budgets, and the absorption of a larger proportion of high-level scientific and technological manpower in war-related work. There are also the costs of distortion of channels of cooperation and communication in an ideologically divided world; and the costs involved in the greater complexity within the country's economic and social organization, which must provide the means for viable policy decisions—both on the domestic use of the increased technological power for equitable economic and social advance, and on the problems of relations with the rest of the world that may be so explosive.

The growth problems of a developed country can be viewed within the context of a combination of technological and economic power, present and prospective; of a variety of accepted goals, and hence of responsibilities; and of the dangers of unforeseen (some unforeseeable) errors and of unavoided (some unavoidable) failures. One may characterize this combination for the United States, recently and currently, as that of enormous power, wide responsibilities, and substantial dangers. The very size of the country's population and economic product, and particularly the large reservoir of its scientific and technologically creative human resources, give it enormous power, currently and in prospect. The responsibilities are wide because the country's decisions—on the directions of basic and applied research, on policy with respect to agriculture and agricultural stockpiling, on nuclear and other energy, on weapon production and sales, on multinational corporations and so on in a long list—have a marked impact not only on its own population but also on much of the rest of the world. The dangers of error and failure are formidable because the power of advanced technology makes errors potentially that much more costly; because so much of the rest of the world needs assistance in its attempts to bridge the gap between attainments and minimum aspirations; and because the destructive potentialities of modern technology are so much greater, particularly in a divided world.

Within the past two centuries, and associated with modern economic growth, there must have been many such combinations of increasingly great technological and economic power, with diverse goals, and the greater dangers associated with errors and failures. Yet, even with lagging adjustments and costly failures, the results, at least in terms of material returns, showed a fairly marked upward trend. Even in this recent twenty-five year period of greater strain and danger, the growth in peace-type product per capita in the United States was still at a high rate; and in the rest of the world, developed and less developed (but excepting the few countries and periods marked by internal conflicts and political breakdowns), material returns have grown, per capita, at a rate higher than that ever observed in the past. And one should note that current problems, still unresolved, always loom larger than those of the past—which have been resolved sufficiently for us to have survived and flourished and for us to be able to view them more dispassionately.

But long-term projections into ranges well beyond those covered by the observed past are subject to wide errors; and the variables and parameters under discussion (and many more should be cited) are too diverse and too crude to permit adequate analysis, certainly within the limits of my competence. The purpose of the brief comment was to emphasize the association between growth of technological and economic power (stemming in large part from new knowledge) occurring under the aegis of the nationalist sovereign state, and the probability of errors of innovation (based, by definition, on incomplete knowledge) and of international strain and conflict.

Aspects of Post–World War II Growth in Less Developed Countries

Introduction

In this paper we deal with selected aspects of economic growth since World War II in developing (less developed, or LDC for short), as contrasted with developed (or DC), market economies, excluding the centrally planned or Communist countries (which in 1972 accounted for some 1.2 of 3.7 billion world population).[1] This exclusion is due partly to difficulties of securing comparable and meaningful estimates for these countries, particularly for the giant among them, Mainland China, but largely to problems involved in the analysis of economic growth in countries in which the tradeoff between economic gain (in output or power) and individual welfare and freedom is so different from that in the less centralized market economies.

The LDCs are the countries in Asia, Africa, and Latin America that are characterized by low income per capita and a production structure that suggests a marked shortfall in exploiting the op-

Reprinted from Anthony M. Tang, Fred M. Westfield, and James S. Worley, eds., *Evolution, Welfare and Time in Economics: Essays in Honor of Nicholas Georgescu-Roegen,* Lexington, MA: (D.C. Heath & Co., 1976), pp. 39–65.

1. The figure for "centrally planned economies" is from the *World Bank Atlas: Population, Per Capita Product, and Growth Rates* (Washington: 1974), p. 8.

portunities provided by modern technology. According to the *World Bank Atlas,* of the 1.85 billion people in the "developing" countries in 1972, close to 1 billion were in low-income countries whose per capita GNP averaged $110; and another 0.27 billion were in countries with "middle income"—i.e., a range of per capita GNP between $200 and $375, and an average of $260. By way of contrast, the average per capita income for developed or industrial market economies, with a population of 0.66 billion, was over $3,500.[2] United Nations estimates, a major source of comparative data, differ in detail of classification from those of the World Bank; but for our purposes, which involve general orders of magnitude rather than detail, the two sets of estimates are fairly comparable.

Our interest is in the growth of the poor LDCs. Not all the countries classified as "developing" by either the World Bank or the United Nations are poor, the striking exception being the oil sheikdoms with small populations and enormous oil revenues. Nor are all the countries classified as "developed" rich, as illustrated by several countries in Southern Europe. There is a twilight zone where a more discriminating classification would place countries that are backward but rich, those that are in the process of movement from LDC to DC status but have not yet attained the latter, and still others that may have regressed from apparent DC

---

2. These estimates of per capita GNP in U.S. dollars are based on modified or unadjusted exchange rates and tend to exaggerate the contrast as compared with the results of detailed adjustments of local currency estimates for purchasing power parity. Yet one should not assume that such far-reaching adjustments reduce the gap to a narrow range. A recent elaborate study yields some illuminating results (Irving B. Kravis, Zoltan Kennessey, Alan Heston, and Robert Summers, *A System of International Comparisons of Gross Products and Purchasing Power,* published for World Bank ((Baltimore: Johns Hopkins University Press, 1975)). In a comparison of India and the United States, to take an extreme example, the conversion by exchange rates yields a ratio of per capita GDP of 2.04 to 100 (for 1970), while using per capita quantity indexes based on international prices yields a ratio of 7.12 to 100 (ibid., table 1.3, p. 8). This is the largest proportional adjustment of the ratios (3.5 = 7.12/2.04). Similar results for Kenya and Colombia are 1.9 and 2.3, respectively. If we assume a proportional adjustment of about 2.5 for all low-income LDCs relative to all DCs, the ratio indicated in the *World Bank Atlas* ($110 to $3,670, or 0.029) would rise to 0.072, and the range between the per capita product of the two groups of countries would still be 1 to 14. A range of this extent surely warrants consideration of the implications of the low per capita product of the LDCs for the vulnerability of their economies to short-term crises and for the meaning of even relatively high rates of growth in their per capita product.

status (possibly illustrated by Argentina). But these intermediate or mixed groups do not loom large enough within the LDC or DC categories to modify substantially the broader parameters of size, structure, and growth. This is especially true when we emphasize, as we should, the population weights in any aggregation of countries for establishing the growth of total and per capita product for large groups.

The broad topic covers a wide field for which, over the last quarter of a century, an enormous body of data, both descriptive and analytical, has accumulated. Indeed, it is hard to exaggerate the explosive acceleration in the flow of data and range of studies in this field, which before World War II was not of primary interest even for the developed countries and practically neglected for the rest of the world. No single scholar can deal with it either comprehensively or with full balance, and particularly within the limitations of time and space warranted on this occasion. The discussion that follows represents an individual's reflections on some of the questions raised by the broader type of aggregative evidence and analysis.

Diversity and Aggregation

DCs AND LDCs COMPARED. For the LDCs as a group, the United Nations has estimated annual growth rates of total and per capita GDP (at constant factor prices) from 1950 to 1972.[3] The growth rate of per capita product was 2.5 percent per year from 1950 to 1960, and 2.7 percent from 1960 to 1972; and the combined rate for the twenty-two years was 2.61 percent per year. If this rate were sustained, per capita product would double in about twenty-seven years, with the further implication that between 1950 and 1975 per capita product must have risen by about 90 percent. For the poorer and most populous LDC region distinguished in the UN estimates back to 1950, East and Southeast Asia (excluding Japan), with a population by 1972 of over 1 billion,

---

3. The estimates for 1950–60 are from United Nations, *Yearbook of National Accounts Statistics,* 1969, vol. II, *International Tables* (New York: 1970), Table 4b; those for 1960–72 are from United Nations, *Yearbook of National Accounts Statistics,* vol. III, *International Tables* (New York: 1975), table 4b. These volumes are referred to briefly as *YNAS,* 1969, II, and *YNAS,* 1973, III.

the growth rates in per capita product for 1950–60 and 1960–72 were 1.9 and 2.2 percent respectively. The combined rate of 2.04 percent implies a rise of close to two-thirds over twenty-five years and a doubling in a period somewhat short of thirty-five years.

Such growth rates are quite high in the long-term historical perspective of both the LDCs and the current DC. While the historical data for the LDCs rarely provide a firm base for judging their long-term growth, the low levels of per capita product that characterize these countries in the early 1950s and even in the early 1960s clearly imply that rates of growth that mean doubling in a period from twenty-seven to thirty-five years could not have prevailed in the long-term past. For such rates, if applied to the years before the 1950s, would have meant impossibly low levels of per capita product and consumption at the beginning of the preceding quarter of a century. And for the current DCs, for sixteen of which we have measures of long-term growth, the observed rates are generally well below those cited for the LDCs in the paragraph above. For periods extending from at least half a century to the long period of their modern economic growth, Sweden, over the last century, and Japan, back to the late 1870s, are the only two of the sixteen countries with growth rates in per capita product that approached or slightly exceeded 29 percent per decade. Indeed, they are the only countries with growth rates above 22 percent per decade (unless one counts Italy, back to 1895–99, with a rate of 23 percent).[4]

A PUZZLE. If growth rates in the per capita product of LDCs over almost a quarter of a century were so impressively high, one may ask why the reactions to them, as shown in the general flow of news about these countries and in the persistent concern about critical conditions with respect to supplies of economic goods, seem to ignore these growth achievements. The news, reactions, and concerns are not sufficiently tangible to be susceptible of easy quantification. Moreover, one cannot take measurements of this sort, even if quantitatively accurate, to reflect economic movements. It may well be that a rise in expectations has produced a negative reaction to economic attainments which otherwise might

---

4. See Simon Kuznets, *Economic Growth of Nations* (Cambridge: Harvard University Press, 1971), table 1, pp. 11–19.

have elicited litanies of praise for economic "miracles." And, indeed, references have been made to such miracles for some limited periods and countries, in contrast to the more prevalent references to acute problems in the LDCs, and to the recurring flurries of concern among international agencies and developed countries over economic deprivation and dangers of collapse in the Third World. Perhaps the emphasis in the flow of news on the troublesome rather than favorable events, combined with the easier accessibility and wider communications, introduced a bias in recent decades that tended to conceal economic advance of major proportions. Still, even if we find, as we may later, grounds for inferring that there has been a change in expectations, and hence in the bases for evaluating the adequacy of modern economic growth, we should still examine critically aggregative measures of the type noted above. They may conceal more than they reveal, and the various kinds of aggregation that yield such measures may contain biases that should be identified, and their magnitude should at least be suggested.

This examination cannot deal with the question of accuracy of the basic underlying data, country by country, or even for a selected sample. The question is particularly relevant to the statistics of the LDCs, where the brevity of the period over which basic data have been collected and the limited scholarly resources for their analysis, combined with the difficulties of proper quantification of processes that do not naturally yield measurable results, limit the accuracy and adequacy of the data. And part of the problem lies in a system of national accounting concepts and classifications which is poorly fitted to the economic life and experience of the LDCs. But, taking note of the limitations, we assume that the basic data, while crude, are of the right order of magnitude for broad findings and inferences—which minimally can be used to generate plausible hypotheses, subject to test and revision as better data and study lead to an improved foundation.

The measures just cited, and widely used, are results of aggregation of: (1) populations, either within or among countries and regions, the products of whose economic activities are pooled together; (2) the outputs of the several production sectors viewed as contributions to, and the different uses of product viewed as drafts upon, that common pool of product; and (3) the movements of total product, or its parts, in relation to population, over the shorter periods within the total time span for which we derive the average growth rates. Because the measures are comprehensive in their coverage of product, of the relevant populations within and among countries, and of the different segments of the time span, the resulting aggregates are effective summaries of the net result of a wide range of interrelated activities over a long span of historical time. But the synthesizing function of such aggregation may involve sacrifice of important differences and variability and be attained along differing lines and with differing costs. These two aspects of aggregation and of the resulting measures will now be briefly discussed, with particular reference to the economic growth of the LDCs since the early 1950s and to the apparent puzzle set forth at the start of this section.

VARIABILITY: TEMPORAL, SECTORAL, AND AMONG LDCs. Let us take the growth rate of 2.6 percent per year in per capita GNP for 1960–72 derived for some sixty-seven LDCs, each with over 1 million population in 1972, and omitting major oil exporters, countries still in colonial status, and those affected by current wars in Indochina. Since the 2.6 percent rate is an average, it may easily be the result of a combination of some countries with no growth or even declines, with others having high growth rates. And, indeed, the *World Bank Atlas,* from which the average rate was derived, lists LDCs (with a total population close to 100 million) with a per capita product growth of less than 0.5 percent per year, and some of them showing no rise or even declines (Bangladesh, Ghana, Afghanistan, Senegal, for example). At the other end, eleven LDCs with a population close to 120 million have per capita growth rates of 3.5 percent per year or more, or an average (weighted by population) of 5.1 percent. Diversity of behavior within a comprehensive average is only to be expected; but this diversity in the growth records of the LDCs has some distinctive aspects, which will be considered after a brief comment on the implications of aggregation among sectors and over time.

Changes in per capita gross product are combinations of changes in per capita product of each of the *n* production sectors, appropriately weighted by the share of each sector in aggregate output. The important point to note in this connection is that the growth rate of the A sector (agriculture and related industries) has been markedly lower than that of the I sector (industry, including mining, manufacturing, utilities, construction, and transport and communication) and of the S sector (services, including trade, government, professional, and personal services). Moreover, in relation to total population (i.e., on a per capita basis), the growth of a basic products sector like agriculture has been low. Thus, calculated from quinquennial averages based on United Nations data for developing countries, the growth rate of per capita GDP over the 1950–72 period averaged 2.3 percent per year; but for the output of the A sector, the average was only 0.56 percent per year.[5] This finding of a low growth rate of agricultural

Short-term changes in subperiods of the time span for which the average growth rate is calculated do not necessarily cluster closely around the average. This is particularly true when total product comprises major sectors in which vagaries of weather from year to year may affect output (as is the case in so many LDCs), or when it is subject to short-term strains of changing markets and demand (as is the case in the smaller LDCs that rely heavily on export). Thus, even for a very large region, such as East and Southeast Asia, the indexes of GDP per capita, which rise over 1960–72, show a drop or stability from 1964 through 1966, and from 1971 to 1972. In other words, three annual rates out of a total of twelve represented contrary movements, while in two others the change output per head in the LDCs is corroborated by a recent study by the U.S. Department of Agriculture, which shows, for 1954–73, an annual rate of increase in per capita production of foods of 0.4 percent per year for the developing countries (compared with a rate of 1.5 percent for the developed countries).[6]

---

5. The underlying annual indexes of gross domestic product at constant factor costs, total and per capita, and of output in the several sectors, particularly the A sector, are from table 6b of *YNAS, 1969*, II and *YNAS, 1973*, III. The earlier volume is used to compute quinquennial arithmetic means of the indexes for 1950–54, 1955–59, and 1960–64, from which the growth rates for the first two quinquennial spans are derived. The later volume is used for 1960–64, 1965–69, and 1970–72, from which the growth rates for the quinquennium 1960–64 to 1965–69 and the four-year period from mid-1965–69 to mid-1970–72 are derived. The averages cited are the geometric means of the growth rates for the four intervals, with due regard to the shortness of the last interval.

6. See United States Department of Agriculture, Foreign Agricultural Economic Report, no. 98, *The World Food Situation and Prospects to 1985* (Washington: 1972), p. 12. The classification into the developing and developed groups is similar to that of the United Nations, but nonmarket economies (excepting Communist Asia) are included.

was a rise of only slightly over 1 percent. The record for Africa, excluding South Africa, shows two declines in per capita GDP, one no-change, and two rises of barely 1 percent (YNAS, 1973, III, table 6b). For individual LDCs, sharp declines in aggregate product per capita and longer stagnation periods can easily be found within the period.

DISTINCTIVENESS OF LDC DIVERSITY. Diversity in per capita growth rates among countries and population groups within countries, in the growth performance of different production sectors, and in the records for shorter subperiods within the total time span could have been expected. However, some aspects of this diversity among the LDCs in the past quarter of a century are distinctive.

First, there is a clear suggestion that among the LDCs the combination of widely disparate per capita growth rates is a common occurrence. This diversity in country growth performance is far more striking than among the DCs. Indeed, of the eighteen DCs listed in the *World Bank Atlas* (excluding Puerto Rico), with a 1972 per capita GNP ranging from about $2,000 (for Italy) to about $5,600 (for the United States), not one shows a per capita growth rate for 1960–72 of less than 2 percent per year (the lowest being that of New Zealand at 2.1 percent). Leaving aside Japan and Israel, whose growth averaged well above 5 percent, the rates for the other sixteen DCs fall within the narrow range from 2.1 to 4.7. With all the DCs included, the average per capita growth rate comes to 3.8 percent (YNAS, 1973, III, table 4b). In general, the world of the LDC market economies seems much more diverse than that of the DCs. The greater heterogeneity is found in the range of per capita product from less than $100 to over $700, in the duration of their existence as independent, sovereign states, in size, and in what might be called the distinctive long-term conditions that determined their historical heritage. The DCs, with their per capita incomes ranging from about $2,000 to less than $6,000, with their common origin within the framework of European civilization (except for Japan), and with the common impress upon them of the social and economic effects of modernization and industrialization, exhibit far less diversity.

Indeed, one could argue that diversity among the LDCs widened in the post–World War II period, if one can reasonably compare the contemporary setting with the earlier decades when most of the independent sovereign states of today in Africa and Asia were colonial possessions of Western powers. The multiplication of new sovereignties, in large numbers and at different dates, with varying degrees of preparedness and with diverse historical heritage that conditioned unity within and viability without of the new states of such different size and endowment, would in itself add to diversity in growth performance over the last two to three decades—setting aside the differences in purely economic factors. The difficulty that many of the new states faced—and still face—in attaining lasting consensus and unity needs no proof. It is evident in the incidence of civil conflicts and wars and in the widespread imposition of military dictatorships as a last recourse in stabilizing internal conditions to permit peace and some growth to occur. One could thus argue that the impressive rise in the *average* growth rate of per capita product among the LDCs, perhaps partly associated with the spread of political independence, has been accompanied by an almost inescapable widening of diversity in the growth rates among these countries. Since the number of units that have become independent sovereignties has increased tremendously, but at different times, during the last twenty-five years, it is not surprising that diversity in growth performance among periods has also grown. Stagnation or decline during some difficult political or other phase was followed by accelerated growth, at historically phenomenal rates, during the next subperiod.

Second, the particularly low growth rate in per capita output of the agricultural sector, and the wide contrast between it and the growth rates of the I and S sectors, raise questions that are specially relevant to the LDCs. To begin with, such differences mean that the weighting of the sectors in arriving at the aggregate growth rate is important. If the price structure is such that the I and S prices relative to A prices are higher than in the world markets, the I-S weights are exaggerated, and the aggregate growth rate is biased upward. A more critical factor is the susceptibility of the A sector to short-term fluctuations and to diversity of its short-term growth experiences among regions of a large LDC. This is the sector that is the major provider of the consumption needs of the populous low-income strata within any LDC. Thus, the sector's low growth rate of per capita output is associated with recurring declines or stagnation of the per capita supply of food under conditions where such recurrent crises pose major organizational and political problems. In this connection one need not go far to find examples in recent years. The possible concurrent growth of industrial output or the S sector at a high rate, total and per capita, is not an effective offset. It is only an indication of the continuity in building the nonagricultural framework to higher levels and would be fully warranted only if long-term recovery of the A sector or long-term prospects of adequate substitution for the domestic supply of the A goods can be expected. Here again, the natural diversity in the conditions of the A sector widens the disparity in aggregate growth experience among the LDCs.

Third, as already suggested, initial per capita product of most populous LDCs was, and is, quite moderate. With the usual internal inequality in the distribution of income within the countries, per capita levels were low indeed for large population groups. Hence, inadequate growth or regression and discontinuities over time are particularly costly in terms of human welfare —as they need not be in countries with relatively high per capita product and ample economic and social reserves for coping with short-term recessions or growth retardation. If diversity has been wide among the LDCs (in growth rates over the full span and in variability of rates from subperiod to subperiod, particularly in the A sector), the combination of a high average growth rate for the all-embracing group of all LDCs with a flurry of crises and deprivations affecting now some, then other, members of the group can be taken as "normal." The broader implications of such partial and temporary crises, particularly for policy choices and understanding of the immediate past and the proximate future, must be inferred from weighing of crises and deprivations against possible gains in the longer run. Such a calculus, admittedly difficult, is required if longer-term policies and prospects are not to be distorted by misinterpretation of partial and temporary difficulties.

THE QUESTION OF WEIGHTS. Given diversity in growth rates of per capita product among the LDCs and their populations, or among sectors within a country, or variability of both sets of growth rates over subperiods, the proper choice of weights used for aggregation and averaging is important. The weights implicit in these summarization processes must, therefore, be examined for their effect on the averages of the type used above to initiate the discussion.[7]

If the levels of per capita product of the several population groups (within countries, or among countries or regions) differ at the start of the growth period, and if the growth rates of the per capitas also differ, the average growth rate for the aggregate will be much affected by the weights used. In the conventional calculations of the type used by the United Nations, the sum of all products is related to the sum of all populations at the beginning and end of the growth period; and the average growth rate is calculated from the changes between the initial and terminal ratios (or along a straight line fitted to the annual ratios). In this procedure, the average growth rate is affected by: (1) differences in the increase of populations with different levels of per capita product, so that if the population of richer LDCs grows relatively more than that of the poorer, the average growth rate in per capita product will be raised; (2) weights for the separate population groups, which are the size of population multiplied by per capita product, or total product. Neither implication of the procedure is defensible. Pooling among the LDCs, which would make the greater population growth of the richer countries meaningful to the poorer, is nonexistent. And there is no reason to assign greater weight to the per capita growth rate of a richer country than to that of a poorer. A more defensible procedure would be to hold constant the shares in total population of groups or countries with different initial product levels and, particularly, to weight each country's or group's growth rate in per capita product by population, not by product. Indeed, for more plausible welfare connotations, one might argue that the growth rates in per capita product for the poorer countries should be weighted by their population raised by a multiple over 1.0, and for the richer countries, by their population lowered by a multiple less than 1.0.

The distinction between the conventional and the population-

---

7. Several of the points raised here have been discussed in greater detail in my paper, "Problems in Comparing Recent Growth Rates for Developed and Less-Developed Countries," *Economic Development and Cultural Change* 20, no. 2 (January 1972): 184–209, reprinted in Simon Kuznets, *Population, Capital, and Growth: Selected Essays,* (New York: W. W. Norton, 1973), pp. 311–42.

weighted averages of growth rates is of particular relevance to the experience of the LDCs in the last twenty to twenty-five years. During this period, the richer of the LDCs (largely in Latin America) had the higher rate of population growth; and even more important, the richer LDCs showed higher growth rates in per capita product than the poorer LDCs, the latter being largely in Asia and Sub-Saharan Africa. Consequently, the conventional procedure yields an average growth rate in per capita product for the LDCs as a group that is biased upward. With the structure of recent growth experience as noted above, the adjustment based on the use of constant population weights is sizeable. Thus, for the sixty-seven LDCs covered in the *World Bank Atlas* for which we used growth rates of per capita GNP for 1960–72 and for which per capita GNP ranged in 1960 (in 1972 prices) from about $60 to about $500, the conventional calculation yields an average growth rate of 2.62 percent per year. The use of the 1960 population weights yields an average growth rate in per capita product of 2.01—a reduction of close to a quarter.[8]

If growth rates in per capita output of the various sectors differ, with that in the contribution of the S sector particularly low, the weights of the rapidly and slowly growing sectors obviously affect the combined product growth rate even for a single country; and we have already alluded to the possible adjustment for overvaluation of the industry and service sectors relative to that of the agricultural sector. But even more far-reaching questions arise concerning the character of some of the rapidly growing sectors—questions that have been discussed for decades in the national income literature. If the share of government (among other services) has grown as it has in so many LDCs in recent decades, indicating a higher than average growth rate for that particular subsector, and if much of it was for development of administrative, defense, and similar maintenance functions, one could· view these outputs as intermediate—as costs of operation, not as final product. With the resulting narrower and purer definition of national product, the growth rate of the aggregate—in which a rapidly growing subsector was now assigned a weight of zero—would presumably be reduced. And this is, in fact, the result if we limit national product to the outputs of the A and I

---

8. Similarly significant differences are shown in ibid.

sectors, and either omit the S sector completely or reduce its weight substantially as compared with its weight in conventional national economic accounting.[9]

There is a related argument in connection with the variability of growth rates in total per capita product or important components over short subperiods. The argument is that an average growth rate over two decades of, say, 2 percent per year means one thing when the annual changes within the period range from 1.7 to 2.3 percent per year, and another when declines in several of the annual intervals are offset by higher than average rates in other intervals. The difference, of course, lies in the special difficulties created by variability over time, particularly in the output of final goods required for "basic" needs, and by changes that are nonsystematic and hence not easily foreseen. One could argue that in averaging annual changes over the span of two decades, the annual declines should be given greater weight and the high offsetting rates given lower weight than their mere arithmetic value—all of this compared with standard weights that would be attached to annual changes that are identical with, or close to, the simple average value over the full period. Use of such a weighting system would clearly reduce the averages for those LDCs for which the record shows a combination of annual declines or small rises in some intervals with explosively high rates in others; and these would be LDCs in which agriculture, sensitive to vagaries of weather, is of great weight, or the large number of those which, during the period since World War II, had major difficulties in establishing a peaceful and viable national state.

Even this brief note on the effects of diversity and variability on aggregation and averaging for the LDCs suggests a Pandora's box of difficult and question-provoking adjustments. It is impossible here, and would be difficult elsewhere, to approximate and test the magnitudes of the warranted modifications. Illustrative calculations in an earlier paper by the author, which did not touch on effects of the variability of growth rates over time, reduced substantially the aggregate average growth rate for per capita product of the LDCs (limited to East and Southeast Asia and Latin America). For the period 1954–58 to 1964–68, the con-

---

9. Illustrations are provided in ibid., particularly section 4.

ventional rate of some 2.0 percent per year dropped to between 1.1 and 1.4 percent.[10] And the effect is all the greater, because for the DCs the application of some of these adjustments raised rather than lowered the average growth rate in per capita product.

With no way of advancing the subject further, one may conclude with three general observations. First, the diversity and variability in the growth patterns of the LDCs, or within the individual countries, are an important datum in judging the significance of the averages for the LDCs as a whole, both for translating the current changes into long-term trends and for any general hypotheses about factors affecting the economic growth of the LDCs. Second, the conventional aggregates and averages tend to exaggerate, to bias upward, the composite measures for the LDCs—which they do not do for the DCs—the main reason being that, at least over the last two decades, the poorer LDCs showed lower growth rates in per capita product and more vulnerability to variability over time than the richer LDCs, an association not found among the DCs. Third, the limitations of the conventional aggregative measures of growth cannot be easily removed by simple adjustments. The choices involved in weighting the several sets of growth rates—for societies at different levels of economic development, for the several production sectors and income classes within these countries, and for the shorter subperiods in any longer span over which growth must be observed—raise difficult questions. The latter can be effectively answered only if they are clearly recognized and the quantitative record explored much further than the conventional aggregates allow.

Population Growth and Institutional Innovations

OUTPUT AND POPULATION GROWTH: LDCs AND DCs COMPARED. The growth of per capita product among the LDCs was attained in decades marked by a high rate of population increase. According to the annual indexes of total and per capita GDP, available from the United Nations for 1950–72, for the LDCs as a group (conventional procedure) the growth rate of per capita product for the twenty-two years was 2.53 per year; that of popu-

---

10. Ibid., table 9.

lation, 2.43 per year; and that of total product, 5.03 per year.[11] For the DCs, the same series show a growth rate of per capita product of 3.29 percent per year, of population only 1.09 percent per year, of total gross domestic product 4.42 percent per year— or almost a third higher, or less than a half, or about a tenth lower, respectively, than those for the LDCs.

It thus appears that failure of the growth rate, conventional or adjusted, in per capita product of the LDCs to keep up with that of the DCs lies in the much higher rate of population growth in the former. And one can easily calculate that with the same growth rate of total product, but much more moderate rate of population increase of, say, 1 percent per year, the rate of increase in per capita product for the LDCs would climb to almost 4 percent per year. Or, as has often been said, population growth has been eating up the fruits of the growth of product, leaving a small residual for the rise in per capita income.

Whatever our judgment of the threatening implications of population increase in the LDCs for the longer-term future, the suggestion that the high rate of population growth is an explanatory determinant of the moderate growth in per capita income is both easy and misleading. In and of itself, the rate of population increase is an inadequate explanation of either the success or failure of growth measured on a per capita level. In this connection, the population growth variable is significant largely in that it reflects the institutional and social conditions of a country.

To begin with, the higher rate of population growth of the LDCs than of the DCs is a recent phenomenon. For decades before the 1930s, and back to the early nineteenth century, the rate of the former was markedly below that of the latter.[12] To be sure,

---

11. For the sources and procedure in calculating the growth rates, see note 5.

12. For a convenient summary of the long-term population growth estimates see United Nations, Background Paper for the Bucharest World Population Conference, *Demographic Trends in the World and Its Major Regions,* 1950–70 E/Conf. 60/CBP/14 (April 1974, mimeographed), table 1, p. 5. The table shows world population estimates by John Durand back to 1950, linking after 1900 with those of the United Nations. Although non-market economies are included, and the distinction between less and more developed regions differs slightly from those used above, the results would not be changed even with adjustment to our classification and exclusion of communist countries.

this was due to a much higher death rate in the less developed regions, which kept the rate of natural increase down despite fairly high crude birthrates—an extremely inefficient method of population control, and one that could not contribute to social and economic productivity. But it is important to recognize that only in the 1930s, and especially after World War II, did the LDCs begin to show significantly higher population growth rates than the DCs. Further, while some birthrates did rise, the trend was due largely to a rapid reduction of death and morbidity rates— one of the first requirements of, and a most important and valuable ingredient in, modern economic growth.

Second, if population, viewed as a collective of consumers, grew more rapidly in the LDCs, and thus can be debited with a greater proportionate draft upon the fruits of economic growth, it also grew more rapidly as a collective of potential workers and should be credited with a greater contribution to total product. One source shows that for a less developed group of regions (Africa, Latin America, and South Asia), whose total population grew from 1.08 billion in 1950 to about 1.75 billion in 1970, or at an annual rate of 2.43 percent, population aged 15–64 and thus classifiable as the potential labor force grew from 602 to 940 million, or at a rate of 2.24 percent per year. In the developed regions, including North America, Australia-New Zealand, Japan and Europe, and excluding Eastern Europe, total population grew from 563 to 701 million, or at an annual rate of 1.1 percent, and so did the population aged 15–64, rising from 361 to 449 million.[13] Thus, the rate of growth of population of working age in the LDCs was more than twice that in the DCs; and one may ask why these additional workers could not have contributed at least to about the same proportional rise in total product in the two groups of countries.

Third, while in comparing LDCs and DCs as groups, we find that while a higher rate of population increase in the former is associated with a lower growth rate of per capita product, at least for the past twenty or twenty-five years, this association does not hold for the individual countries within the LDC group. Using the sixty-seven LDCs, with the records for 1960–72 found in the *World Bank Atlas,* we classified them by their rates of popu-

---

13. Ibid., tables 2 and 8, pp. 7 and 18.

lation increase over these twelve years, which averaged 2.5 percent per year (weighted by 1960 population). For twenty-nine, not counting India, the growth rate of population was 2.5 percent or less. Their population was 356 million in 1960, and their population-weighted average growth rate in per capita income was 2.1 percent per year. India, with a 1960 population of 432 million, had a growth rate of population of 2.3 percent per year and of per capita product of 1.1 percent. In the remaining thirty-seven countries, with a 1960 population of 413 million, the growth rate of population was more than 2.5 percent per year, and the population-weighted growth rate of per capita product was 2.9 percent per year. Thus, the association among the LDCs between the rate of population increase and the growth rate in per capita product was, if anything, positive rather than negative, reflecting in large part the difference in growth rates between Latin America and the other LDC regions. It would not be difficult to suggest specific explanations, but the finding is cited merely to indicate that over recent decades other factors tended to outweigh the high rates of population growth, at least among the LDCs.

Fourth, the acceleration in the rate of population increase in the LDCs has been marked because the rate of decline in the death rates was extremely high—about five times as fast in the two to three decades as the decline of mortality rates among the DCs in their comparable population-transition phase. And since the decline in birthrates has lagged behind that of death rates in the past experience of the currently developed countries, it is assumed that the lag in the case of the LDCs is only to be expected. But historical analogies may be misleading; unless there is a tested explanation and an indication of the operative mechanism, references to lags are just descriptions of still to be explained events. This comment is particularly relevant because in many LDCs in Latin America, long-term declines in death rates have been accompanying long-term rises in per capita product, and yet there has been no indication of a responsive fall in crude (or age-of-women standardized) birthrates.[14] One would expect that

---

14. A valuable collection of long-term series is found in O. Andrew Collver, *Birth Rates in Latin America: New Estimates of Historical Trends and Fluctuations,* Institute of International Studies, University of California, Research Series No. 7 (Berkeley: 1965). Two monographs by Eduardo Arriaga in the same research series provide valuable data and discussion on

thirty to forty years of substantial decline in mortality, including that in infant and children's mortality, would lead to some contraction of birthrates, assuming that the high level of the latter in the past may have served in part to offset the deaths of infants and young children. The persistence of high birthrates, therefore, calls for an explanation.

PERSISTENCE OF HIGH LDC BIRTHRATES: HYPOTHESES. Some tentative hypotheses to try to account for the persistence (and components) of high levels of fertility in the LDCs in recent decades have been presented elsewhere.[15] But they should be summarized here, if only because they interpret the pattern of demographic behavior as a reflection of economic and institutional conditions that have a major bearing on economic growth in the LDCs.

The relevant hypotheses were noted under three broad heads: (1) technology of birth control; (2) possibly lower costs of bearing and rearing children in the LDCs; and (3) possibly higher returns from larger numbers of children in the LDCs. The technology of birth control was viewed as affecting some segment of the population of the LDCs, the group that wishes to have fewer children. However, even for this group, a variety of birth control methods, which, in the long-term past, had led to control of population numbers (e.g., postponing the age of marriages of females), were still available. Since the group did *not* have to depend on the *modern* means, the significance of the technology factor is reduced. Nor is it clear that the desire for fewer children affects a substantial proportion of the population of the LDCs in their childbearing ages. The lower absolute costs of children in the LDCs are clearly recognized; but one may question whether these costs, relative to the economic level of the parental population, are so low, compared with their costs in the nuclear families of the developed countries. Furthermore, costs cannot be effectively discussed without consideration of returns, and it seemed

---

death rates and their declines. They are: *New Life Tables for Latin American Populations in the Nineteenth and Twentieth Centuries,* Research Series No. 3 (Berkeley: 1968); and *Mortality Decline and Its Demographic Effects in Latin America,* Research Series No. 6 (Berkeley: 1970).

15. See my paper, "Fertility Differentials Between Less Developed and Developed Regions," *Proceedings of the American Philosophical Society* 119, no. 5 (October 1975): 363–96. Reprinted in this volume, pp. 194–256.

warranted to place the burden of explanation on the returns from children. The implication, then, is that in the LDCs, families, in their own responses, and possibly reflecting the norms of blood-related collectives and societies wider than the family, view children as an investment—as a source of wealth, defined broadly as economic and social power—under the conditions determined by economic and social institutions within which they live.

Three aspects of this investment in children can be spelled out. "One is the economic, labor pool aspect, the desire for more children because under the rural or small family business conditions of the LDCs, children are a supply of labor at the disposal of the family that, after some years, provides economic savings and advance far greater than any that could be generated by the same family unit with fewer offspring." [16] The second aspect of investment in children may be designated the genetic pool aspect, relevant to those societies among the LDCs in which economic and social mobility is blocked by monopolization of economic and social power by a few families. Hence, limiting the number of children and giving them greater training or education is no assurance of future economic or social rise. "Under such conditions, advance for the offspring of the lowly is a matter of success based on personal characteristics or endowments, on a kind of genetic lottery that may turn up a dictatorial corporal or general, or a successful athlete, or the female consorts of either, so prevalent in many LDCs." [17] Here a rational calculation would call for as many children as will survive to maturity, as many more tickets in the genetic lottery.

The third, and perhaps most far-reaching, aspect of the investment in children is that of security—not merely or primarily the economic security of parents who, in their old age, have to rely on the help of surviving children, but much broader, encompassing protection against natural and social calamities, protection not provided by the government or other non-blood-related organs of society. The pressure in many preindustrial societies (e.g., for centuries in China) for larger families and a wider blood-tie group has been associated with the weakness of the government and the need to rely on family ties for security of the

---

16. Ibid., p. 394.
17. Ibid., p. 395.

individual members. As long as governmental and other non-blood-related organizations remain weak in this respect, an adequate increase of those related by protective blood-ties will be a high priority goal, despite possible short-term disadvantages.

RATIONAL RESPONSE AND RETURNS CONSIDERATION STRESSED. Two aspects of these tentative hypotheses advanced to explain the high fertility levels in the LDCs, and thus high rates of population growth, should be noted. One is that emphasis on returns from children as the main factor is corroborated by the structural characteristics of the high fertility rates in the LDCs. These characteristics are the entry of females into marriage at early ages; the continuation of childbearing to much more advanced ages of married women than in the DCs; the importance of high parity births; and the high proportion of children born to aged mothers and particularly to aged fathers (beyond forty years of age), despite the presence of a number of surviving siblings. All of this seems to suggest, although it does not prove, that the production of large numbers of children is a systematic and planned activity, rather than a reflection of impetuous and uncurbed passion or of blind adherence to some traditional and increasingly irrational pattern.

The second, and more important, aspect of the hypotheses is the emphasis on fertility rates as rational responses of the population to the economic and social conditions, implying that major declines in fertility are not likely until these conditions are changed.[18] The emphasis is then on economic and social struc-

---

18. Lest it be thought that continuation, for some time, of high rates of population growth proves impossible because of physical or technological limits, it should be noted that the United Nations population projections do envisage such trends for the remainder of this century. Yet these projections of population volumes are considered sustainable—barring, of course, catastrophes of the nuclear holocaust type—with declining death rates. The brief explanations of the assumptions in the two sources cited below clearly indicate the implications and the key roles particularly of those relating to the modernization of the economic and social structures.

The magnitudes projected should be noted, using the "medium" (of several) variants that can be viewed as more plausible than the others. In *World Population Prospects as Assessed in 1968* (New York: 1973), the population of less developed regions (defined again to include South Asia, Africa, and Latin America), which grew at the rate of 2.8 percent per year in 1965–70, would keep growing at roughly the same rate to 1985, and then the rate would gradually decline to 2.2 percent by the end of the

ture, and the key factor suggested as setting limits to the economic growth of the LDCs is then the capacity of the societies for institutional innovations—for changing the existing economic and social institutions so as to take advantage of the potentials of modern (i.e., more advanced) technology. In their specific form, these potentials would differ from country to country depending on the historically conditioned endowments and the changing stock of available technology.

This implication is of particular relevance in the present connection. It may be amplified by suggesting that just as population growth cannot be treated as an exogenous variable determining growth rates in per capita product but must be viewed as the result of human decisions in roughly rational response to economic and social conditions, neither can we assume that there are some rigid technological constraints on the growth of the LDCs that would explain their limited achievements in the way of increased

---

century. For the developed regions (defined to include Europe, excluding Eastern Europe; North America; Japan; and Australia-New Zealand), the growth rate for 1965–70 of close to 1 percent would remain at that level to 1985 and then decline to 0.8 percent by the end of the century. The stability, at high levels, of the growth rate for LDCs through 1985 is the result of a decline in birthrates offset by an almost equal decline in crude death rates (e.g., for South Asia a decline in birthrates from 44 per thousand in 1965–70 to 37 per thousand in 1980–85, almost matched by a decline in death rates from 17 to 11 per thousand for the same two quinquennia, ibid., table A.3.1, p. 68), with the further decline in birthrates outweighing the diminishing decline in death rates. For the DCs, the movements of crude birth and death rates are much slighter, as is the change in the absolute level of the low rate of population increase.

In *World Population Prospects, 1970–2000, as Assessed in 1973,* working paper, mimeographed, ESA/P/WP/.53 (New York: March 1975), the 1970 population totals have been revised slightly downward, and so have been the projected growth rates (due largely to unexpectedly sharp declines in fertility in the DCs and failure of death rates to decline as rapidly as projected earlier). However, the general patterns of persistence of high growth rates in the LDCs through 1985, and only moderate declines thereafter, and the contrast between these levels and those for the DCs (at about half to a third of those for the LDCs) remain (see, e.g., ibid., table 1.1, p. 12).

This brief summary of UN population projections indicates that, even with substantial advance in modernization, a realistic prognosis suggests continuation of high rates of population growth in the LDCs, peaking in the decade 1975–85 but remaining at fairly high levels to the end of the century, and exceeding the population growth rates in the DCs by wide margins. The possible consequence for the difference in growth rates of per capita product between the LDCs and the DCs as well as the possible persistence and widening of the gap, is clear.

per capita product in the recent past. In particular, one must resist the tempting argument that because these LDCs are poor, they cannot generate sufficient savings to finance the capital formation necessary for higher growth rates. The proportional magnitude of material capital required for growth rates higher than those achieved would not be large even in economies with relatively low product per capita if a backlog exists in technological opportunities and effective utilization of productive factors is assumed. With flexibility of factor proportions, facilitated by choices in the rate of utilization of both capital and labor, relatively low capital-output ratios can be attained. Of course, an abundance of capital can be used in a trade-off for greater inefficiency; but this possibility does not justify the view that capital shortages are a key factor in limiting growth rates in the LDCs. That view is widely prevalent, despite the experience of not a few LDCs that managed to reach high levels of growth in per capita product with high rates of population growth and with adequate domestic savings proportions (low average incomes notwithstanding), and despite similar experiences in the past of a number of current DCs.

THE KEY FACTOR LIMITING LDC GROWTH. One must look, then, for the key factor in the capacity of LDCs to adjust their economic and institutional structure in order to provide optimal, or at least adequate, channels for growth. Such adjustments may easily be constrained for noneconomic reasons—for example, by resistance to the abandonment of wasteful practices that have assumed quasi-religious significance—and represent no special interest of any group. Or it may be that institutional changes adversely affect some groups while benefiting others, and the consensus for such changes is absent. Or it is possible that a higher rate of economic growth, with its disruptive (as well as productivity-raising) effects, would, if forced, upset the basic consensus and threaten the unity of the country, causing unavoidable delays in economic advance.

For this reference to innovations in economic and social institutions, and to the difficulties of sustaining them, to be more than a shift of focus to a rather vague concept of "capacity for modernization" calls for careful examination of individual LDCs. By this approach, those countries that have delayed the adjustment, that have adopted limited growth-promoting policies, that have not removed the obstacles to an effective program, and that have suffered breakdowns, can be compared with others of apparent success and the specific antecedents to that success. Such an attempt would have to rely on the rapidly growing literature on the LDCs, whose diversity was emphasized earlier; and it is certainly beyond the scope of a brief summary. Even so, one may argue that, barring conditions of political subjection, a sovereign LDC, seen as a unit in a diversified world and with many technological opportunities, cannot properly be viewed as having the limits on its growth set, within reasonable magnitudes, by factors exogenous to its economic and social conditions—i.e., factors associated with either its genes, its demography, or some aspects of technology (with the possible exception of Eskimos in the Arctic wilderness, or nomads in the desert). And one can cite evidence from both recent and past history on the difficulties that the currently developed countries experienced in organizing themselves for modern economic growth by establishing a unified state that could channel such growth effectively. If one thinks of the rapid succession of internal conflicts in the two recent decades in Pakistan, Nigeria, the Congo, and Ethiopia, and if one reflects on the rapid changes in political regimes, frequently ending in military dictatorships or one-party governments, in many LDCs (including those in Latin America which have been politically sovereign for many years), one can see that setting and maintaining the basic conditions for economic growth is a demanding and never-ending task. The solutions to this task can vary greatly in terms of adherence to or sacrifice of principles highly prized by many societies (individual liberty, equality, or cooperation in loss and gain). It is the difficulty of easing this task that must be identified, in the first instance, as the proximate cause of the shortfalls in growth among the LDCs—shortfalls that may be viewed as avoidable.

The difficulty is exacerbated by two consequences of the low per capita product of the populous LDCs. One, already noted, is vulnerability to short-term calamities (whose frequent occurrence in LDCs is due to dependence upon less advanced agriculture and to greater difficulties in coping with natural disasters such as earthquakes, floods, etc.) because of lack of reserves to deal with emergencies and because of weakness of transport and other means of mobilization. The other consequence that deserves mention is the technological distance between the low-income and even middle-income LDCs and the developed countries from which they could borrow technology and secure assistance. The technological distance means that while, in general, there is a substantial backlog of accumulated technology that has not been exploited by LDCs, the current supply of technology and technological opportunities available in the DCs may be of little value to the LDCs. To illustrate, LDCs may need better small-scale transport or economical water pumps rather than complex computers, nuclear installations, or supersonic airplanes. The flexibility of choice of capital and labor apparently open to the LDCs may thus be limited by the nonavailability of a better technology that would suit their particular needs and the scarcity of technical talent to generate the adaptive uses of what can be selectively borrowed from the DCs.

These two consequences provide a partial explanation of the finding that the poorer LDCs in Asia and Sub-Saharan Africa, with their low per capita incomes, showed a lower growth rate of both total and per capita product than the richer LDCs, particularly in Latin America (excluding the oil-rich units from all groups). It is only a partial explanation, because so many LDCs in the Asian and African regions have only recently attained their political independence. Many of these faced particular difficulties in establishing a unified, and viable, new political entity, with an incidence of civil conflicts and political breakdowns; and in some of them, the resulting constraints upon economic performance and growth have continued. But even allowing for these major struggles in initial formative stages of a nation, it may still be true that the greater vulnerability of the lower-income LDCs and their greater technological distance from the DCs contributed to a lower growth rate in recent decades than was obtained in those LDCs whose higher initial per capita product and greater extent of industrialization reduced their vulnerability to short-term calamities and made adoption of modern technology easier.

Evaluation of, and Response to, Economic Growth

CHANGES IN EXPECTATIONS. Assume that, with the adjustments suggested earlier, the growth rate in per capita product of the LDCs over the last quarter century averages between 1.0 and

1.5 percent per year, which means a total rise over the period of between 28 and 45 percent. Consider also that an increase in real return per head is indicated by such evidence as the marked reduction in death rates over the period by between a quarter and a half, rising per capita consumption, and higher levels of education and health. Has an evaluation of, and response to, this undeniable economic advance of the LDCs, and for most of them after a long period of stagnation, been affected by changed expectations? And if so, why and how did expectations change?

In observing evaluation of economic growth in the DCs, three characteristics can be suggested, at least as related to modern economic growth. First, growth appears larger in prospect than in retrospect: quantity indexes weighted by beginning-of-period prices yield appreciably higher rates than the same indexes weighted by end-of-period prices. This difference is due to the fact that new, innovation-related products are priced much more highly in the earlier years—before their widespread and rapid growth and the associated improvement in production efficiency and reduction in costs—than in later years when these products become cheaper quasi-necessities. Second, all innovation-powered economic growth eventually generates problems of adjustment and undesirable externalities—many unforeseeable in the early stages because of inadequate knowledge of the properties of the technological innovation and of the social innovation that it may bring into being. This is an almost inevitable result of some "new" elements in an innovation, which by definition is a venture into the partly unknown. Third, since current events are always much more heavily weighted than past ones, the evaluation of economic growth tends to be biased downward, resulting in the deflation of the initially high values of the positive contribution of innovations and in the concentration on the current problems generated by them. The beneficiaries of electric power or of the internal combustion engine, for example, tend to take them for granted, while justifiably complaining of either pollution or failure of centralized sources of energy affecting millions of people. They forget the older days of confinement in equally or more polluted cities without a chance to escape to the suburbs, or of dependence on sources of light and energy far less efficient than centrally provided electric power. Similarly, in the field of health, the beneficiaries of reduced mortality in the younger ages are concerned

about the degenerative diseases of older people and the prolongation of life to ages when it can be neither pleasant nor productive.

If tempered by consideration of the longer-term contribution of
past economic growth, such emphasis on current problems (i.e.,
an implicit downward bias) may be justified. It becomes a necessary stimulus for overcoming the problems, or at least mitigating
their effects. But the important point is the relevance of these
observations to the view held by the LDCs of their economic
attainments and growth in relation to their distance from the
DCs. For with respect to the latter the LDCs are, in a way, like
earlier versions of the DCs embodying the earlier generations
who appraise growth in prospect rather than in retrospect; and the
price weights of the LDCs are an analogue of the beginning-of-
period prices used in weighting the quantity indexes. This analogy
is confirmed by the recent study of comparative purchasing power
on an international scale. To illustrate, when we compare consumption per capita in India and the United States, using Indian
price weights, the ratio of quantities (India to U.S.) is 1 to 22.2;
whereas when we use the U.S. price weights, the ratio is 1 to
12.0.[19] Similar results can be found for the U.S.-Colombia and
U.S.-Kenya binary comparisons. In other words, the LDCs, using
their own standard to evaluate the levels of the DCs, appraise
them more highly and find the distance to them greater than
would the DCs, using their standard and appraising the distance
to the LDCs. Likewise, one could suggest that not having fully
experienced modern economic growth, the LDCs are much less
aware of (or concerned about) some of the maladjustments and
negative externalities that it brings in its wake. Thus, the LDCs
would evaluate growth much more highly than the DCs. Furthermore, if in their evaluation of their own growth at least a part of
the yardstick is formed by the attainments of the DCs, the distance to be at least partially reduced and the gap to be closed
loom wide indeed.

We come now to the question of the bases of evaluation of economic growth in the LDCs—an evaluation within those countries
as to the adequacy or shortfall of the growth attained. As already
indicated, we deal here with intangibles, not susceptible of quantification or hard evidence (at least not at hand). Yet the judgment

---

19. Kravis et al., op. cit., table 13.5, p. 174.

involved is an important factor in the response to economic growth that has already occurred, possibly inducing change-provoking action if growth is found to be significantly short of the minimum goals. In concluding this paper, it would be tempting to speculate on the yardstick, the expectations that may be applied, and on the changes in such expectations that may have occurred in recent decades. But even such speculation involves review of various goals (greater output, more equity, minimum assurance of defense power in the divided and hostile world, adequate individual freedom, and so on). A review of such goals, some competing, some complementary, is beyond my scope and competence.

SOME ASPECTS OF GROWTH PERCEPTION. Instead, one may point out some aspects of the evaluation and possible response that are apparent from the discussion. First, if in evaluating economic growth the emphasis is not so much on the rise that may have been attained but on the distance to some minimum goal, the judgment will depend on the distance between the goal and the initial economic position of the country, as well as on the tolerance of interruptions and delays. To illustrate: if a country begins with a per capita product of $100, and has also previously suffered from short-term failures, the goal of growth may be set at $500 as a desirable level that would also act as protection from short-term disasters or, at least, minimize their impact. If, then, it is assumed that a fair target is to reach this level in fifty years (or thereabout), an average growth rate in per capita product of about 3.3 percent per year is expected. If, over a twenty-five-year period, growth has, in fact, raised per capita product by 50 percent, the movement was only an eighth of that necessary to cover the total distance—even with the target remaining fixed (and it is likely to move upward over time). For such a calculation, the comparison of the actual growth rates in the LDCs, either with those in their own past or those in the past records of the DCs, is not relevant. In the history of these LDCs, particularly those that were not free to plan their own destinies, such economic goals were overshadowed by the goal of political freedom and independence. And in the history of the current DCs, even of the follower countries, initial levels were much higher (except perhaps for Japan) and the distance between these levels and the goals set was narrower, so that the growth rates viewed as feasible and acceptable might have been distinctly below those that the recent post–World War II growth experience warranted.

Second, the same argument applies to distributive aspects of growth or to effects on inequality in the distribution of returns—which we did not touch upon partly for lack of space, but largely for lack of reliable data, despite prolific discussion in the recent literature. If the goal is to avoid, under given aggregate growth, deterioration of economic position of large, lower income groups, the requirement of some significant advance applies not only to the country as a whole but to subgroups of the population. The failure of crops affecting farmers, or unemployment and underemployment affecting large proportions of a labor force augmented by rapid population growth, represent shortfalls—even if the overall advance of the country may have been impressive by past standards.

Third, it may be realistically argued that the expectations, the yardsticks by which economic growth is evaluated, have changed in recent years. Goals are more ambitious, and delays are less well tolerated than probably was the case in the pre–World War II past. The increased technological power of man and the rapidity with which devastated countries recovered and forged ahead after World War II, the success in reducing and wiping out disease and ill health the world over, and the high rates of economic growth achieved by so many countries had an effect similar to that ushered in by modern economic growth when it emerged in the pioneer and early follower countries in the late eighteenth and the first half of the nineteenth century. The effect was to strengthen the view of man as master of his destiny. It served to create a vision of the vast potential power of man's advancing knowledge in providing economic abundance, once the needed adjustments of social structure were made. And through the widening·ties of communication in the world, it had the further effect of spreading man's new view of himself to countries that had previously failed to exploit adequately the potentials of modern technology. These two views—of the dominant power and potential of modern technology (and of the stock of useful knowledge behind it) and its accessibility to any human society willing (and presumably capable) to make the needed adjustments in social and economic structure to channel this power properly—

have certainly been strengthened and spread more widely in the world in the post–World War II decades, both by a denser network of communication and by examples of extraordinarily high economic performance bordering on miracles.

Fourth, the spread of political independence to so many national units in the world, which proceeded at such a phenomenally rapid rate after World War II and is still continuing, created many more foci of responsibility for economic growth. Accompanying the process was the tacit assumption (sometimes overt in the propaganda literature for political freedom) that the new sovereign powers would be capable of adequate response to the challenge of economic growth or would, at least, be more responsive than when they were colonies. In that sense, adequate economic growth was viewed as a promise, as a first priority task, by those many and populous LDCs that attained sovereignty only after World War II. So it has become for all states, with the recognition that what is crucial is the social response, not natural resource, not genetic endowments, not even the existing stock of material capital. In the case of the poorer LDCs, the challenge was, of course, much more acute, because they lacked reserves for ameliorating the effects of short-term relapses and of temporary stagnation.

Fifth, the multiplication of sovereign units represented, and naturally contributed to, the strengthening of nationalist tendencies and positions in the world—if only as a matter of establishing more firmly the new identities and developing a consensus on the basis of a feeling of common belonging. But this was also a divisive tendency; and in the newly established national units, there has often been room for strife within (among divergent ethnic, tribal, or religious groups) and conflict without. Economic growth was, consequently, sought to provide not only adequate economic returns to the population but also the sinews of strength in establishing viable unity within the country and in assuring an adequate defensive posture vis-à-vis the outside. The intensification of industrialization in many LDCs, particularly the larger ones, sometimes to the neglect of agriculture, was clearly motivated by the need for some minimum domestic supply of tools that, however useful in peace, were indispensable in the case of armed conflict. And this made judgment of adequacy of economic growth dependent not merely on progress toward peaceful goals but on its provision of the minimum power for self-protection in a divided and hostile world.

Conclusion

These brief comments, which could be elaborated by numerous illustrations taken from the record of events in the last few years, are sufficient to indicate that the evaluation of economic growth attainments in the LDCs, by the people involved (insofar as one can judge from the outside), may be in terms of high expectations —i.e., yardsticks that involve fairly ambitious goals. It is the application of such yardsticks that may explain the tension and strain and the search for modifications of national and international structures. This would be only a natural response to the judgment of inadequacy of the growth attained so far and in light of the dominant theory that potentials of modern technology and modern economic growth are accessible and available to all once the necessary modifications of economic and social structures, at home and abroad, are made.

Such a response is not without danger. If economic growth problems of the LDCs can effectively be met only by changes in internal social and economic structure (possibly requiring concurrent changes in the international framework that channels relations between the LDCs and the rest of the world), it is also true that each change or modification has its specific cost—short-term for the groups that are affected adversely and long-term for the whole society. And no calculus is available for measuring the balance of costs and gains, short-term and long-term, in order to provide guidance in seeking to maximize returns for the society or societies involved.

The difficulty is that economic analysis of economic growth, in terms of inputs and outputs, both the conventional and the more expanded (including inputs into human capital, valuation of leisure, etc.), is still too limited to encompass the costs and returns from modifying the economic institutions, let alone the social. How do we value the cost of shifting from the status of independent worker to that of employee, even if we can estimate the difference in average income? How do we measure the costs of displacement of rural population from the land and of the migration to the cities for a long period of acclimatization and adjustment to urban life? Or in the case of more violent modifications of social structures, how do we compare the costs of forceful reeducation campaigns (including concentration camps) with the additions of a fraction of a growth rate in GNP or in the product of heavy industry? The questions are not irrelevant, for these various alternatives have, in fact, been followed, with differing results in terms of conventional economic product; yet they obviously represent situations in which even the expanded economic calculation yields only a narrowly partial answer. And emphasizing such partial analyses, as something we can do, in the hope that they will shed some light on some aspects of the problems may mean a dangerous neglect of unmeasured major factors. We would, thereby, provide badly biased answers for situations in which the total costs are markedly different from those measured.

Since the widespread and far-reaching change in economic and social structures is a condition, part and parcel of modern economic growth, economic analysis of growth in its present state is severely limited. However, this is no argument either for neglecting the need, in a variety of situations, for such economic and social changes or for not pushing the study of economic growth toward a broader approach in which the application of quantitative analysis and direct consideration of the changes, past and present, in the institutional framework could be combined. Even if the combined measurement of economic costs and costs of social change may prove impossible, the very identification of changing aspects of social and economic institutions should be helpful both in refining the narrower economic analysis and in widening its use for aspects of economic growth neglected until now.

Technological Innovations and
Economic Growth

I. Technological Innovation: Definition and Phases

Technological innovation is defined here as application of a new element in material technology, i.e., in man's knowledge and capacity to manipulate the natural environment for human ends. Since human ends, and means to attain them, are diverse, we focus our discussion by limiting it to material technology as related to production of economic goods. The new element may be an invention, or a discovery of previously unknown properties of nature, directly usable for economic production. Application may be just sufficient to test economic promise; but we deal here with innovations that had a perceptible economic impact, with application on a fairly wide scale. Finally, we distinguish material technology from social technology, i.e., the capacity of men to organize for various social purposes, economic production among them. Obviously, both social and technological innovations can, independently of each other, contribute to economic product. But, as will be argued below, such independent contributions of the

Completed in 1974. Reprinted from Patrick Kelly and Melvin Kranzberg, eds., *Technological Innovation: A Critical Review of Current Knowledge* (San Francisco: San Francisco Press, Inc., 1978 [photo-offset]), pp. 335–356.

capacity to control nature and of the capacity to organize society are possible only within narrow limits.

The new element in a technological innovation may yield several types of economic contribution, and of widely different magnitude. In economic analysis, innovations can be classified in various ways. Those that yield new consumer goods, in which the basic choices are made by entrepreneurs (private or public). Those that are cost-reducing for established goods (producer or consumer) can be distinguished from those that yield new products (producer or consumer). The typology can be further complicated by identifying the sector of production most directly affected, and by recognizing the social adjustments required to exploit the economic contribution of specific innovations. A cost-reducing innovation will have a different effect in an industry with product of low long-term income and price elasticity. A process innovation that raises appreciably the scale of the productive unit (plant) requires individual and social adjustments different from an innovation that does not affect the scale of production. Innovations can be cost-reducing, but relatively more capital-saving or more labor-saving. The above classifications distinguish innovations by type of economic contribution, by their effects rather than by their causes or sources (the latter are touched upon briefly in a later section); but even this typology is incomplete, and could hardly be exhaustive. The purpose of these brief comments is to suggest the pervasive effects of technological innovations on different industries, different population groups, different requirements for social change. Yet such pervasiveness is combined with unequal impact on the different production sectors: at any given time innovations tend to be concentrated in a few sectors, and the identities of the latter change over the long stretches of historical time.

In addition to diversity in *type,* the diversity in *size* of the economic contribution made by the technological innovations should be stressed. The literature in the field commonly distinguishes between "major" inventions and routine, "improvement" inventions,[1] and one would expect that major inventions would

---

1. See e.g., Jacob Schmookler, *Invention and Economic Growth* (Cambridge, MA: Harvard University Press, 1966), particularly pp. 18ff. and the lists in appendices C-F.

lead to major innovations, and minor inventions and improvements to minor innovations. But the distinction is a rough one, complicated by difficulties in defining the unit of innovation properly. Should a single innovation be associated with a single invention or a single useful discovery? If so, how does one treat the thousands of inventions (patented) that never reach the application stage; or that, having reached it, prove commercial failures, or make a useful but quite minor contribution? How does one treat the major inventions that, in the course of application, generate a host of subsidiary minor inventions, and make a revolutionary contribution to economic production? Can one usefully employ a unit that covers, on the one hand, an invention that improves the method of producing toothpicks and, on the other, a revolutionary change in the structure of the steam engine like that contributed by James Watt?

The answers to these questions depend partly on existing tools and knowledge in the field, partly on the purpose of the analysis for which a unit of technological innovation is defined. Given the extreme difficulty of measuring the specific contribution of a technological innovation, we cannot hope to calibrate innovations by their magnitude, within the wide range that measurement would probably reveal. Nor can we assume a supply of even rough data on innovations that have never reached the commercial stage; or having reached it, had only a minor success. And, in a discussion of the role of technology in economic growth, we must define the relevant unit of technological innovation much more specifically than if the field of study were more broadly defined. We limit our discussion below to successful technological innovations, and to those that may be considered major—in the sense of representing a marked advance and substantial economic contribution. We thus exclude both unsuccessful attempts at innovation, and minor improvements and innovations. It is only for relatively major innovations that we have some qualitative and quantitative information. It is only for them that we can observe the interplay of technological and social factors in the relatively long process of cumulative contribution to economic product and economic growth. This limitation follows a common practice in the field; although the persisting scarcity of quantitative measures for various innovations necessarily means that current classifications are partly arbitrary and that it is difficult to secure a base for improving them.[2]

Three comments with respect to this choice of major innovations as the basic unit are relevant here, comments that apply also to the lists of major innovations discussed and analyzed in the literature. First, a successful *major* innovation is defined as major because it makes a perceptible economic contribution; and, if it involves a substantial departure from existing practices, it is applied because it has proven economically successful. Aborted or unsuccessful innovations must, by definition, be minor—in terms of inputs into them and of effects produced. Second, a major innovation, whether or not associated with a major invention, ordinarily involves a host of minor inventions and improvements; in the course of application and diffusion, it usually provides opportunities for gains from subsidiary inventions, improvements, and the very process of learning. This implies that minor inventions and improvements that are part and parcel of the major technological innovations are included in analysis and measurement. Only such minor inventions and improvements as are not associated with, and are not a part of, a major technological innovation, are omitted. Third, while the designation "major" implies a minimum-size contribution to economic growth and often implicitly a minimum-size addition to technological knowledge, the unit employed here is intermediate—between minor inventions and improvements, on the one hand, and large groups of major inventions-innovations closely related to some basic and widespread contribution, on the other. If the definition excludes a minor innovation such as the modification of a plow sulky (for which numerous U.S. patents were issued in the nineteenth century), it

2. In addition to Schmookler's monograph cited in footnote 1, see also his, *Patents, Invention, and Economic Change* (Cambridge, MA: Harvard University Press, 1972); John Jewkes, David Sawers, and Richard Stillerman, *The Sources of Invention* (London: Macmillan, 2nd ed., 1969); Universities-National Bureau Committee for Economic Research, *The Rate and Direction of Inventive Activity* (Princeton: Princeton University Press, 1962), particularly part III, pp. 279–360; Edwin Mansfield, *The Economics of Technological Change* (New York: W. W. Norton, 1968); and the recent National Science Foundation studies, particularly Sumner Myers and Donald G. Marquis, *Successful Industrial Innovations,* NSF 69-17 (Washington, D.C., 1969) and *Interactions of Science and Technology in the Innovative Process:* Some Case Studies, NSF-C667 (Columbus, Ohio: Battelle, 1973).

does include introduction of the condenser (and such related changes as the air pump and cylinder closure) in Watt's stationary engine—separately from the development of high-pressure stationary steam engines, and from the use of such engines in railroad transport. The interdependence of even *major* technological innovations, their coherence into large technologically and economically revolutionary entities (grouped around a single source of industrial power, or a single source of power for communication, or a single industrial material, or a single mechanical manufacturing function) is of key importance in analyzing the role of technological innovations in economic growth.

A major technological innovation implies a substantial new element in technology, and an opportunity for a sustained, substantial contribution to economic product. This means a systematic succession of distinct phases, in which the emergence of one phase depends upon the completion of the preceding one. These phases constitute the life cycle of an innovation; and while only roughly defined in the literature, they may be combined into a suggestive sequence.

This sequence begins with an open-ended, pre-conception phase—in which existing scientific and technological elements can, in retrospect, be seen as having supplied indispensable ingredients for the new technological conception underlying an innovation. The contribution to technological preparedness, not the emergence of demand, is stressed: the demand, eventually satisfied by the innovation, *may* have emerged during, or even before, the pre-conception phase and stimulated the search for a solution; or it may have always been present (e.g., the demand for easier long-range transport or communication, or for labor-saving processes). Without the scientific and technological preconditions, the demand might never be satisfied—at least as effectively as by the innovation. This phase is open-ended because the process of scientific and technological advance is continuous and it is difficult to establish the breakthrough basic to the innovation. For example, the scientific bases of electrical innovations were laid down in the early nineteenth century, but they did not give rise to innovations until late in the century; and even then one may ask whether they were conditioned by still earlier knowledge. In practice, the decision to limit the backward extension of this phase is usually pragmatic. It is assumed that if the period is long, the net contribution of earlier developments to a much later specific technological conception embodied in the innovation cannot be large.

The first complete phase that follows is that between the conception of the technological innovation as a feasible task and the date of its initial, clearly successful, application (what the NSF study, "Interactions of Science . . .", cited in footnote 2, calls the "innovative" phase, and what we designate, for convenience, the initial application, or IA, phase). Frank Lynn subdivided this phase into the incubation and the commercial periods, setting the former between the date when "technical feasibility of an innovation is established" and the date "when its commercial potential becomes evident and efforts are made to convert it into a commercial product" (p. II-38).[3] More elaborate subdivisions are discussed in Mansfield and others.[4] In general, it is difficult to date the initial conception of the innovation, as distinct from development to successful initial application; and while the period from conception to first successful commercial application averages about twenty years in the Lynn sample, the variance is extremely wide and is associated largely with the incubation period. This is only to be expected, for the dating depends upon identifying an adequate perception and judgment of technological feasibility and economic promise; and only rarely is firm evidence available for such perceptions and judgments.

The completion of the IA phase implies, given the successful initial application of the major innovation, that there will be diffusion from the pioneer to other producers—as well as improvement, as the use of the new element in technology becomes more widespread. The beginning of this diffusion (D) phase is set by the date at which the first successful application is completed. To diagnose the *termination* of the D phase, however, requires that a limit be set, at which the diffusion process is completed. In the literature, the limit is narrowed for practical, and often analytical, reasons. Thus, the analysis usually deals with diffusion in use in a single country, not in the world at large. If the world were

3. See his "An Investigation of the Rate of Development and Diffusion of Technology in Our Modern Society," in National Commission on Technology, Automation and Economic Progress, *Technology and the American Economy*, Appendix volume II (Washington, D.C., February 1969).

4. See Edwin Mansfield and others, *Research and Innovation in the Modern Corporation* (New York: W. W. Norton, 1971), chapter 6, particularly pp. 110–15.

used, the diffusion phase of hardly any modern technological innovation would approach even the half-way mark. Furthermore, if the major innovation is strictly and narrowly defined, it helps to set limits to the diffusion process. The practice is justified if innovations A and B, defined narrowly, are, in fact, sufficiently different so that the latter is not merely an imitation (thus, in "Interactions of Science . . .", hybrid small grains and Green revolutionary wheat were classified as innovations distinct from that of the earlier hybrid corn, not as diffusion of the underlying hybridization process that began with corn). However, difficulties persist in defining the limit to the diffusion process of a major innovation. They arise partly from the improvement component of innovation and diffusion.

Consider the simple cases in the United States of diffusion of narrowly specific machines or processes among the economic units that could employ them as substitutes for older machines or processes (summarized in Mansfield, *Economics of Technological Change,* pp. 114–119). The rate of diffusion is measured as the change in the percent of U.S. firms introducing the new machines, or in the percent of total acreage of corn planted to hybrid seed. The process is completed when the percentages reach 100, i.e., when all firms in the industry have introduced the new machines, or when all acreage has been planted with new seed. However, the diffusion of the innovation, as far as economic contribution is concerned, may be, even at this 100 percent point, far from complete. The new machines, representing a recent innovation, are being continually improved, possibly well beyond the point when the 100 percent level is reached, and the same is true of hybrid seed. The likelihood is that in all such cases the rate of improvement, even beyond the 100 percent mark, will be, at least for a while, greater than that in those sectors of the economy that have not been blessed with recent innovations. Hence, even in these cases the diffusion process is much longer than that suggested by the measures (which averaged about twenty years). The case is even stronger for large unit-cost consumer durables. Even if we could set some absolute limit to the number of cars, or refrigerators, or television sets, per family in a country, diffusion would not be completed when this number is reached, since substantial *quality* and *cost* improvements in the new product would still be possible. This would mean further diffusion in the sense of a continued spread of the contribution of the innovation. Unless we assume that the net contribution of an innovation, stemming either from quality or cost changes, is fixed when the first successful application is completed—an untenable assumption—diffusion is a function not only of the first successful breakthrough, but also of the improvements that follows; and may extend well beyond the diffusion in mere numbers.

Conceptually, the D phase is completed when some approximate upper limit in numbers (per unit of the universe of users) and some lower limit in the yield of further improvements (quality or cost) are reached, indicating that innovation effects have been exhausted. These upper limits on numbers and lower limits on improvements would ideally have to be determined for each innovation. A clear case of termination of the diffusion phase is one in which a later innovation, yielding products and processes that sharply compete with the older innovation, closes off drastically the economic grounds for further spread of numbers or further improvements of the older product. But in other cases, the closure by obsolescence, introduced by competitive pressure of technological progress, is not as clear. The only reasonable observation at this point is that the diffusion phase of major innovations is fairly long; and that further study is needed to distinguish important subphases within it, since the early periods of the phase may well witness much higher rates of diffusion and improvement than the later periods. Moreover, the pattern of movement within the long diffusion phase may differ among types of innovation, particularly between innovations yielding new specific producer goods, the broader innovations relating to power and materials, and innovations bearing on consumer goods that may affect long-term location and consumption patterns.

The completion of the diffusion phase means, in a sense, the end of a technological innovation as an innovation. But an identifiable component in the economy, usually of substantial magnitude and often far larger than originally expected, remains—and can be associated with the specific innovation. The subsequent development of this component may, in another sense, be viewed as the next phase in the life of a given technological innovation. This phase may give rise to some major economic and social problems; and may be affected not only by policies adopted during the period, but also by policies acted upon in the earlier

phases. A change in the diffusion phase may postpone and miti-
gate the problems of the following phase, which, for obvious reasons, may be designated as that of slowdown and obsolescence
(SO). It is thus necessary to stress the inevitability of the SO
phase in its eventual emergence in the history of any specific
technological innovation.

The course of economic change in the SO phase of an innovation differs widely, depending upon the nature of the original
innovation and the patterns of technological progress elsewhere.
To illustrate, in the case of canals and steamboats on internal
waterways, the competitive pressure of steam railroads, a later
innovation, caused a sharp contraction not only of growth rates
but also of absolute volumes of activity. A similar pattern is seen,
in recent decades, in the use of steam railroads as passenger and
to some extent as freight carriers. Steel output, a major innovation
that is close to one hundred years old, is still rising. But whether
reflected in a sharp contraction of volume, or in a slowdown in the
rate of technological improvement, diffusion, and growth, the SO
phase raises major problems of adjustment—to change in growth
potentials, to displacement of previously effectively employed resources, to general loss of position within the economic and social
structure. For some innovations, this phase is complete, in the
sense that the obsolescence results in contraction of absolute
volumes to minimum or negligible levels. For others it remains
open-ended—if the end is defined as relatively complete displacement—despite the fact that the pace of growth is far lower than in
the preceding phases, and far lower than those of more recent
innovations in the same or other fields.

Some aspects of the rough phasing of the life cycle of a major
technological innovation are touched upon in later discussion. But
at this point, three general comments are relevant. First, the time
spans are long: about twenty years for the initial application
phase, and much more than twenty years for the properly defined
phase of diffusion. Thus, even if we disregard the less determinate
time spans of the phases of pre-conception and of slowdown and
obsolescence, the periods are of half a century or longer. The
spans are long not merely because of the time required to solve
the purely technological problems in breaking through to an
effective invention and resolving the difficulties in development,

prototype production, etc., but also because of the time required to make the complementary and other organizational and social adjustments that would assure adequate diffusion and economic success. It is in the interplay of technological advance and organizational, economic, and social adjustments that the crucial feature of the innovation, the *application* of a new technological element, lies.

Second, the duration of the life cycle of an innovation is partly a function of its magnitude, for both the technological task and the process of social adjustment are the more formidable, the greater the departure from established technological practices and the greater the potential diffusion of the innovation. This makes it all the more important to emphasize that even major innovations come in large, coherent groups; and that for both a firm and an economy, the analysis of the innovation process and of the contribution of innovation to economic growth must take account of this *clustering* pattern. For such clusters or groups, the interplay of technological, economic, and social factors covers long periods, and contains multiple inputs and feedbacks among the various aspects. Well over a century elapsed between the time when the first steam engines were shown to constitute a major technological advance and the time when diffusion of steam power was reasonably complete (from the 1770s to well beyond mid-nineteenth century, in the *developed* countries of the world). The time span was much shorter for narrower and more specialized innovations like the zipper, and even the sewing machine.

Finally, while the definition of phases and the classification of periods within the life cycle of a major technological innovation are crude and subject to revision with further study, the concept of the sequence of distinct phases and of a life cycle pattern seem crucial in analyzing the contribution of the innovation process to economic and social change. Phase distinction is essential to the study of the emergence, diffusion, and obsolescence of an innovation, in view of the duration, complexity, and cumulative changeability of the process. And any consideration of policy intervention into the process must be oriented, in the first instance, to significant phases. Obviously, policies relating to pre-conception conditions would differ from those applying to the incubation subphase: and the latter would differ from those relevant to the development and initial successful application subphase; and so on along the sequence. Furthermore, consideration of all the phases, including the expected phase of slowdown and obsolescence, is important in that policies affecting one phase would also have some consequences for the next phase. Thus, prevention of monopolistic ossification in the diffusion phase might yield obvious benefits in both prolonging diffusion and alleviating, in the later stage, the effects of obsolescence.

II. Contribution to Economic Growth

By economic growth we mean a long-term rise in the capacity to supply economic goods, capacity defined within a specified social context and supply evaluated in terms of costs and returns to the human carriers. The growth of a firm, an industry, or a country is subject to constraint by basic rules of social and economic organization. And in the evaluation of such growth, the augmented flow of goods must be offset by all the costs impinging on men as producers and consumers. The observation is particularly important in discussing the contribution of technological innovations to economic growth, because the innovations involve changes in the rules of economic and social organization; and may carry with them costs and returns that do not appear in the conventional economic calculus. We shall discuss the contribution of technological innovation as suggested by the long stretch of modern growth in the developed market economies, since the late eighteenth century —omitting the difficult problems of the peculiar role of technological innovations in the growth of dictatorially planned economies of the Communist type.

One, apparently simple, way of gauging the contribution of technological innovations to a country's economic growth is to identify both new final products (as final products are defined in national economic accounting) and the new processes or tools that affected significantly the costs and supply of older final products; and then to calculate the country's final output that is accounted for by the "new" components. The identification of new would require knowledge of the date when the innovation was introduced; and definition of the period within which the product or process, once introduced is to be counted as new. Definitions of that period, and judgments of the effect of the new tools or processes on the economic base of an old final product (like corn), may differ. But experimenting with periods of different duration might, in itself, prove interesting: it might indicate the variation in the proportion of new with the changing duration of the backward extension. And the attempt to ascertain the specific contribution of new technology to old final products would yield insights of its own.

Of course, such a count of new components, and the proportion of aggregate national product for which they account, would, if practicable, suggest only the *gross* contribution of technological innovation. It would not reveal the loss involved in the obsolescence of older products and techniques, and the additional costs sustained in introducing the technological innovations (compared with undisturbed continuance of old ways). This point is discussed at length later. Here we should note that the identification of new final products and new production tools and processes may be extremely useful in revealing the effect of technological innovation on patterns of work and life, and implicitly patterns of social organization. If by new we mean innovations introduced during the last century (i.e., back to 1873), removal of these new components would leave the country without electric power, telephones, automobiles, airplanes, movies, radio, and television—let alone the major transformations in educational and medical services, reflecting the new components within them. Nor would we have highly organized large plants, automatic controls, computers, and the innovations in the biological processes. The list could easily be extended by scholars more familiar with technological innovations of the last century; and would be sufficiently impressive even for the last half century.

Two broad comments are suggested by this new-components identifying approach. First, it reveals the large contribution of modern technological innovations in the way of new consumer products —as distinct from modification of methods of producing old and established products. Consequently, not only conditions of work, but also conditions of life in general, have been widely affected; and the present generation uses, and is surrounded by, consumer goods quite different from those of the preceding generation. By identifying these new products, as well as the old ones that they replaced, we secure an insight into the nature of the change, which cannot be conveyed by the anonymity-imposing calculations of inputs and outputs weighted by market prices in the national economic accounts or in the analysis based upon them. Thus, the replacement of candles or oil lamps by electric illumination within the households had consequences over and above the large reduction in cost per illumination unit—some positive, in making population less dependent upon nature and its illumination; others negative, in making them more dependent on a single source of power, and the danger of breakdowns. The result was not merely an economic gain in dollars and cents, but a change in the quality of the good and in the corollaries of its wide adoption by households. A similar statement can be made regarding the new production processes—which required different patterns of work. And this means that in addition to the quantitative gap in economic levels among succeeding generations of consumers and workers, there is a qualitative gap of obvious relevance to the problem of measurement and analysis.

Second, since new components displace old, whether in consumer goods or in producer tools, the older options disappear. By and large, the process becomes irreversible, particularly since prolonged success and diffusion of the new component removes, for a long period, incentives for further improvement in the old, displaced component. Consequently, technological innovations may not mean a much wider choice, either for the consumer or the producer. Unless a consumer is exceptionally powerful, in economic and social terms, he is free to choose only what the majority of consumers choose (and thus create an economic base for an effective technological innovation). A consumer who prefers candles for illumination may find it difficult to get an adequate supply of good quality today; and the same may be true of a consumer desiring "natural" ice, or other types of old-fashioned consumer products (not to mention the less developed countries, which would find it difficult to secure an older technology, most suitable to their factor proportions). The disappearance of the old options is a result of various constraints that are typical of modern technology. These and other corollaries must be taken into account in a quantitative approach to the estimation of the *net* contribution of technological innovations to economic growth—which must be net, since the measures of economic growth are also based on the *net* balance of output over input of relevant production factors.

A major technological innovation often requires, for its efficient channeling, a scale of production, a stock of fixed capital, continuity of operation and hence of work, and a relation between the human and other factors of production that are quite different from those characterizing the earlier technology. The amount of fixed capital, the impersonal character of the operating firm, and the personal relations within the firm, needed to operate a steam railroad are vastly different from those of the horse and carriage transport of earlier times. The needs of the modern petroleum refining firm and of a tractor-producing plant are far different from those of the hay and feed, and horse farm, of the past. This means that older patterns of organization of production must be modified —with consequent changes in conditions of participation of men as workers, entrepreneurs, or capital owners. Indeed, much of the diffusion phase of a major innovation can be described in terms of a gradual crystallization of the institutional conditions for increasingly efficient application, even allowing for minor subinventions and technical improvements. The inflexible demands of a technological innovation may involve new characteristics of organization of the productive plant and firm, new methods of recruitment of labor force, new conditions for participation of management and of capital owners—in short, a variety of innovations in organizational and social technology. The variety of such innovations is quite extensive—ranging from new legal devices associated with the modern corporation and other modern organizations, to basic shifts in the allocation of jobs among the labor force, to shifts in recognized power relations among the various groups involved in industries affected by technological innovations, with consequent countervailing pressures.[5]

Some of the changes just noted are part and parcel of the technological innovation proper—because many new inventions, tools, and products would not be feasible unless there is a change in scale. Steam power could not be used economically in minor doses, and the increasing advantage of high-pressure engines meant a minimum scale of operation that far exceeded that prevailing in

5. On organizational change, see A. A. Berle and Gardner Means, *Modern Corporation and Private Property,* rev. ed. (New York: Harcourt Brace and World, 1968), particularly book II, chapter 1; and Kenneth E. Boulding, *The Organizational Revolution* (New York: Harper, 1953). On the labor force, see Bert F. Hoselitz, "Social Structure and Economic Growth," *Economia Internazionale,* vol. 6 no. 3 (August 1953), 52–77, reprinted in his *Sociological Aspects of Economic Growth* (Glencoe, Ill.: Free Press, 1960), pp. 23–51.

the past; and this is true of the innovations in metallurgy and in the fabrication of standardized products. But if large scale had to be introduced, and if, in controlling large charges of power, fixed capital, the envelope, had to be massive, the older type of firm unit, an individual or family-entrepreneur owner, could not be preserved. This meant also the legal and institutional changes that brought the modern corporation with its separation of ownership from management; the impersonal character of its organization; and the contrast in power between individual workers and the firm unit, until the workers could find strength in the modern labor union. Thus, a direct thread of connection runs from the major technological innovations, with their scale and other constraints, to a variety of organizational and institutional changes. One major problem in measuring the net contribution of a technological innovation to economic growth lies in identifying the *indispensable* social and institutional changes; distinguishing them from other concomitants that were discretionary; and measuring the magnitude of the former, in terms of the costs or returns that may have been involved.

If through their effects on scale and character of the production process, technological innovations changed the conditions of *work,* the latter, in turn, brought about changes in patterns of life required to meet them. If new production processes required scales of output that made urban centers indispensable, migration from the countryside and a shift from country to city patterns of living were called for. If the scale of production meant that employee status would become a dominant feature of the labor force (instead of small-scale entrepreneurship or work on own account) and recruitment would be largely based on overtly tested skills and qualities, the whole life cycle phase of preparation for a job of the current and next generation would be affected. Such preparation is clearly a large part of a pattern of consumption and living, consumption as now defined in the national economic accounts and in much of our analysis. And the combination of what might be called production-requirements-of-work-participation with an existing scale of consumer wants and priorities, may create imbalances that, in turn, would be resolved by technological innovations in consumer goods—which, once made, would further affect patterns of living. Thus the desire to combine participation in work in the high employment and income potential fields of new technology—which meant working in cities—with living in the more pleasant rural-like surroundings (the desire enhanced by shorter working hours, leaving more time for leisure) had several consequences. It induced the spread of commuting; created a wide demand for automobiles; led to the development of dormitory suburbs; and had other positive and negative consequences. To be sure, the urbanization-compelling change in production scale, necessitated by technological innovations, was only one factor in the combination. Yet it made an important contribution, and this contribution to changes in patterns of consumption and life should be included in evaluating the net yield of technological innovations.

The organizational changes and those in conditions of work and living, just noted, were complementary adjustments, in the sense that they were needed, and some indispensably, for effective channeling of the technological innovations. But the latter may have had also other, negative, impacts: on the capital and labor resources engaged in the old technology displaced by the new; and on natural resources, taken here to include all major environmental aspects of nature. We comment briefly on these *dislocative* effects.[6] Regardless of the rate of adjustment of displaced labor and capital to other opportunities, the displacement and readjustment costs must be debited to the particular technological innovation that is their source. And the impact on natural resources, either by way of enrichment or depletion, must also be taken into account—even though such an impact may not appear directly in the firm's or nation's calculations of costs and returns. At present, neither the deterioration of the environment and the depletion of natural resources, nor the enrichment of these resources by discoveries and additions to our technological knowledge (except to the extent of actual *input* of labor and reproducible capital) enter the calculations in the national economic accounts.

It follows that the net economic yield of a given technological innovation (or of a group of them) must involve not only a comparison of the economic value of output and input as conventionally measured, but also an evaluation of the required changes

---

6. For more detailed discussion, see my paper, "Innovations and Adjustments in Economic Growth," *The Swedish Journal of Economics,* vol. 74, no. 4, December 1972, 431–461, reprinted in *Population, Capital and Growth* (New York: W. W. Norton, 1973), pp. 185–211, which covers several of the points touched upon here.

in conditions of work and life, of both the complementary and the dislocative adjustments. Obviously, the specific contributions of a given technological innovation under the various heads distinguished—let alone their combination into a single measure of net yield—cannot be easily ascertained; and the difficulties are enormous. Yet it is useful to know what a *full* evaluation of the return from a technological innovation involves; and the discussion suggests a few general observations on the evaluation, first, of individual innovations, and then of their combined flow in the course of economic growth.

In evaluating the contribution of a single, or coherent group of technological innovations, the phases over the long sequence seem particularly important. The nature and magnitude of the conventional and nonconventional costs and returns would vary greatly among the several phases. The relation of output to input would differ markedly between the IA phase, when the breakthrough occurs but when the total realized contribution is probably far short of the accumulated inputs or costs, and the D phase, when the effects of mass spread of the innovation are realized. Likewise, the requirements, with whatever costs and returns they signify, would have to be met in the early stages in the life cycle of an innovation —if the latter is to realize its potential. The competitive impact on older components rendered obsolescent by the innovation, presumably moderate at the beginning, would become acute as the innovation diffuses to large market magnitudes, but might cease with the reabsorption of the displaced labor and capital long before the diffusion of the innovation is completed. Some negative externalities, in the way of pollution or impairment of the environment, hardly perceptible in the earlier and middle stages of the life cycle, might become increasingly pressing as the innovation reaches the later subphases of the diffusion process and constitutes an increasingly massive component within production processes and the pattern of life of the country's population. Such variation in the nature and magnitude of costs and returns among the successive phases and subphases, would mean a corresponding variation in the magnitude and sources of the *net* contribution to a country's economy. The greatest contribution might well come, not in the early stages of an innovation's life cycle, despite rapid increases in productivity; but later, when the innovation has reached large volumes, relative to countrywide product, but is still growing at substantially higher rates than the older sectors. Sustained study of the life cycle of technological innovations is still in the future; and when the results accumulate, the definitions and structure of the sequence of inputs and outputs may have to be revised.

In an evaluation of the type discussed in the preceding paragraph, two questions arise—in addition to that of combining measurable conventional inputs and outputs with the nonconventional ones so difficult to measure. How far back do we trace the contributing inputs? How far forward do we trace the possible indirect outputs? The first question is associated with our earlier comments on the open-end pre-conception phase in the life of an innovation. Difficult as it is to set a stopping date in the backward extension in the search for the sources of a given innovation, it is even more difficult to identify the antecedents so as to estimate the costs that should be debited as an input appropriate to the given innovation. Likewise, if, as will be argued below, a major innovation, in its spread, provides opportunities and pressures not only for related innovations but also for new tools, insights, and puzzles for scientific study, and leads to further advance of science, how far forward should we trace such effects so as to measure the output attributable to them? Given the nature of the questions, the answers must be pragmatic, depending largely upon a judgment of the yield, in the way of additional debitable costs and creditable returns, of the pursuit of further antecedents and more indirect consequences. And the problems are aggravated when we shift to the flow of technological innovations in their *aggregate* contribution to a country's economic growth.

Finally, given the long life cycle of a major innovation (and even longer spans for coherent clusters of them), the novel and unforeseen in the new element of technology, the changing interplay with the required social innovations and adjustments, and the dependence of a single major innovation in the longer run on the unfolding of the cluster of which it is a part, it is difficult to discern the eventual shape and estimate the magnitude of an innovation in its positive and negative aspects. The projection and prognostication may become increasingly successful as, with the passage of time and development, the broad contours of the innovation emerge more clearly. But history is full of cases in which even the inventors and the initial entrepreneurs had only a dim notion of the eventual nature and magnitude of the innovation that they were successfully promoting. And there are many cases in which experts and active workers in science and technology were blind to the implications and consequences of research and inventive efforts in which they were engaged. To be sure, such errors in prognosis are much larger for the major technological innovations, and particularly the clusters of these, than for the minor inventions and improvements that can be diagnosed and projected more successfully, once their market value has been tested. But it is the major innovations and clusters of them that substantially change, both directly and through the opportunities that they provide for minor improvements, a country's capacity for higher levels of economic performance and higher rates of economic growth. Here again the forward evaluation of a major technological innovation will be improved only as further studies of inputs and outputs during the successive phases in the long life cycle yield better understanding of the social and technological interplays in the sequence.

When we consider the contribution of the *whole* flow of technological innovations to the country's product and economic growth, the questions raised in connection with the evaluation of a single innovation assumed different aspects and parameters. The requirement to trace the inputs and outputs attributable to a *specific* innovation is no longer operative, but the task of evaluating total inputs and outputs, conventional and nonconventional, remains. And the questions concerning distant antecedents and the more indirect consequences, now emerge as part of the problem of allowing for a time lag between all contributing inputs and all resulting outputs. The aggregation of several innovations means that new, recent, and older innovations enter the current flow, adding their contributions in different phases of their life cycles. The life cycle pattern of a single innovation disappears, and is replaced by a potentially more stable and continuous pattern of the absolute or proportional contributions of all technological innovations, major and minor, to the growing product of a country's economy. But this aggregate net contribution, and the underlying inputs and outputs, may be subject to a swing, with a much longer duration and a much narrower proportional amplitude than that of a life cycle of a single innovation or a group of them. This swing might be observed if in a pioneer or early follower country, the pace of growth accelerates with the initiation or adoption of a broad new technology and then slows down as later follower countries enter the process and reduce the comparative advantage of the pioneer or early follower.

Current aggregative analysis has benefited from the great additions to national economic accounts data in recent decades, developed as an empirical counterpart to theoretical structure of the economics of allocation of resources, production, and pricing. The comparisons of the combined growth rates of inputs with those of output derived in this analysis leave a positive residual, which is due, largely if not entirely, to the contribution of technological change. This is a net contribution, since all the relevant inputs have presumably been accounted for and since the total output is presumably complete and unduplicated. Even on the assumption of total inclusion of both inputs and outputs, the residual may reflect factors other than technological change, e.g., improvements in the quality of human resources (not due to any inputs) or trends in natural or political conditions having little to do with technology. But it is reasonable to assume that technological change is an important, perhaps the dominant, component in this unaccounted-for residual.

Several groups of problems have emerged in the development of this approach: of inclusiveness of the inputs involved in the production process, with particularly reference to possible investments in human capital (now treated as consumption in conventional accounting); to the depletion of natural resources, now not covered; and to the changes in patterns of life and consumption imposed by the new technology that do not represent pure consumption. There is further a problem as to how the inputs are to be combined to derive the proper magnitude of the growth of total inputs, with reference to effects of scale and nonlinearities in the relations. Then there is the question whether the coverage of output is inclusive, either with respect to some positive items (e.g., the value of increased leisure) or to negative items (e.g., pollution and general impairment of the environment). Different solutions to these three groups of problems—inputs, weighting, and outputs —would mean differences in the magnitude and pattern of the unaccounted-for residual. And for the remaining residual there would still be the fourth problem, viz., how to distinguish the contribution of technological innovations from that of other factors

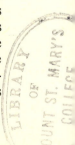

(positive and negative). An enormous literature has grown up in recent decades on the first three groups of questions, in a field of national income and productivity that has had a long history, going back to the foundation of the discipline.[7] Although it cannot be summarized effectively here, some comments on the recent trends, and on the problems, at least as one investigator sees them, may be appropriate.

If labor inputs are measured in hours, with allowance for age and sex composition of the labor force; if the net stock of reproducible capital is used to gauge capital inputs; and if labor and capital are weighted by the rough proportions of labor and capital shares in total factor income, factor inputs can be estimated. The results, for a number of developed countries over long growth periods, are clear: the combined factor inputs account for a small fraction of per capita product, leaving a large unaccounted-for residual. This residual, well over three-quarters of the growth in per capita product, is presumably due largely to underlying technological innovations, which permit larger outputs with unchanged amounts of labor and reproducible capital. The inclusion of land, or similar stocks of nonreproducible resources, would only raise the proportion of the residual in the growth of per capita product. Revision of the inputs, or of the weights for combining them, or of the output, would have to be large, and in the direction of raising the growth rate of input and decreasing that of output, in order to account for the unaccounted-for residual.

The recent efforts at amplification and revision of the productivity calculations, and the implicit revisions of input and output, give the impression of two tendencies. The first is to reclassify some consumption items as prerequisites of higher productivity,

7. It is practicable to give here only a few selected references. The collections of' papers in three volumes of the Conference on Research in Income and Wealth, *Studies in Income and Wealth, vol. 25* (Princeton: Princeton University Press, 1961); *vol. 31* (New York: Columbia University Press, 1967) and *vol. 38* (New York: Columbia Columbia University Press, 1973) are useful; as are those in *The Review of Income and Wealth,* series 18, numbers 1 and 2, for March and June 1972, dealing with factor input and productivity. M.I. Nadiri presents a comprehensive review in "Some Approaches to the Theory and Measurement of Total Factor Productivity: A Survey," *Journal of Economic Literature,* vol. VIII, no. 4, December 1970, 1137–1177. The empirical studies by E.P. Denison and J.W. Kendrick are repeatedly referred to in these sources.

either as investment of human capital, or as changes in consumption required by the new technology and yet representing no additional consumer welfare. The second is a bias, in considering the social and other adjustments to technological innovation, toward emphasizing the negative or problem aspects and neglecting the positive aspects (also excluded from conventional measurement). This is an individual observer's reaction; and can only be illustrated, not proven. Yet one *should* start with a natural suspicion. If aggregative analysis and the underlying theory yield a residual in the form of unexplained total factor productivity, it is a natural inclination to reduce the residual by *ad hoc* reclassifications of older components, before considering whether the underlying analytical system should be revised to permit integration of a novel element, such as technological innovation, so far exogenous to the analysis. Also, if with rapid growth, as conventionally measured, there are associated discomforts and negative aspects, it is a natural inclination to concentrate on them and introduce them as improper omission, without allowing at the same time for the omission of *positive* elements.

The comments just made are not intended to condemn critical consideration of inputs and outputs in conventional economic accounts. Consumption, as now defined, should be critically examined and any capital investment or hidden cost identified and excluded; outputs should be examined and both the positive and the negative byproducts included. The argument is rather for a broader view of the issues. Thus, if formal education is found to have increased and to be positively associated with incomes of individuals, informal education, on the job or through some apprentice system, may have declined in relative proportion. Can we say with assurance that fewer years were spent on education (formal and informal) by a farmer in medieval times than by a farmer in modern times? Or can we say that the gross capital stock, including land, per farmer, was much lower in medieval than in modern times—and sufficiently so as to explain the vast differential in agricultural productivity between the two epochs? Similar questions can be asked concerning a medieval craftsman, who presumably went through over eleven years of training as apprentice and journeyman, as compared with a modern blue-collar worker. To be sure, the former's capital endowment was lower than that of a modern industrial worker, but the difference would hardly account, in conventional economic terms, for the immense difference in productivity. We put these questions to suggest that it is not education, and not material capital as such, but accession of useful knowledge and its innovative application that is crucial; and the *indispensable* inputs in modern education, to use one component in which the consumption element can be quite large, may not, on a per capita basis, much exceed that in earlier times.

Similar questions can be asked about changes in conditions of life and negative externalities. Assuming that we find urbanization raising the cost of living as compared with that in the countryside, can we also assume that there was no consumer preference for the cities that warranted greater outlays without allowing for romantic notions about the countryside (in its "pure" form, unameliorated by proximity of cities)? If we find pollution and other forms of depletion of the environment resulting from some components of economic growth, do we also recognize the enormous positive effects of modern technology on health and longevity (not included now as positive components in conventional economic accounting)? If we identify the pressures of modern life as a negative externality, do we also recognize the enormous increase in leisure made possible by the advanced technology underlying modern economic growth?

To be sure, emphasis on neglected negative byproducts is a useful goad to reform and change; and much of analysis in the economic and social literature appears to be aimed at diagnosing and remedying problems, not at a balanced presentation. But if we are to consider the *net* contribution of technological innovations to economic growth, it is a balanced view, including both positive and negative aspects, that we must seek. Attaining such a balance is difficult because measurable items, like the components of inputs and outputs conventionally defined, cannot be readily combined with evaluation of major changes in conditions of life, work, and in organizational structure of society and man. For this reason, it is all too easy to advance a selective, yet unbalanced view —with resulting controversies for which there is no simple resolution.

Under the circumstances, no fully acceptable measure of the *net* contribution of technological innovations to modern economic growth is at hand. However, it is possible to attempt a variety of experimental adjustments to current conventional measures, in which additional costs and returns are estimated, along the lines illustrated by the recent Nordhaus-Tobin study.[8] Further work in the same direction will at least enhance our appreciation of the magnitudes involved, and may limit the range of disagreement in the field. But for our purposes, a simple summary of the contribution of technological innovations to modern economic growth can be suggested. First, technological innovations produced a thoroughgoing transformation of conditions of work and of life, while increasing enormously the volume of final goods and changing substantially some of their characteristics. Indeed, the novel elements in modern economic growth, that distinguish it qualitatively from the past, are largely due to technological innovations and adjustments to them. Second, mass application of technological innovations had, inevitably, some negative consequences. All material technology is disturbance of the natural ecological balance; all technological innovations also have elements of the unexpected, some negative; and, given the complex sequential interplay of technological and social innovations, timely prevention of these negative consequences is unlikely. The current critical reaction to economic growth and technological innovation is a natural response to the negative consequences, the adjustment or amelioration of which has been delayed. Third, while it is difficult to reduce the contribution to a single quantitative estimate, net of all the costs involved in conventional inputs, nonconventional requirements, and negative by-products, one cannot avoid the conclusion that the net contribution of technological innovations must have been positive and large. The nettest definition of economic product, flow goods to households, omitting any components that may be suspect as hidden capital goods, (e.g., technical education), and allowing for offsets to additional costs or discomforts of living imposed by technology, would still show a rapid increase per head, against fewer working hours. This increase cannot be at the expense of capital stock in the aggregate, even including natural resources (the stock

---

8. See William Nordhaus and James Tobin, "Is Growth Obsolete?" in *Economic Growth,* Colloquium V of *Economic Research: Retrospect and Prospect* (New York, National Bureau of Economic Research: Columbia University Press, 1972), pp. 1–80; and discussion, pp. 81–97.

has in fact grown on a per capita basis). The finding suggested by aggregative economic measures is amply supported by related measures of health, longevity, nutrition, supply of mechanical energy, and of a variety of consumer goods, on a per capita basis, for the economically developed countries. Such a great increase must be due largely to the application of new knowledge, technological innovations and their social complementarities.

That the net contribution is large also explains the pressure and striving, against obstacles, for the useful application of new knowledge. Inference of a negative or minor contribution would mean that innovating societies were foolishly misled, time after time, as to the ultimate consequences of the innovations that they encouraged. To be sure, given the organization of the modern world, societies were compelled to modernize and adopt technological innovations, if they were to retain independence. But judged by current experience, this element of compulsion was of secondary importance. The basic datum is that the modernizing societies wanted modern economic growth, and the technological innovations that were its substance.

Underlying the broad conclusion above is the assumption of a social consensus within modern society, favorable to economic growth. The net contribution of technology to economic growth would have been evaluated quite differently by early Christian ascetics, who considered that only a *minimum* supply of economic goods were needed. That group's estimate of economic growth and product would be far smaller than our conventional one; and its judgment of the effect of technological innovation would be negative, for its contribution to economic goods would be viewed as unnecessary and its influence on holy life pernicious. And a similar judgment might prevail in a society that puts a low valuation on material welfare. Some groups, even within modern society, may deviate from the dominant notions, in their judgment of the value of material welfare in the specific forms contributed by modern technology; or in their appraisal of effects of modern technology on capital stock, viewed broadly as capacity for desirable growth in the future. But if we consider the effective consensus of a modern society, through its successive generations, the estimate of the net contribution of technological innovation is positive and high; and likely to remain so with better balancing of conventional and nonconventional costs and returns.

III. Contribution of Economic Growth to Technological Innovation

The discussion above centered on the contribution of technological innovations to economic growth, stressing their dominant role in the increase of per capita product, in the major transformation in conditions of work and of life, and in the institutional structure of modern societies. But the association is two-directional: economic growth contributes to a greater flow of technological innovation. The combination of a contribution of growth to further innovation with the contribution of past innovations to growth forms a continuous and self-reinforcing mechanism—subject to limits, but sustainable by continuous feedback between growth and technological change. In this section we comment on the contribution of growth to the flow of technology, the latter again largely viewed as the flow of major innovations.

In its IA phase, a major technological innovation is initiated by a fairly clear perception of a need, requiring some new element of technology, and of the capacity to supply this element effectively. It is marked by a subphase, in which the technological task posed is worked out. It terminates with the first economically successful application. The ingredients, present in different proportions throughout the IA phase, are technological knowledge servicing inventive capacity, an overt or potentially large need or demand, and entrepreneurial ability to mobilize and manage the economic resources involved. It is in the diffusion phase that many of the necessary social and institutional adjustments are made, a host of minor improvements and inventions emerge, and other effects assume substantial magnitudes, with their specific characteristics more fully revealed. In dealing with the contribution of economic growth to the enhanced flow of major technological innovations, we shall be concerned with the impact of the former on additions to knowledge in the pre-conception phase, and on the supply of technological capacity, perception of need, and supply of entrepreneurial talent in the IA phase—not with the diffusion phase.

In discussing the effects of economic growth on further technological innovation, the initial argument may be put simply. If modern economic growth is due, in good part, to the productivity-raising effects of technological innovation, and if the societies involved recognize this connection and consider its results desirable, they will presumably use resources, augmented by past growth, to induce further technological innovation. The societies will base these uses on several judgments. Given ever-present large or potential demand for more goods, they will consider the value of enhancing the stock of basic knowledge and thus the broader technological base from which inventions and improvements can be made. They will judge the value of increasing the supply, and strengthening the motivation, of would-be inventors and discoverers. They will weigh the value of stimulating the supply and facilitating the emergence of necessary entrepreneurship. Both the pioneer and follower countries in modern technology and modern economic growth would certainly incline toward such uses of resources—the follower countries modifying the available technological innovations to suit their own resource endowment, and then attempting to pioneer in new fields to catch up with or surpass the leader. Assuming that such uses of resources by modern societies, and the policies adopted, are well conceived, the resulting enhancement of the rate of additions to the stock of useful knowledge, to inventive capacity, to entrepreneurial talent should, all other conditions being equal, augment the flow of further innovations.

This two-way connection between the contributions of technological innovation and economic growth is obvious enough. All societies that recognize a high positive yield of any given use of resources ordinarily attempt to employ part of the proceeds to enhance such advantageous uses. And the literature of economic history, and of history of science and technology, is full of references to attempts by modern societies, since the seventeenth century, to further the growth of natural sciences and useful arts. They have encouraged academies and scientific organizations, established new universities for the natural sciences, rewarded inventors with prizes and patents, and instituted a host of measures based on a recognition of the connection between economic growth and the widening application of a growing stock of useful knowledge to production problems. There has been a long evolution in the social recognition of this connection between the technological innovations and economic growth, and in the changing institutional and ideological framework that conditioned social attitudes to science, technology, and innovations. But practical problems of optimal selection of means of enhancing further technological innovation aside, the linkage between the growth-promoting experience of past innovations and the innovation-promoting consequences of past growth is quite obvious in modern societies.

A related general argument would stress the effect of accumulated *experience,* and institutional innovations, through which modern economic growth may stimulate further technological innovations. The experience with past innovations has presumably yielded new ways of handling not only the organizational problems involved in the movement from conception to first successful application, but also those involved in the development of basic science and its connections with applied science. Hence, all other conditions being equal, the experience yield of technological innovation-based economic growth should facilitate a greater flow of further technological innovations in the future. If the obstacles to such further innovation that may also be the result of past economic growth are not increasing, the observation provides another general argument for expecting that economic growth will enhance the further flow of technological innovation—even apart from the greater volume of resources for that purpose and the public policy designed for that end.

But modern economic growth influences further technological innovation in other ways. A somewhat less obvious, but crucial connection, is indicated by the major role that wide application of new technology plays in yielding a variety of tested knowledge and new tools not previously available, relating to the particular aspect of nature that underlies the new technology. Modern science, characteristically, has always been stimulated by new data and new tools. If we recognize that applications of new technology (or of old in new combinations) provide science with new data, new tools, and new puzzles; that, in response to these stimuli, science may generate new discoveries and new insights; and that, on the basis of the latter, new technological opportunities relevant to potentially large demands may be glimpsed, to be realized in new inventions and technological innovations—we observe another connection between past technological changes in their introduction and diffusion in economic growth, and a flow of new technological innovations. That this later flow is likely to be at a greater rate than the earlier does not follow directly from the preceding argument. But it would follow if we argue further that, in modern economic growth, cumulative advance of applied technology means a greater flow of new data, new tools, and new puzzles—and thus a greater stimulus to the advance of science, and to the related further advances in invention and technological innovation.

In view of the importance of scientific knowledge in modern technology and some tendency in the literature to draw a sharp line of division between science and technology, assuming separate lines of cumulation in the two, it may be useful to restate the argument just advanced.[9] The argument consists of the following theses. First, modern science, in its attention to data and puzzles yielded by practical production problems is distinctive; and a connection may be drawn between the observation of production practices and some major scientific discoveries. To cite an early illustration: observation of the limited capacity of pumps led (in the seventeenth century) to the discovery of the earth's atmosphere and its pressure. Second, whatever science discovers or generalizes about, and it does so about tested aspects of behavior of nature, is grist to the mill of technology, for the latter is essentially manipulation of the forces of nature for man's purposes. Hence, no matter how variable the gap in time may be between scientific discovery and technological application, the greater knowledge about behavior of nature will eventually be found relevant to some practical application. Third, once successful application in the form of a major technological innovation is made, it is usually found that the knowledge of the process and material involved in the earlier science discovery is *incomplete* from the technological

---

9. These comments on effects of the wide application of technological innovations on further growth of science (furthering, in turn, more technological innovation) are the reflections of an amateur: no economist is competent to deal with such connections. They are based on general reading, not expert knowledge. Yet in this important, still to be cultivated, field, even amateur conjectures may be useful in suggesting intriguing connections and perhaps stimulating more thorough consideration.

In addition to many of the books and studies mentioned in footnotes 1 and 2, and general references in the history of science and technology, I was much influenced by three monographs not mentioned so far: I. Bernard Cohen, *Science, Servant of Man* (Boston: Little Brown, 1948); W. Rupert Maclaurin, *Invention and Innovation in the Radio Industry* (New York: Macmillan, 1949), particularly chapters I–IV, dealing with the movement from scientific discovery to technological application (and effects of the latter on increased knowledge); and D.S.L. Cardwell, *From Watt to Clausius: The Rise of Thermodynamics in the Early Industrial Age* (London: Heinemann, 1971). No claim to even a moderately wide coverage of the field is intended.

standpoint, although no additional knowledge was needed in establishing the original discovery or finding. Fourth, such additional knowledge, and new tools made economically possible through mass application of the innovation, may, and usually do, provide new data, new insights, new puzzles. Thus, the use of the Savery and particularly the Newcomen atmospheric engines, a technological application of the discovery of the atmosphere in the preceding century, led to the basic improvements by Watt, which replaced the atmospheric with a true steam engine. The development of the latter to a high pressure type and the observation of increased efficiency at higher pressures led to puzzles, which in their scientific resolution yielded the thermodynamics branch of modern physics (with its laws of conservation of energy, and of entropy). A similar learning process in the course of mass application can be illustrated in other fields by the Edison effect, or the discovery of the way short rays are transmitted via the ionosphere—with obvious stimuli for modern physics and astronomy. Fifth, the further advance of science provides bases for new technologies; and so the chain continues to mass applications, more data, more tools, more puzzles, and so on.

The argument above is not in contradiction with the observation of differences in characteristics between scientists and technologists; or with the historical fact that some countries, like the United States in the nineteenth and early twentieth centuries, made no great contributions to basic science and yet were leaders in invention and technological advance; while others, like France, were much greater contributors to basic science than to new technology. The differences in the approach to problems between scientists and technologist-inventors, and the corresponding differences in their personal characteristics and backgrounds, are, if anything, in partial support of the proposition above that mass application results in much new knowledge. Apparently the setting of the problem in basic science often does not require fully tested knowledge about *technologically* important characteristics—even though the latter, when established, do provide food for further scientific thought. Thus Hertz, establishing the existence of short rays, in accordance with the prediction of Maxwell's theory, was not induced to inquire precisely how these rays were transmitted through space. Nor is the difference in national identity of the locus of advance in basic science and in technology surprising:

given the transnational character of science, any nation that is capable of understanding it can build on it; and the new technology, even if it is based on new science, may well be more easily developed in a country other than the pioneer in the scientific advance. The same difference may occur between the locus of technological advance and of science based on the knowledge yield of the former; thermodynamics was formulated in France (by Carnot), in Germany (by Clausius), and only partly in England (by Joule and Kelvin)—and yet England was the major developer of the steam engine. The argument is simply that in the development of modern technology, the common base of the economic growth of developed countries, an important feedback relation exists between development of science and technology and economic growth, and between economic growth and further development of science and technological innovation. The argument holds on an international scale, with allowance for time lags and for differences in national locus between the several links in the connection.

The hypothesis just advanced bears also upon the question whether, with enlargement of scale, the activity yielding additions to new knowledge and new technology is subject to diminishing or increasing returns. Evidence is available showing that modern societies devote an increasing proportion of their resources to augmenting the supply of scientists and technologists. The growth in numbers, and in level of advanced training, of scientists, engineers, and high-level technologists—the group capable of adding both to the growth of natural science and to the flow of inventions, improvements, and other ways of advancing material technology, has been rapid. Indeed, this growth has been greater than that of almost any other occupation (except that directly connected with a completely new branch of production, e.g., computer specialists). If these augmented talents were engaged, in increasing density, in a circumscribed field of science or technology, diminishing returns could be expected. But scientific discovery moves from one field to another, and it is induced to shift its focus and sometimes revise its theoretical structure by an accumulation of new data, new tools, or new puzzles provided by the unexpected lessons of mass application of major technological innovations, themselves perhaps resulting from an earlier scientific advance. Invention and innovation also tend to move from sector to sector, not only because of stimuli from the new scientific discoveries but also because of the exhaustion of cost-reducing opportunities and of demand responsiveness in sectors in which technological innovations of earlier days had time to diffuse widely. The richer promises are elsewhere and are often provided by new types of demand connected with changed conditions of life and work. These points, relating to the need or demand component in the triad involved in major technological innovation, are discussed below; but here, in dealing with the rate of return to an increased supply of providers of new knowledge and new technology, we note the tendency, and inducement, to shift from one field to another. This shift should help to avoid diminishing returns that could be expected with increasing supplies in a narrowly circumscribed field of science or technology.

The answer to the question of the dynamics of returns (diminishing, constant, increasing) to increased supply of participants in the process of adding to basic and applied knowledge and to technological advance, and to a greatly increased flow of material resource input into the tasks, depends partly upon the tests one would apply. The *impression* is one of great acceleration in the nineteenth and twentieth centuries in the rate of discoveries in natural sciences, in the marked multiplication of disciplines and cross-disciplines, and in the flow of major technological innovations. Furthermore, the greater density of the network of science and modern technology provides more favorable conditions for the generation of new ideas and inventions more rapidly. The closer relation between science and technology, reflected in the technological breakthroughs by scientists addressing themselves to technological tasks, can be illustrated by the development of nylon and of the transistor. But all these are impressions, and no proper measure of output and input, particularly of the former, are available. Such data as counts of scientific papers, or lists of major discoveries, inventions, or patents, are all limited by the wide diversity in the magnitude of the unit and the difficulty of interpreting a consensus on "major" in terms of a narrow range of magnitude. Such measures as numbers of persons engaged, with adequate levels of training, and even of material resources input, run into difficulties because of possible variance in selectivity and innate capacity of the people involved—surely an important aspect in a production process in which creativity is a major component.

No firm answer can, therefore, be given. Still a moderate statement can be made: despite the large increase in the supply of people and resources to the knowledge-augmenting and technology-enhancing activities, diminishing returns, if present, did not prevent the continuance of a vigorous rate of flow of discoveries, inventions, and technological innovations. This observation applies in the international field of modern science and technology—not necessarily to any one country. As already indicated, in some countries the flow of technological innovations did accelerate with entry into modern economic growth; in others, the rate of technological innovation, compared with earlier phases of their economic growth in modern times, may have declined.

What are the effects of modern economic growth on further technological innovation, in so far as demand for its products and supply of requisite entrepreneurship are concerned? An initial examination of this question suggests several impeding effects. As already noted, reduction in costs of a final consumer good, through preceding innovation, may be such that even marked cuts through further innovation cannot be expected to stimulate greater demand. Thus the need, or market for, further innovations may be damped by effects of past growth. Or, second, economic growth based on past technological innovations and resulting in marked enlargement of the scale of the plant and the firm, may make for entrepreneurship more conservative with respect to further innovations—particularly if the industries are oligopolistic or monopolistic. Finally, modern economic growth, in market economies, has resulted in a substantial rise in the share of the governmental, public sector in total product and resources; and the responsiveness of the public entrepreneur to further technological innovations may be more limited than that of entrepreneurs in the private sector. The three observations just made cover wide and complex topics, on which substantial literature exists. We merely offer a few comments to stress that, as usual, the process even of modern growth has not only self-sustaining but also self-curbing elements.

To illustrate the first observation, consider the case of cotton textiles. The technological innovations, which extended from mechanization of spinning in the 1770s to mechanization of weaving in the 1830s (the two most labor-consuming operations), combined with various auxiliary and complementary innovations, resulted in the conversion of cotton textiles from what was a high-priced luxury to a low-unit-price, mass-use commodity. Once the new technology of producing cotton textiles was established and improved, further technological innovations could reduce the low cost further—and particularly provide some competitive advantage to the pioneering firms. But, by and large, opportunities for substantial gains from further technological innovations, in *that* field, were decisively narrowed; and were certainly much narrower than opportunities for technological advance and innovation in other fields, in which current technology and the high costs of final product left much room for gain from an innovation. This did not mean that technological advance in the light textiles industry ceased. But much of it came as diffusion of technological change in other fields (e.g., automatic controls over the spindles and looms) or in the form of different textile products, such as rayon and later nylon. There was no pressure for further major technological innovations within the cotton textile industry proper.

Several aspects of this illustration deserve note, because it typifies the slowing down of incentives to further innovation in industries that reach technological maturity within a given framework of current technology. First, the loss of incentives to innovate was *relative,* not absolute—in the sense that potential returns from further innovation became more promising in other sectors. Thus, assuming a stock of uncommitted inventive and capital resources seeking promising opportunities, the comparative advantages of using them in the mature industry would be far lower than in the past when it was growing. Second, relevant technological innovations that do occur, may originate elsewhere and be introduced into the industry; or may provide a base for the production of a different product, serving the same purpose, thus setting up a new, different, and competing industry. Third, the relevant innovations that occur at this stage are not usually managed by the entrepreneurial talent within the mature industry. The developers of rayon and nylon were not the entrepreneurs in the cotton textile industry. With the latter reaching maturity, and lack of great potential returns from technological innovations within the old technological framework, the successful entrepreneurs might seek other sources of greater returns—either in the protected markets of the colonies, or by raising the protective barriers of the large domestic market, or by shifting the industry to regions with appreciably lower labor costs and easier labor supply. The last statement illustrates an important point. Maturity of an industry generally means large economic magnitudes, and the power to exert political pressure within the economy or to exploit differentials in supplies of productive factors. These powers are not operative, or are of lesser importance, in the early phases of major rapid technological changes within a new industry.

As already indicated, economic growth means large scale of plant and firm, with the structure of fixed costs and marginal returns leading to monopoly or oligopoly in many modern industries and to public regulation of some. What are the consequences for entrepreneurial response to invention and innovation? As MacLaurin indicated (see p. 251 of the volume cited in footnote 9 above), in a truly competitive industry there would be no research, for there would be only windfall profits; and returns from an innovation could be derived by a pioneer only if protected by a patent (or secret), i.e., by monopolistic power. And it is true that a large-scale firm and monopoly provide opportunities for internal research (e.g., DuPont work on nylon) that are not available to smaller and competitively pressed units. But in the case of monopoly, or even oligopoly, technological innovation can be slowed down by absence of competitive pressure. Monopolistic concerns, unlike others, can delay innovation even when its technological and long-term economic feasibility is established. Such a delay, while avoiding the destructive effects on capital and labor in uses that would be displaced, does represent a slowing down in the rate of technological *innovation*. Finally, the rigid rules under which the regulated public utilities must operate may well inhibit adventurous entrepreneurship that is often required for particular types of innovation, or at least inhibit it more than in industries not subject to this special type of regulation.

The comments above should have been put in the form of questions, for no clear answer can be provided here. But one may suggest a similarity to the effects of slowing down of demand for a consumer good that is the product of past innovations. In the latter case we observed that a loss of incentives for further innovation in the *given*, "mature," field, results in the focus of vigorous technological innovation shifting to another field. This may be true also in the slowing down of technological innovation in a given field because of the existence of a monopoly or oligopoly in it. Unless they are strictly regulated, the dominance of the large concerns in a given field need not prevent them from technological innovation and from research and development outlays in *other,* possibly (but not necessarily) related field. The two sets of cases are parallel in the sense that relaxation of pressure for technological innovation—either because of slowing of demand, or because of attainment of a relatively protected position—may retard the flow of technological innovation in a specific field. But with resources available for innovation, the focus may shift, with accelerated growth following in another field. One may still ask whether this combination of retardation due to dominance in a given field, perhaps before the maximum reduction of real costs through technological innovation has been reached, with a shift of resources for innovation to another field, is an optimal outcome. Policy remedies would depend upon the answer. But the answer would involve difficult comparisons of lost or delayed opportunities in one field with accelerated opportunities in others.

The growth in the share of government—in product, labor force, capital—in the market economies in the course of modern economic growth was due to several factors. Urbanization created situations in which basic services to urban population—in much greater volume than required by the more thinly spread rural population—had to be provided by the public sector rather than sold on the market (police, sanitation, health, etc.). Certain types of capital investment, which could not be handled by, or entrusted to, the private sector, had to be taken over by government (highways, port facilities, and in many countries the railroads, shipping, and airlines, atomic energy, space exploration). Education and health services, not geared to the paying capacity of the recipients, were an ever-growing responsibility of government in a modern society. Finally, the participation of *developed* countries in acute armed conflicts meant devotion of large material resources to defense. The question posed here is whether an increasing proportion of resources in the public sector, without the profit motive and without competitive pressures for efficiency, has not meant a lack of stimuli for significant technological advance. In that sense development in the market economies might have narrowed the area for further technological advance.

The question is strictly relevant only to the civilian part of the government sector. One may assume that international competition and tension provide sufficient pressure so that the incentive for technological innovation in weaponry and other components of defense production has not diminished; and is probably not inferior to the competitive pressures within the private sector. And the evidence on the major technological breakthroughs, associated with the war and defense industries, some of large value for civilian production in the longer run, is impressive. It is hardly an accident that World War I accelerated the spread of the internal combustion engine in automobile and airplane transportation; or that World War II is associated with the development of atomic power, radar communications, electronic controls and computers, and the space industry. Two sets of questions may still be raised concerning the war- and defense-related industries. The first is as to the level of efficiency, in the absence of cost controls and economic pressures as great as those in the private sector. The second is in regard to the *net* contribution of an advance in military fields to technological innovations relevant to peace-type production and needs. We are in no position to examine the first set of questions, which would involve detailed quantitative analysis under properly set control conditions. The second should be examined in the light of the fact that defense purposes emphasize technology of transport, communication, power, and strength of materials—all areas of technology potentially and directly relevant to civilian use. One last point: it is distinctive, and indispensably typical, of modern economic growth that the developed countries are ready to devote large material resources to defense purposes, substituting the material for human resources as much as possible. And this explains the extremely high technological level sought under the competitive pressures of international strain among the *developed* countries (the pressure would not be as great in the strain between developed and less developed countries).

The question about the effect of the increasing share of government on incentives for further technological change relates more properly to the civilian components of government product. The answer would involve an examination of the functioning of the civilian government, and the inducements to technological entrepreneurship that are provided. One would also have to examine both the relatively limited segments of the public nonmilitary activities that are specifically directed at basic and technological research—as a common service to society; and those that encourage higher education, a prerequisite for much of research and technological advance. The question is raised to indicate its relevance in the wider field of inquiry that would deal with feedback effects of economic growth, stemming largely from past technological innovations, on further flow of the latter.

In discussing the effects of economic growth on further technological innovation, we stressed the positive feedback of what might be broadly called *learning* aspects of economic growth—learning about benefits of past innovations as a rationale for more resources and better policy to encourage them, learning by experience better ways of generating and successfully channeling technological innovations, and, particularly important, learning from the new data, new tools, new puzzles generated in the mass application of innovations. In contrast, in dealing with the effects via demand and entrepreneurial responses, we tended to stress only the *inhibiting* ones. However, we also indicated that the common response in the private sector to such limiting consequences of economic growth on further technological innovation was a shift in focus. Even in the public sector, within the nonmilitary component, there has been a movement toward greater technological innovation in fields in which the new technology, either because of its dangers or because of its greater social rather than private return, had to be handled by the government (as with atomic energy, space exploration, or geophysical research).

In connection with shifts of technological innovation to new fields of consumer demand, we have already noted that economic growth did have some effects that constituted a positive feedback. But we should add a further note about several aspects of economic growth that constitute positive contributions to further technological innovation of the type that yields new consumer goods. Thus, for one thing, the concentration of population in urban centers, one of the corollaries of modern economic growth, exposed consumers to a demonstration effect not found in the countryside. Also, the anonymity in the cities, contrasted with personal knowledge and status identification in the more settled society of the countryside, permitted consumer choices uninhibited by traditional status restraints. Furthermore, the availability within modern cities (and eventually in the countryside) of sources of industrial power for consumer purposes encouraged the invention of new consumer goods that would use such power. A clear illustration is the proliferation of new consumer durable goods dependent upon a continuous supply of electric power, originally provided almost exclusively for illumination purposes. Thus, the shortages of domestic labor, associated with cessation of migration from the country-side, created a demand for substitutes for cooking, cleaning, wash-ing, and similar purposes. This demand that might otherwise have been met (and was partly met) by development of commercial cooking and baking, commercial laundries, commercial cleaning establishments, etc., stimulated technological innovation which supplied fractional electric power equipment for many domestic services (and later even for recreation devices, ranging from the gramophone, to the radio, to television). Finally, one should note that it was part and parcel of the social and ideological corollaries of modern economic growth that material welfare was assigned a high priority; and that consequently the consumer was quite re-sponsive in recognizing the advantages of a new consumer good when it emerged in the course of a technological innovation. De-mand was thus created by supply without a substantial lag; and often with a speed far exceeding the expectations of the innovators.

IV. Concluding Comments

This paper dealt with relations between technological innovation and modern economic growth, against the background of the his-torical experience of non-Communist developed countries. By technological innovation we mean application of new elements in material technology, i.e., in the knowledge and capacity to manip-ulate nature for human ends—more specifically here, for eco-nomic production. By economic growth we mean the sustained rise in the supply and diversity of economic goods to the population, under acceptable rules of social and economic organization. Be-cause of the wide scope of the subject, the difficulties in establish-ing quantitative weights, and the limitations of space and com-petence, the discussion was perforce too brief; and at some points only raised questions, or merely noted a particular aspect of the problem. Far from attempting to represent an adequate summary of the state of knowledge as found in the literature, the discussion was limited to reflections by an observer who has worked on quantitative aspects of modern economic growth, while entertain-ing a strong interest in the contributions of technology to it.

Given the brevity and uneven character of the discussion, a detailed summary is hardly necessary. But it might help to list the major observations.

1. Technological innovation played a key role in the rise of product and productivity in modern economic growth; and also induced major transformations of conditions of work and life.

2. These transformations were required to channel new technology effectively, and meant organizational changes in the earlier institutions that governed production. The resulting changes in conditions of work for the active participants were a major element in changing conditions of life. Thus, technological innovations required innovations in social structure and even in prevailing attitudes. They also required adjustment to resulting displacement of resources in earlier, and obsolete, uses.

3. A major technological innovation, i.e., one with a substantial economic impact, involves a sequence of phases stretching over a long life cycle. It takes time to pass from the perception of a new technological possibility to economic mass production, requiring economic and social changes; and to reach the period of slowdown and obsolescence. Of the four phases suggested—pre-conception, initial application (IA), diffusion (D), and slowdown and obsolescence (SO), the IA and D phases alone account, on the average, for half a century. The phase sequence, the differences in input-output relations in the different phases, and the phase differences in the interplays between the technological, economic, and social adjustments, bear clearly upon analysis, policy consideration, and prognosis.

4. The clustering of even major technological innovations into groups of related changes (stemming from exploitation of one source of power, or from a new industrial material, or from the interrelation of functions within a production process), combined with the interplay between innovations and the social and institutional adjustments to them, lengthens the sequence of distinctive phases and adds to their complexity.

5. The focus of technological innovations shifts over time from one sector of the economy to another, and creates new sectors. Their immediate impact is always unequal among sectors, and hence among social groups in the economy. This inequality of impact is itself a social and economic problem that requires adjustments.

6. Because of the combination of conventional economic inputs with required changes in conditions of work and life, and because of the combination of conventional economic outputs with possible nonconventional byproducts of technologically-induced economic growth, an adequate quantitative gauge of the *net* contribution of technological innovations to economic growth is still to be established. Current measures of total factor productivity, while possibly reflecting largely technological changes, are either limited to conventional input and output, or involve a variety of *ad hoc,* and not fully tested, assumptions as bases for inclusion of nonconventional inputs or byproducts.

7. Such a net measure may not be of much value, since a variety of elements, in both inputs and outputs, is needed to give meaning to the comparison. Yet the search for such a net measure helps to focus the analysis. Provisionally, one may justifiably argue that the social valuation of technologically-facilitated, modern, economic growth is high and positive; with the critical reactions reflecting responses to temporary lags in adjustment.

8. Technologically-induced economic growth, having been attained, stimulates further technological innovation. Society is stimulated through the learning of past benefits, and the effort made to allocate more resources and provide more favorable institutional conditions for further innovation. Past experience with technological innovations may make for better ways to develop successful innovations in the future. A particularly important stimulus is the learning, through mass application of recent new technology, yielding new data, new tools, new insights and puzzles to natural science, and helping to widen the base provided by the latter to further technological breakthroughs and innovations.

9. Economic growth hastens the maturity of the older fields by slowing down growth of final demand for their products. It may also limit the conditions for responsive innovative entrepreneurship in the established and modernized fields because of the large scale of the firm, and possible dominance of a few in an oligopolistic or monopolistic situation. Furthermore, the rise in the share of the public sector is a factor, since in its nonmilitary areas it may not be easily responsive to technological innovation. The slowing down of the older sectors, once modernized through technological innovation, helps to shift the focus of innovation to other sectors. And these shifts to new sources of power, new materials, new types

of producer equipment, and, in an important way, new types of consumer goods, help to maintain a high or increasing pace of technological innovation; and a high or increasing pace of economic growth.

We conclude the paper with brief, tentative impressions of the current state of the field, insofar as it bears on the study of economic consequences and origins of technological innovation; and even more tentative suggestions regarding directions of further work.

The importance of both science and technological innovation for modern economic growth must have become apparent by the middle of the nineteenth century (if not earlier), when the development of steam power and its application to railroads, besides other less important technological innovations, were seen to provide new bases for rapid growth and transformation of modern societies. The policies of some governments in planting technological institutes and otherwise encouraging science and technology testify to this recognition. Yet, in both the classical and (implicitly) the Marxian schools within the economic discipline, technological progress was viewed as a feeble barrier to the expected exhaustion of natural, non-reproducible resources (acting via pressure on profits and capital accumulation, and via limitation on reduction of labor inputs into required means of subsistence). The failure of the resulting long-term prognoses of both schools, apparent by the last quarter of the nineteenth century, only led to extruding the subject of economic growth (and the related topic of technology) from the accepted corpus of the discipline. Economics concentrated on the problems of limited means to various ends, within a short-term framework in which technology, institutions, tastes of consumers, were all supposed to be given, i.e., fixed. With few exceptions, of which Schumpeter's monographs just before World War I were most conspicuous, the problems of economic growth were neglected, until their reintroduction, largely after World War II. And the short-term orientation of the economic discipline led to a neglect of empirical and quantitative work on long-term trends and macroquantities. Such work was kept partly alive in the concern with business cycles and then revived, with impressively explosive growth, in the late 1930s, and again largely after World War II.

The explanation of these past trends in the treatment of problems of economic growth, and the associated problems of technological change, is less important here than the consequence for the field of our interests. The consequence was obviously a failure to accumulate economic data relevant to the effects and origins of technological innovation and a limited stock of analytical studies, most of them recent. In particular, there has been no attempt to link technology to the basic output and input statistics of the developed countries. Subclassifications relating output, labor force, capital, etc. to technological innovation are missing from our aggregate measures. The number of economists engaged in the study of technological aspects of economic growth has been, and is, quite small. Even the studies in economic history that would provide systematic accounts of the emergence, development, and phasing in the spread of innovations (single, or in clusters) are few. If there is now a really serious concern with the contributions and sources of technological innovation, with the prospects of specific policy action in the field, then much systematic work must be initiated on the quantitative aspects of the problem, and implicitly on the analytical formulations that would be needed for, and then modified by, such quantitative analysis.

In this development of further quantitative work, linkages with the already accumulated and established measures, country-wide or industry-wide, would be particularly important. The possibility of distinguishing within total output, labor force, and capital of the country or of an industry, components associated with recent, not so recent, and much older technology, would add immensely to the quantitative base for the study of the interrelations between technological innovation and modern economic growth. A more systematic analysis of the accumulated experience with research and development outlays and of the costs of innovations would be possible. And systematic historical accounts of the emergence and spread of clusters of major innovations should be encouraged. Such an account of the spread of steam, or of electric power, or of the automobile, each of which meant a major addition to the productive capacity of modern societies, major transformations of conditions of work and life, and much social innovation in the process of adjustment, would illustrate the complex interrelations and the sequential phases involved.

The list could easily be expanded, but would then run the danger of conveying, unwarrantedly, an impression of careful selection and testing. These are only *ad hoc* suggestions, can be no more than that, and are hardly worth multiplication. The main burden of these comments is to stress the long neglect of the field, and the consequences for the current state of our knowledge. The illuminating and intriguing monographs of the handful of economists who have worked on technological innovation are only a beginning. A more sustained volume of systematic quantitative analysis, closely linked to the flow of basic data, and of monographic work on the complex interrelations susceptible of historical study, would add to our understanding, perspective, and to the stock of empirical findings needed for adequate analysis and policy consideration.

Notes on the Study of
Economic Growth of Nations

1. Introduction

The recent quarter-century has witnessed an explosive rise in the
flow of basic data on the economic performance and growth of
nations and an enormous addition to the stock of descriptive and
analytical studies in this field—one that has been neglected in the
discipline of economics since the second half of the nineteenth century. The international compilations, such as the United Nations
Demographic Yearbook and the *Yearbook of National Accounts
Statistics,* are bulging with detailed demographic and economic accounts for scores of nations for which hardly a single statistic was
available in pre–World War II days. Rich complementary flows
have come from the specialized international agencies (ILO,
FAO, WHO, IMF, IBRD, and many others, including the regional UN agencies), let alone the statistical accounts and yearbooks of individual countries—young and old, developed and less
developed. Many new journals in the field have emerged and
flourished, with the present journal an outstanding example. New
courses relating to economic growth, modernization, etc., have
evolved and augmented the offerings by university departments

Reprinted from Manning Nash, ed., "Essays in Economic Development
and Cultural Change in Honor of Bert F. Hoselitz." *January 1977 Supplement to Economic Development and Cultural Change*, vol. 25, pp. 300–313.

of economics, sociology, and political science, and a large mono-graphic literature has developed. As a result, the old field has been revived and reinvigorated. Moreover, this flow of new data and new studies was concurrent with a rate of economic growth in both developed and less developed countries that was significantly higher than that in the past—qualified though this growth experience may be by its shortcomings relative to some desirable goals.

A fair summary of, or a balanced reflection on, the major results of this explosive addition to our data and knowledge would make insuperable demands on the expertise and judgment of any one scholar. By contrast, one could much more easily point out the flaws, gaps, and limitations of both data and analysis. This is only to be expected, considering the immensity and diversity of the field, the enormous demand for a wide variety of adequate data, the limitations of the analytical tools, and the changing pressures of public concern. Still, if the comments below may suggest that I succumbed to the temptation of an easier choice, I maintain that it may be appropriate on this occasion to concentrate on the tasks ahead indicated by the gaps in our present, tested knowledge. These loom large precisely because past work, with its variety of findings, has taught us a great deal and has exposed major lacunae that were not apparent before.

The brief discussion that follows reflects judgments of an individual scholar on the major gaps and difficulties—as I see them—that lie ahead in the further development of the field. While the restrictive choices may fail of acceptance and the positions taken may seem to be inadequately formulated, the comments at least implicitly reveal the limits of our present knowledge in the field of comparative growth of nations.

2. Supply and Quality of Data

A major problem arises in the collection of adequate data. In the first place, comprehensive and articulated measures (and I shall concentrate on them) of a country's performance and economic growth require data that can be supplied only by the country's government, assisted as it may be by private corporate bodies or individual scholars. Second, the capacity to supply such data of acceptable quality and adequate range is partly a function of the country's social and economic development and partly a function of the value placed by government on unimpeded supply and interpretation of such data. The former is obviously more limited in the less developed countries (LDCs); and the latter is far more limited under dictatorships, Communist or other, than in democratically organized countries (allowing for a range within this dichotomy). Third, it follows that the supply and quality of the data required as raw materials for such basic economic measures as national product, consumption, employment, and the like, with the requisite industrial, occupational, income size, and other categories, are likely to be much more limited for the LDCs than for the economically developed, and more limited for countries with restrictive governments than for democracies in which flow of information and attempts at interpretation, critical or favorable, are not inhibited.

The import of these brief statements is fully recognized if one realizes that even in economically developed, democratic societies, the supply and quality of data needed for the basic economic measures are not without limitations. As to quality, much of the information is provided by fallible individuals, corporate bodies, and the like, and, consequently, biases of ignorance or of reluctance to provide full information will persist. Moreover, the data are collected and processed by bureaucrats who, despite their high educational level, may not be fully responsive to the demands of inquiring scholars. And the data, a costly product, will not always be provided, even if the scholarly analysts manage in good time to demonstrate the critical need for them. But in economically developed countries (DCs), one can at least count on easier quantifiability of the economic activities and on greater correspondence between the analytical concepts in the economics discipline and the real processes. If these societies are also democratic, one can count on the ready appreciation of the need for the data by the respondents and hence on their cooperation, and on the contribution of free scholarly analysis and discussion in resolving problems that arise in reconciling observational raw data with analytical concepts. If, even so, existing data are inadequate for newly emerging problems and needed revisions of concepts, the available intellectual resources may be applied to some illustrative or ad hoc solutions, pending the long-term accretion of the relevant basic statistics.

Contrast this with the situation in an LDC. In such a country, with the distinction between economic activity and life in general not clear-cut, much of the former is not easily quantifiable—particularly in terms of analytical concepts and classifications usually geared to developed economies. Resources, particularly intellectual, are scanty, as is the experience with collection of quantitative and nationwide information in the past. Even if full and free discussion of the results is encouraged, the necessary expertise is possessed by all too few, and this limits the range of the analysis; and, furthermore, native intellectual resources are subject to a substantial brain drain. The accumulation of studies bearing on economic performance and growth of the country, which might provide some guidance in the use of data to derive meaningful economic measures, is almost nonexistent. Thus, even assuming freedom of information and a genuine interest in the broader aspects of economic performance and growth, the supply and quality of data for most LDCs are quite deficient. Since much of what is published and made available rests on flimsy foundations, its use is subject to critical caution.

The situation has been complicated in recent decades by what might be called politicization of the whole field of national economic and social accounts and their analysis—whether in demography, economics, or sociology. This may take the milder form of viewing demographic and economic national accounts, no matter how poor in quality, as indispensable perquisites of national sovereignty—but with sensitivity to such political implications as led to conflicts about regional population totals in the successive censuses in Nigeria; or those involved in claiming credit for successful economic performance and in offering excuses for economic failure. Or, in the restrictive Communist dictatorships, it may take the more extreme form of viewing basic economic and social data as weapons in the international ideological struggle—so that tight limits are imposed on their availability, let alone on the freedom of evaluation and critical review. Furthermore, in the field of economic data (perhaps less so in demographic), adherence to Marxian concepts means exclusion of various economic activities (largely services), which are viewed in an ideologically less restrictive approach as important components in total economic product; and such exclusion obviously results in a paucity of data relating to the omitted activities.

When basic social data are viewed as weapons in conflict-prone social and political issues, with conviction and conflict varying only in strength, the situation in the supply of these data is similar to that in some natural science fields in the past centuries of religious conflicts and constraints. Thus, the very drives that concentrated so much attention on economic growth and contributed greatly to the increased flow of relevant data have paradoxically also sharply restricted the supply of data for some regions and adversely affected the quality of the data and of the measures derived from them for many parts of the world outside the range of economically developed democracies.

To illustrate these statements, I refer briefly to the impressive recent compilation by the United Nations of national economic accounts.[1] Turning to the most comprehensive summary table 6A of volume 3, pages 132–33 (for gross domestic product, omitting the services of general government and private organizations), we find that it still excludes several Communist countries (China,[2] Democratic Republic of Korea, Democratic Republic of Vietnam, and Mongolia), which, however, account for almost a quarter of the world's population. Furthermore, in order to combine the estimates based on different definitions for the Communist and the non-Communist countries, crude adjustments were made in the more elaborate accounts of the market economies rather than in those of the Communist countries (which would be more difficult, for lack of adequate data).

For the market economies, summary data in volume 3 are plentiful. For example, table 1A, for gross domestic product, total and per capita, for selected years, covers 49 countries in Africa, 40 countries in America (North and South), 35 countries in Asia, 18 countries in Europe, and 9 countries in Oceania. And volumes 1 and 2 contain more detailed accounts for over 100 market economies ranging alphabetically from Argentina to Zambia and with respect to per capita product from the United States to Upper Volta. But how reliable are the underlying data and the

---

1. United Nations, *Yearbook of National Accounts Statistics, 1973,* vols. 1 and 2, *Individual Country Tables,* vol. 3, *International Tables* (New York: United Nations, 1975).

2. This means also the exclusion of Taiwan, which, for political reasons, was omitted from all recent United Nations reports and statistical documents. Yet, for the analysis of economic growth of LDCs, Taiwan is most relevant, for its statistical data are relatively rich and apparently of far more acceptable quality than those for many other LDCs.

resulting estimates for many LDCs? To use a specific illustration, volume 1, pages 201–20, contains tables on gross domestic product for Ethiopia for selected years 1960–72, by industrial source, and in current and constant prices. This is for a country that has never had a complete census of population, in which internal communication and transportation channels are still quite limited, and which has been relatively isolated from, and neglected by, world scholarship. It is far from clear what the estimates, submitted to the United Nations by Ethiopia's government, are based on—estimates that, according to table 4B in volume 3 (p. 108), yield growth rates over the 1960–72 period of 4.2 percent per year in total GDP and 2.0 percent per year in per capita GDP.[3] Similar skepticism is warranted with respect to the more synthetic indexes in volume 3 for less developed regions dominated by countries that, given their history and current level of economic and social development, are not likely to generate a sufficient flow of data of adequate quality.[4] The reasons that may induce governments to submit to international agencies economic estimates that are based on flimsy foundations are a matter for speculation, and are perhaps not relevant here except as reflections of the politicization trend noted above. More important is the fact that the explosive rise in the flow of basic data and of economic measures based on them has, in extending the coverage to the less developed and the Communist countries, seriously affected the quality and comparability of the data and measures. The resultant problems, because of the magnitude of the task involved and the recency of the development, are still to be adequately faced in the study of comparative economic performance and growth of nations.

As indicated, the concentration of the comments above on the LDCs and the ideologically restrictive Communist societies does not mean that the supply and quality of data for the economically

---

3. Curiously, the *World Bank Atlas* (Washington, D.C.: International Bank for Reconstruction and Development, 1974) shows, for gross national product (which would not differ much from gross domestic product) per capita, a growth rate for the same period of 2.6 percent per year (see p. 7).
4. For a discussion of the resulting disagreements among international agencies in their estimates of growth rates for such regions, see my paper "Problems in Comparing Recent Growth Rates for Developed and Less Developed Countries," *Economic Development and Cultural Change* 20, no. 2 (January 1972): 185–209, particularly sec. 2, "Scope and Reliability."

developed democracies are fully adequate. It is important to realize that, in the nature of the sources of social data, empirical analysis in the field always requires adequate knowledge of, and a variety of judgments on, the limitations of observational data in relation to the analytical concepts used. The point of my emphasis is that in the quantitative study of economic growth, in which the comparative approach (over time and in space) is central, the difficulties raised by the supply and quality of data in the case of the LDCs and the Communist economies are particularly formidable.

To be sure, broad aspects of the comparisons may not be significantly affected by the difficulties just noted. Undoubtedly, the per capita economic performance of most LDCs is much lower than, and their industrial structure quite different from, that of most DCs—the two groups properly defined. But for narrower and more interesting questions, for example, in establishing growth rates or changes in industrial structure over recent periods among groups of LDCs, the limitations of the data may prove serious. In that case, a major effort must be invested in critical scrutiny of the data for individual countries as a basis for acceptance, modification, or rejection. In the longer run, the quality and supply of any body of observational data depend, in large part, on their use and the critical examination to which they are subjected in their continuous conversion by scholars into counterparts of analytically defined concepts and categories. In short, the data must be tested for adequacy for major analytical uses. This is a continuous task in any empirically founded research field and, in the case of the comparative quantitative study of economic growth, a task that, for most LDCs and many Communist countries, is only in its early phases.

3. Innovations, Growth, and Transformations

The high rate of rise in per capita product and the rapidity of structural changes of the economies affected by modern economic growth are associated with application of new knowledge to production problems, that is, technological innovations. The latter affect conditions of work, and hence conditions of life, and often require, for proper channeling, modifications in economic and social institutions that may involve institutional or social innovations.

These could be better designated as transformations, including changes in both structure and institutions. Technological innovations, in any given decade, have a major impact in only a few industries and sectors. Their focus shifts from one generation to the next, from one set of "growth" industries to another. With this differential impact on production sectors, and hence on regions within a country, these innovations also affect relations among countries, altering transport costs, terms of trade, and differential resource endowments.[5]

To realize the pervasiveness of technological innovations in modern economic growth, we need only observe how much of the current output in a DC is either new final products not known a century ago or products created by new processes that employ new tools, materials, or sources of power radically different from those available in the past. The magnitude of the contributions of technological innovations to growth per capita is indicated by the large proportion of the latter accounted for by approximations to total factor productivity. It would be even more marked if one took into account, as is not done now, the effects of the increasing scarcity of natural resources that would have prevailed if there had been no technological progress and had population increased as it has. The concentration of technological innovation at any given time on a limited range of industries of a DC is observed in the changing identity of "growth" industries from one quarter-century to another. And the changing conditions of work and life are revealed by the shifts in the distribution of population and labor force between country and city, between self-employed and employed status, or by levels of education and specialization. The changes in institutional patterns and devices, geared partly to changes in conditions of work and partly to changes in conditions of life, are the subject of a vast historical and disciplinary literature in the social sciences.

Despite the key role of technological innovation in modern

---

5. For a related discussion of technological innovations and adjustments to them in economic growth, see my paper, "Innovations and Adjustments in Economic Growth," reprinted in *Population, Capital, and Growth: Selected Essays* (New York: W. W. Norton, 1973), pp. 185–211, and "Technological Innovations and Economic Growth," in *Technological Innovation: A Critical Review of Current Knowledge,* ed. Patrick Kelly and Melvin Kranzberg, (San Francisco Press, The, San Francisco, 1978). Reprinted in this volume, pp. 56–99.

economic growth, its treatment in economic analysis has been peripheral and has been neglected in the customary collections and treatments of economic data. Adequate analysis and measurement are obviously difficult: here we have a source of increase in production and productivity that yields *results* which we can, although with some effort, approximate. However, the *inputs* into it cannot be easily assayed in meaningful economic terms. Thus, one can estimate the increase in productivity due to supply of illumination services provided by electricity, calculating the inputs of direct and indirect labor per lumen—and comparing them with per lumen inputs of the older illumination industries. But this is clearly an incomplete calculation. Is there a meaningful *economic* relation between the enormous increase in productivity thus calculated and the inputs into the technological innovation—ranging, perhaps, from Faraday's work on electromagnetic induction through a series of major inventions in the later nineteenth century? To be sure, we can say that the resulting savings greatly exceeded the total inputs into the scientific discovery and invention related to the technological innovation (and not included in the conventional measure of inputs). And it is no accident that scientific discoveries are not patentable, for their contributions to output may prove to be incalculably large, if any calculus at all is possible. But this is hardly a basis for adequate treatment of such a productive factor in any analysis, in which determinate relations between input and output must be established.

In some cases, inventions and technological innovations emerge, perhaps after a long search, in response to obvious demand—so that necessity becomes the mother of invention, as was said of the mechanization of cotton spinning in England in the eighteenth century. But even in such cases, a base for adequate analytical treatment is lacking. For there is still the question whether there is a determinate relation among input into search for invention as a response to observably unsatisfied demand, the timing of the response, and the results of the innovation once applied. Casual observation of the historical record casts doubt, since in the case of successful innovations, the results often far exceed the unsatisfied needs as envisaged earlier; and we know so little about the input into unsuccessful innovations. Nor should we overstate the frequency with which major technological innovations are responses to clearly felt needs; and we should not be ready to identify an invention once successful and satisfying obvious needs as a response to antecedent demand that may not have been there. Thus, in view of the relative efficiency of the Newcomen engine and the relatively limited demand for steam power at the time, one may argue that James Watt's major innovations did not come in response to a pressing need but were, rather, the results of the application of a brilliant, inventive mind to a major technological problem, which utilized essentially scientific methods to define the problem. Yet Watt's contributions opened the way to a long series of further major innovations in the application of steam power. Their magnitude far exceeded the magnitude of the "need" as seen not only by Watt's contemporaries but even by scholars of the mid-nineteenth century, John Stuart Mill among others.

This is not the occasion to comment on the difficulties that classical and Marxian economics had in dealing properly with such an incalculable production factor as technological innovation, or on what followed—the exclusion from the corpus of economic analysis of technological changes, as well as of changes in institutions, tastes, etc., as exogenous factors. Only in recent decades, after long neglect (interrupted by Schumpeter's analysis of entrepreneurially directed innovations as the source of economic growth but viewed largely as disruption of a static equilibrium), has analytical work on the economics of technological innovation been resumed; and in more recent years, increasing attention has been directed to the statistics and economics of research and development activities. But even today we do not fully understand the determinants of technological innovations, of the possible connection of the latter with scientific discovery and changed technological potentials, on the one hand, and with entrepreneurial perceptions of possible demand, on the other. Nor are we adequately aware of the feedback from the mass application of technological innovations in the course of modern economic growth, via the emergence of new tools and greater knowledge of the underlying materials and processes, to the basic and applied sciences, stimulating further discoveries and providing new bases for further technological inventions and innovations. Much still remains to be learned from historical data and historically observed connections before any generalizing theoretical hypotheses can be formulated. Such learning may compel the attention of scholars in the economics discipline to processes and events beyond their traditional area of interest. Yet, given the major contribution of new knowledge and technological innovations to the substance of modern economic growth, such ventures outside the discipline cannot be avoided. The need for them is as obvious as that with respect to another neglected field of economic analysis, the economics of population composition and growth.

A related complex of topics may be described as the economic and social corollaries of technological innovation. And here the scope is enormous. It ranges from *complementary* adjustments— new patterns of life and new institutional forms evolved in response to technological innovation and required to channel the latter effectively into mass application—to *compensatory* adjustments, usually in the older sectors within the country (and sometimes abroad), to the destructive effects of technological innovations in their successful competition with older sectors for resources or markets. The expansive, as well as the disruptive, effects of technological innovations, in their steady succession in the course of modern economic growth, are much of the sum and substance of that growth process. The latter should perhaps be viewed in terms of the struggle between current beneficiaries and current victims of technological innovation, a struggle that seems more relevant than that between economic classes distinguished by their control of assets (particularly if the latter include, as they should, investment in education and human capital). A vast amount of data, qualitative and quantitative, has accumulated on changes in economic and social institutions and in conditions of work and life of the population. Much of the data could be traced as corollaries of historically given specific complexes of major technological innovations.

Yet few systematic studies have been made of the relation between a given complex of major technological innovations (e.g., those relating to steam power, or to electric power and various components of it) and the various responses in economic organization and social institutions that they elicited. Perhaps the divisions among the social science disciplines and a lack of expertise in the field of technology, particularly when associated with basic or applied science, have militated against this type of study. In such a study, connections with some distinctive characteristics of the given complex of technological innovations would be traced to various social and economic effects, including those on the longevity and space distribution of the population; the narrower economic consequences, such as shifts in relative costs and prices; the institutional consequences, such as the emergence of a new legal form of organization (which then assumes a life of its own); and the political consequences, that is, how the relation between the population and its government will be affected.

A meaningful analysis of modern economic growth requires more tested knowledge of the determinants of technological innovation and of the various social effects engendered, whether positive or negative (the latter a subject of much clamorous discussion in recent years). Obviously, such analysis is a primary need of developed democratic nations, which have to rely for further growth on a continued stream of technological innovation. It should also bear on the determinants of original (not imitative) technological innovation in restrictively planned Communist economies, particularly those that, given their level of economic development, could have been expected to contribute to the advance of science and technology. Their record should be particularly scrutinized in an attempt to discern the magnitude and direction of their contributions, as a possible reflection, in comparative analysis, of the specific effects of the distinctive organization and orientation of these countries. Such study should also have bearing on the LDCs, for the potentials and conditions of diffusion of more advanced technology to these countries cannot be understood without more knowledge of the technological and social complex that characterizes the developed societies and economies.

I am not at all sure how such studies of the determinants of technological innovations, and of their social and economic corollaries, could be pursued so as to yield comparable and generalizable results. Nor is there assurance that the tools for the requisite analysis of these long-drawn-out complexes of interrelated changes in so many different fields of human activity are at hand. All one can say is that the topics, perhaps not fully articulated in the brief notes above, are important to our understanding of modern economic growth; that the research already completed by a few scholars on the economics of technological change (Jacob Schmookler, Edwin Mansfield, and Nathan Rosenberg, among others in this country) has yielded interesting and illuminating results, as have some recent monographs on the history of technology, particularly in its relation to, and interplay with, the development of science. A vast amount of data has also accumulated on modernization and changes in economic and social institutions in the DCs. It should provide abundant raw material for tracing the connections between at least some changes in conditions of work and life and in institutional structures and the historically bound, specific complexes of technological innovations. To be sure, the suggested attempts at synthesis—of a variety of data on sources and determinants of technological innovations and of an even greater variety of disparate data on social and institutional changes viewed as responses to requirements and disruptions associated with technological changes—offer great challenges and limited promise of addable results. But one may hope that such attempts at wider synthesis will be made, no matter how tentative or methodologically primitive they may have to be at first.

4. LDCs and the Gap

The group of economically less developed countries, designated "underdeveloped" in the early collections of international income statistics by the United Nations but "developing" in more recent years, comprises a wide and somewhat changing list of countries. To clarify the discussion, I narrow the definition by excluding the major oil exporters with small populations and inordinately high per capita incomes derived from control of a raw material made valuable by Western technology. I also exclude countries in the twilight zone between the DCs and the LDCs— some in southern Europe (such as Greece, Spain, and Portugal) and others in the temperate zone of Latin America (Argentina, Uruguay, and Chile). I also set aside the Communist LDCs, dominated by Mainland China, for which the data supply and quality and the characteristics of economic and social organization are so different from those of the other LDCs. It is to be hoped that specialists will succeed, in the coming years, in preparing adequate measures and acceptable analysis of the experience of Mainland China (and its satellites) within a proper historical and comparative perspective.

We are left, then, with the less developed market economies in Asia, Africa, and Latin America with per capita product in 1972 that ranged from less than $100 to about $800 but with a heavy concentration of the population in the low per capita income brackets. Of the total of some 1.6 billion population in these LDC market economies, over 1.2 billion were in countries with per capita product well below $400; and the arithmetic mean for these 1.2 billion in 1972 was about $140.[6] These, then, are largely relatively poor LDCs that differ widely in historical heritage, in location, in duration of political sovereignty, in the population-land ratio, and the like.

The limitations in the supply and quality of data available in the LDCs, mentioned in section 2, are relevant here, as is the wide diversity among these countries in size, political history, and historically determined social and natural endowments. Moreover, most of these societies lived for centuries practically isolated from western Europe. They did not participate in the revolutionary developments in science and technology that originated in Europe; they were eventually subjected to the aggressive dominance of western European developed countries; and they were finally freed from it at different dates within the last century to century and a half, most rapidly since World War II. Since these societies had little continuous contact with the West in their long history, and since colonial status superimposed distorting effects on their heritage, little tested knowledge of them is available. And yet it is not an ethnocentric illusion to judge tested knowledge by the canons of Western-originated scientific activities and patterns: statistical tests, quantitative formulations, and logical structures are in order in studying both developed and modernized countries and traditional preindustrial societies.

We must keep in mind these difficulties in securing tested knowledge when we view the rapid extension of statistical coverage to the LDCs and the vigorous accumulation of monographic and comparative studies that has occurred over the last 2 to 3 decades. Without claiming adequate knowledge of the literature, I am sure that a variety of relevant questions remain to be answered and that the difficulty is not in finding topics for further research in the field but in selecting the few that seem central and of high priority in the next phase of scholarly work. This,

---

6. These data are from the *World Bank Atlas* (n. 3 above). A better adjustment for comparative purchasing power of the currencies might double these averages, but they would still be indicative of very low levels of per capita economic performance.

like the rest of this paper, represents an individual scholar's judgment, affected largely by what I have learned and the unanswered questions that I perceive.

One may begin by asking why, given the low per capita economic performance, and the availability of a large stock of technology still unexploited by the LDCs, the growth in their per capita product over the last 25 years has fallen significantly short of that for the DCs—so that the initial wide gap between the two groups has grown even wider. And to reduce emphasis on comparisons that may not be too meaningful, I limit the question to the LDCs that attained political independence before or at the very start of the post–World War II period, and compare shortfalls in the growth record not with the DCs (whose growth rate might have been unusually high after World War II because of transient circumstances) but with presumably feasible and desirable goals of a sustained, significant growth in per capita product, without breakdowns and alarms of critical short-term shortages. According to the record for the last quarter-century, many populous LDCs, particularly those with low initial per capita product, showed either zero growth or very low rates by modern standards and frequent short-term breakdowns and failures.

The question is difficult, not for lack of answers, but, rather, because of a profusion of them in past analytical discussions dealing with obstacles to economic growth in the LDCs and with the various policy alternatives that were deemed suitable for overcoming them. The difficulty lies partly in the multiplication of competing or complementary hypotheses without much opportunity for effectively testing them or for weighing their relative contributions, but even more in the proximate character of the determinants suggested, in that they are only the immediately observable variables, not the more deep-seated, underlying factors.

This last point is particularly important in considering further work in the field, and deserves a few illustrations. Thus, one could argue that the available stock of more advanced technology is not really suitable for use by the LDCs, not being fitted to their resource endowments; and that the required capital financing sources are not available in the poor LDCs, with their meager savings. But then one could ask why these two difficulties could not be overcome—the first by selection and adaptation adjustments of the kind made by those current DCs that were follower countries in the past (e.g., the United States and, particularly, Japan) and the second by effective utilization of domestic savings (whose net proportions in many current DCs in their earlier past were not much above 5 percent of GNP), particularly by economical utilization of capital. Thus, one could argue that population grew at explosive rates in the LDCs in recent decades and might have slowed down the growth rate in per capita product. But even if one accepted this argument and did not ask why the resulting higher rate of labor supply could not be effectively used to sustain high growth rates, one could at least ask why, despite presumptive benefits to the population and the country of fewer, better nurtured and educated children, no fertility reduction policy was pursued by households or governments. (Technical means have always been available, if only by raising the age of marriage of the female.) Thus, one could argue that economic policies that emphasized industry and neglected agriculture, or concentrated on capital-intensive producer goods industries rather than on labor-intensive consumer goods industries, disregarded the sound and balanced foundation for sustained growth and adequate food supply. But then one may ask about the rationale of such policies or why they were not quickly abandoned, given the prompt indication of their undesirable effects.

One major assumption is implicit in these illustrative comments: a politically sovereign LDC of an adequate size, coexisting with developed countries, aware of a transnational stock of knowledge and technology, living within a tolerable natural endowment (not in the Arctic wilderness of the Eskimos or the desert of the nomads) should be capable of a satisfactorily high and sustained growth rate of product per capita. Given internal freedom and rational pursuit of desirable goals, the country should be able to make the adjustments and choices that would yield the desirable growth rate, with a minimum of undesirable concomitants. If these adjustments and choices are not made or are delayed for too long, one should look for a rational explanation. Several reasons may be suggested. One may be that pressure of other goals is greater than that for economic growth (e.g., military strength for protection, or survival of values, religious and other). A second may be the resistance of some groups whose direct current interest may be adversely affected by growth-promoting changes and adjustments, resistance which the sovereign government and society are unable to overcome while maintaining internal consensus. Third, the sheer combination of the various necessary adjustments and policy changes may not be accepted at a rapid rate by the society without intolerable pressures that may affect the nation's unity and viability.

The emphasis above is on the modernization capacity of an LDC. Can it initiate and sustain growth-promoting changes in economic and social structure? Can it channel the disruptive impact of modern economic growth when it occurs so as to avoid the loss of effective social consensus and thus its viability? That the building up of such modernization capacity among modern nations has been far from easy is indicated by the long, and often turbulent, record of nation building among the current DCs since the late eighteenth century. And the difficulties of establishing viable sovereign states among the newly independent LDCs in the 2 to 3 recent decades (and in many whose political independence dates back to the nineteenth century), with the frequent internal and external conflicts, clashes among hostile tribal or other groups, and forcible expulsion of foreign minorities despite their rich economic contributions, are too fresh in our memory to need emphasis. It may well be that relatively slow economic growth is to be expected among the LDCs in the early stages of their lives as sovereign nations as they build up consensus and viability. Only then, perhaps, will accelerated growth become possible. When the foundation of community of feeling and resulting unity is strengthened, more radical shifts in economic and social structure may be accepted without the risk of losing freedom and flexibility through sharp centralization of internal power and forceful imposition of a minority choice.

Economic analysis of economic growth has always assumed the existence of a viable and coherent state, with different roles at different stages (reflecting some divergence in the respective weights of the private and public sectors) but with a minimum capacity and cohesion throughout. For the LDCs, or many of them at the lower end of the economic range, this assumption of a viable and coherent state structure may be an oversimplification that disregards the crucial role of the process by which such a viable state is built up. Clearly, much of the diversity in the growth record in the post–World War II decades between DCs and LDCs, and among the latter even when limited to market economies, can be traced to different levels of development of the structure of sovereign nations as cohesive units. If this observation is valid, we need to study the political and social structure of nations in terms of their capacity to make decisions required for adequate and sustained economic growth, without drastically sacrificing internal liberty and ignoring varied group interests. And such study would mean a shift from economics to political economy, in a sense a return to the emphasis in classical and Marxian economics on the role of the state but with reference to a much wider range of forms and structures—and, one may hope, a greater appreciation of the variety of trade-offs between economic and political power in the short run and the loss of choices open to a nation's population in the long run.

Any consideration of the political and social envelope of economic growth among the LDCs would have to face the complications created by the striking decentralization of decision authority that has occurred with the multiplication in recent decades of small, newly formed sovereign states. The drive for the creation of mini- or microstates, with relatively small populations, appears to be growing, perhaps in response to the privileges of sovereignty and the presumption of special powers and rightful claims bestowed by the recognition of such sovereignty. Or it may be in response to an urge toward social coherence so strong that it prevents the extension of consciousness of kind to larger, somewhat more heterogeneous communities. This movement raises the question of whether the sovereign nation is still the proper unit in the study of economic growth. A basic argument in favor of the latter is that a sovereign nation represents a sufficiently large population to allow for extensive internal division of labor, a diversified structure of production, and sufficient independence even when developed, despite substantial foreign trade proportions. Does such a definition still apply to units like Hong Kong and Singapore, with their highly specialized interstitial functions among much larger units; or would it apply to an enclave of a few hundred thousand population almost fully dependent on a much larger neighbor or patron? But this is only one facet in the wider problem, particularly acute for LDCs: strengthening the nation's capacity for modernization, in its various components, thus facilitating exploitation of the production potentials of modern economic growth.

Population Trends and Modern Economic Growth: Notes toward an Historical Perspective

Introduction

1. Birth and growth, youth and maturity, senescence and death, frame—somewhat differently for males and females—the life span of an individual as a member of society. Demographic processes and structures, while resting on a biological base, have far-reaching social implications. Fertility, growth, mortality, and the resulting sex and age distributions of changing numbers, condition the division of labor in society and the sequential roles—economic and social—of the demographically distinct groups. Conversely, economic and social processes and structures have far-reaching demographic consequences—affecting fertility, family formation, and the life cycle of dependence, education, maturity, occupation, and retirement.

2. The economic growth process of a given historical epoch, characterized usually by distinctive major sources of increased capacity, must have specific effects on the demographic processes and structures. These effects are associated with the *opportunities,* economic and social, provided by the epoch's sources of growth

Prepared for United Nations Symposium on Population and Development held in Cairo in June 1973. Reprinted from United Nations, *The Population Debate: Dimensions and Perspectives, vol. I* (New York, 1975), pp. 425–433.

and development, and with the *requirements* that the current material and social technology imposes. Modifications of the basic demographic processes, introduced by economic growth and social development, then become the bases that condition the further stages in the economic and social growth process.

3. The discussion below concentrates, for greater relevance, on the interrelations between *modern* economic growth as exemplified by the process in the currently developed countries over the last one and a half to two centuries, and the major trends in their demographic processes. But a similar interplay between population and economic growth (including concomitant social development) could be traced for premodern stretches of history in the presently developed countries, or for those regions of the world in the recent past that have been relatively free of the impact of modern economic growth.

Interrelations between Population Trends and Modern Economic Growth

4. The major demographic trends observed in the developed countries (largely Europe, the European offshoots overseas, and Japan) over the long period since they entered modern economic growth are familiar and do not call for lengthy discussion.[1] Of prime importance was the marked reduction in mortality, which raised life expectancy at birth from forty years or below to close to seventy years. It had major impacts on the mortality of infants and young children, on the mortality (and associated morbidity) from infections and related diseases, and on mortality in the cities, which had previously suffered from much higher death rates than the countryside. This reduction in mortality was ac-

---

1. The summary of population trends presented is clearly selective, and cannot be viewed as an adequate survey. In addition to many United Nations sources, ranging from the 1953 report, *The Determinants and Consequences of Population Trends,* to the two major population bulletins, no. 6, 1962 (on mortality), and no. 7, 1963 (on fertility), to the background papers, prepared for the 1965 World Population Conference, on mortality (by C.C. Spicer) and on fertility (by George W. Roberts), and to the most recent *Population Studies* (no. 47), *The World Population Situation in 1970* (New York: 1971), I found particularly helpful the summary by D.V. Glass and E. Grebenik, "World Population, 1800–1950," chapter 2 in H.J. Habakkuk and M. Postan, eds., *The Cambridge Economic History of Europe,* vol. VI, pp. 60–138 (Cambridge: Cambridge University Press, 1965).

companied, but not simultaneously, by a decline in fertility. The crude birth rates declined (in the older countries of Europe) from over 30 to 1,000 to well below 20, a trend that largely reflected intramarital fertility and was a result of decisions by the families to limit the number of children. It was not the result of any genetic changes, or of involuntary reaction by the human species to changes in the material conditions associated with economic growth. The combination of low mortality with low fertility—while still allowing for a much greater long-term rate of natural increase than that over the preceding centuries of high birth and death rates—was new and unique. It had to be new because the opportunities for reducing the death rates to the low levels attained were new and unparalleled in the past.

5. The above comments may suggest both a close timing relation between modern economic growth and the downward trends in mortality and fertility; and a distinction between the long-term trends in mortality and fertility, in that the element of human choice and decision was absent in the former and of great importance in the latter. Neither suggestion is valid. In many European countries crude death rates declined in the eighteenth century and were in their low 20s by the second quarter of the nineteenth century—*preceding* the initiation of modern economic growth by several decades. By contrast, in many countries there was no further decisive decline of death rates until late in the nineteenth century, with most of the reduction concentrated in the current century—several decades after modern economic growth was initiated. Urban death rates were substantially higher than rural even in the first decade of the twentieth century, in the European countries and in the United States. Likewise, in the older European countries (but not in the United States), fertility did not begin to decline until well into the last quarter of the nineteenth century—with a substantial lag after the initiation of their modern economic growth. Despite the connection between the delay in the decline of birth rates and the delay in the decline of mortality (and the latter provides only a partial explanation), and despite the connection between the delay in the decline of mortality and the effects of rapid urbanization on the aggregate death rate, it still remains true that the timing of the broad association between modern patterns of mortality and fertility and

modern economic growth, is *not* close. The economic growth processes undoubtedly provided opportunities for reducing mortality and raised the inducements and requirements for lower fertility. But the opportunities were not so free of obstacles, nor the inducements and requirements so dominant in the early stages of the industrialization process, as to effect a prompt response in the demographic trends.

6. Nor was a strong element of social, or even individual, decision absent from the proximate factors that made for the reduction of mortality, and for the delay in its decline in the nineteenth century. Granted that for an individual, the decision to postpone death is not usually a matter of choice, the views on mortality—particularly of children—changed slowly. The acceptance of their death as "usual" or even as an offset to the "improvidence of the poor" persisted. But it was the socially determined implemented decision that was more telling. If the reduction in death rates before World War II was due, as has recently been argued, to better nutrition and living conditions, and to public health and sanitation measures, far more than to advances in medical care and knowledge,[2] the role of social decisions becomes patent. The provision of means of subsistence and of housing, of generally improved living conditions, reflects policies on income distribution, prices of necessities, housing and treatment of the poor. Public health measures, involving political decisions on uses of funds and on regulation of the private sector and of individuals, clearly rested on a social consensus that was slow in coming. A delay in the latter would have delayed even further the decline in the urban, and hence aggregate, death rates. The long struggles of the public health reformers through much of the nineteenth century clearly indicate that even when the sources of high mortality were known, much effort had to be expended to secure the social decisions needed to reduce their impact.

7. The opportunities and pressures produced by modern economic growth led to decisions important in the reductions of the death and crucial in the declines of the birth rates, and affected

---

2. See T. McKeown, R.G. Brown, and R.G. Record, "An Interpretation of the Modern Rise of Population in Europe," *Population Studies* (vol. 26, no. 3), November 1972, pp. 345–382; and on public health in Great Britain, most of the issue of *Population Studies,* (vol. 17, no. 3) March 1964.

family formation, location and migration, and the life cycle sequence of education, occupation, and retirement. For a better understanding of these we note some distinctive features of modern economic growth. The reference must perforce be brief and simple. But the features are sufficiently conspicuous and persistent, and many of them amply documented, to minimize misunderstanding.[3]

8. First, the permissive basis for the great rise in per capita product, combined with high rates of population growth, was the rapid increase in our tested knowledge of natural processes, applied to problems of production technology. This increase took the form of successive technological innovations, which in their spread into mass use raised product and productivity. They also led to further knowledge concerning the properties of nature and to invention of additional tools, which facilitated new discoveries—and thus led to further applications. The reinforcing connections between discoveries, inventions, innovations, applications, further learning, more discovery, and so on, permitted the sustained pressure toward higher production levels. But the key link in this chain was the mass application of innovations for wide use—which meant that knowledge was directed toward agreed-upon useful ends, among which the provision of goods for ultimate consumption was paramount. It was hardly an accident that innovations relating to final consumption and consumer goods were just as prominent as those relating to producer goods; and that the growth of consumption per capita was almost as great as that of total product per capita. This orientation of knowledge to useful ends and of production to ultimate consumption obviously has bearing on mortality—life and health being prime consumption goods. It also has bearing on fertility, in that the orientation toward greater consumption for the existing and next generations would, other conditions being equal, lead to the choices of fewer

---

3. For a summary of the characteristics of modern economic growth see my Nobel Memorial lecture, "Modern Economic Growth: Findings and Reflections," in *Les Prix Nobel en 1971* (Stockholm: 1972), pp. 313–32 (reprinted in *American Economic Review,* June 1973). A more detailed discussion is given in the earlier monographs, *Modern Economic Growth: Rate, Structure, and Spread* (New Haven: Yale University Press, 1966), and *Economic Growth of Nations: Total Output and Production Structure,* (Cambridge, MA: Harvard University Press, 1971).

children. These implications will become clearer as we consider some other distinctive features of modern economic growth, closely connected with the one just noted.

9. Second, a high rate of growth of product per capita, fed by successive technological innovations and their mass application, was, perforce, accompanied by rapid changes in the production structure of the country undergoing modern economic growth—the structure of the sectors in which the active economic members of the population were engaged—with consequent changes in the occupations and the geographic location of these participants. These rapid changes in the country's production structure were partly due to shifts in domestic demand, reflecting different income elasticities of demand for various goods; partly to the tendency of the focus of innovations to shift from one sector to another, as the potentials of economic advantage of new applications shifted; and partly to the effects of innovations in transport, communication and the natural resource advantage among nations. *Industrialization*—the movement of output, capital, and labor shares from agriculture to industry—has been the most prominent of these changes in production structure; but the shifts within the nonagricultural sector, particularly of labor toward the service- rather than commodity- producing industries, have been equally important. One implication of these rapid shifts in production structure for our theme is that they widen the possibility of intergenerational breaks—with sons being attached to industries, occupations, and locations different from those of their fathers, to a far greater extent than in a more slowly changing, traditional, economy. The effect on formation of families and, in general, on the ties of authority of the older over the younger generation, is obvious. Moreover, it is reinforced by other aspects of this shift in production structure that have markedly influenced population trends.

10. One of the two most relevant aspects is the sharp rise in the proportions of capital and labor engaged in large-scale, nonpersonal enterprises—as contrasted with the decline in the proportions attached to small-scale, personal, or family units. The other is the sharp rise in the educational and other skill requirements of labor. The rise in the size of the productive plant was associated with the economies of scale of modern technology.

These economies were the results of technological properties of new sources of industrial power, of better controls over precision in fabrication and of major improvements in intraplant communication—technological and social. The growth of the large-scale enterprise (the economic, not the production, unit) was also facilitated by the revolutionary changes in communication, and by the organizational innovations feasible with a technology the rules of which could be overtly formulated and easily and widely communicated—impossible on the basis of earlier personal master-apprentice relations. The requirements for more formal education and greater skills were partly a direct consequence of the larger scale of productive units and enterprises, which demanded adequate communication and understanding within the organization; partly a reflection of the increasing reliance of society on the production of new knowledge as a source of further growth; and partly a result of the need for *formal* education as the basis for judging the equipment of would-be participants—given the system of recruitment into economic activity associated with modern economic growth, to be touched upon below.

11. The rapid shifts in production structure, the emergence of large-scale production plants and economic enterprises, and the rise in educational requirements of the economically active groups in the population had striking effects on the location of population, internal migration, family formation, and the typical life cycle of an individual or family unit. Describing these population trends as consequences or corollaries of modern economic growth, or responses by individuals and families to changing opportunities and changing conditions of exploiting these opportunities associated with economic growth, is partly a semantic problem. The important point is the *coherence* between the economic growth and the population trends, a basis for evaluating the current situation in both developed and developing countries.

12. Industrialization was associated with intensive modern urbanization because the former was accompanied by a rise in the scale of the productive unit to a point where the economies of scale demanded concentration of production and large bodies of workers, and induced the formation of new or larger cities. Even without economies of scale, the movement away from agriculture would have furthered urbanization: the emergence of specialized

crafts in the Middle Ages led to some urbanization in the European countries, even though the scale of handicraft production and trade was relatively small. But it was primarily the rapidly rising scale of modern technology and the successful resolution of the problems of communication and organization that powered the movement toward the cities and their rapid rate of growth in the nineteenth and twentieth centuries, *pari passu* with the accelerated rate of growth of product and population. An additional, and key, permissive factor lay in the marked rise in labor productivity in agriculture, which made it possible for a small fraction of the labor force (well below 10 percent in recent years) to produce enough agricultural goods to satisfy, at a high per capita level, the other nine-tenths of the population. The rapid movement, suggested by these fractions, to high levels of urbanization, is clearly a product of modern technology and economic growth—much of it in response to economic scales of production and enterprise. And the recent emergence of dormitory suburbs in the developed industrialized countries, an attempt at adjustment permitted by greater affluence, only confirms the element of economic pressure involved in the urbanization process in earlier decades.[4]

13. Given the parameters of modern economic growth, particularly those of the growth of sectoral demand for labor, and the more limited parameters of population growth, rapid urbanization and rapid structural changes within the production system could not have occurred without vast internal migration. With modern economic growth characterized by rapid structural changes, which imply wide differences in the growth rates of the various parts of the structure, the disparities between differential rates of population increase and differential rates of growth of demand for labor were bound to become wide. When the de-

---

4. For a summary of data on urbanization and discussion of concepts see United Nations, *Growth of the World's Urban and Rural Population, 1920–2000* (New York: 1969), and the references there to historical studies. Current worldwide data on the structure of labor force by sectoral attachment can be found in International Labour Office, *Labour Force Projections, 1965–1985*, parts I–V, (Geneva: 1971). Historical data on industrial attachment of labor force are given in P. Bairoch and others, *The Working Population and Its Structure,* Institut de Sociologie, Universite Libre de Bruxelles (Brussels: 1968).

mand for labor in some new industries grew between 5 and 10 percent per year, and that in the older industries located elsewhere hardly grew at all, the differential in natural increase rates could not accommodate itself to such disparities. In addition, there was, through most of the period, a higher rate of natural increase in the countryside—where additional employment opportunities were limited—than in the cities—in which such opportunities grew more rapidly. Urbanization reflected only the major disparities between rates of natural increase and rates of growth of employment opportunities, and the internal migration implicit in it was only part of the stream augmented by intercity and interregional flows. (In some countries, the United States for example, immigration contributed to the adjustment by its differential flow into those regions where demand for labor was particularly active.) Such vast internal migration and immigration is important for our theme. It broke the ties between the participant in economic activity and his family origins; it made the migrant more receptive to economic opportunities; it changed the conditions of life and work, with whatever effects they may have had on family formation and fertility; and it reinforced the increasing separation between family and economic activity, which has been a most important consequence of modern economic growth.

14. Migration only reinforced the separation between the family and economic activity that was imposed by the increase in scale of production and of the economic enterprise. Unlike a farm, a handicraft shop, a small store, or an individual service activity, a modern large-scale plant cannot be contained within a household. A large economic enterprise, demanding large amounts of fixed capital and with a perpetuating future not dependent on any one person's or family's life, cannot be effectively operated as a personal or a family firm. It demands an overt, impersonal, and effective organization in which the roles, responsibilities, and privileges are explicitly formulated and legally enforceable. The control and organization of large-scale production demand that it be separated from the household. The individual participants must perform their tasks within the plant or the office, away from their families and households. They thus become members of a group whose practices and discipline have only limited contact with the life of the individual participant as a member of a household or a

family. As a result, a large volume of economic activity formerly carried on within the households of traditional farmers, craftsmen, shopkeepers, has been removed from family activity. Moreover, the function of the family as an institution transmitting economic experience and skills from one generation to the next has been severely limited. And while the process began with the removal of market-oriented activities from most families, it was followed by mechanization of household services, by professionalization and hence removal from the family of many educational services, and by the shift out of the family and into the organized labor markets of an increasing proportion of domestic labor resources that previously had provided services within the family.

15. The removal of the full-time economic activity from the family and household and the resulting separation between the production plant and the home were accompanied, and eventually reinforced, by the revolutionary changes in the practice and criteria of recruitment of individuals into economic activity. Given the large scale of the modern plant and enterprise, the large numbers of active participants involved, and the migrant origin of much of the available labor, it was impossible to recruit on the basis of personal knowledge of candidates and their family origins (although this approach was followed in the recruitment of unskilled immigrants through the ethnic compatriot boss system in some early phases of U.S. growth). Furthermore, the requirements of rising education and other skills to handle effectively rather complex production tasks involving costly capital equipment, made personal knowledge of an applicant far less important than knowledge of his testable equipment, whether it was manual dexterity, ability to relate to people, or general or professional formal education. The large numbers and the large economic magnitudes involved in adequate resolution of recruiting and staffing problems warranted a concerted and prolonged effort to develop an effective classification of the production tasks within the plant and enterprise, and to formulate criteria of satisfactory selection. These were bound to replace the traditional type of recruitment based on personal knowledge of workers and of their family antecedents. The shift from recruitment on the basis of status, closely connected with family origins and warranted in earlier times by lack of better ways for judging the suitability of

individuals for their economic tasks, to recruitment on the basis of a person's objectively tested capacity for performance, specifically formulated to a well-defined range of production tasks, was a revolutionary change in the modernization of society in adjustment to modern economic growth. And it had far-reaching effects on population and the life cycle of its members. Economic activity and preparation for it occupy much of the life of an individual, from childhood through maturity; and major changes in conditions of entry, and implicitly in the criteria for rise *within* the economic system, that occurred in the shift in recruitment, were bound to have multiple and far-reaching consequences.

16. One immediate consequence was the rise in the level of formal education and the spread of formal certification. The educational system became increasingly involved in screening individuals, and in channeling them to more advanced levels roughly on the basis of ability—even if qualified by parental position and by surviving patterns of discrimination. A growing proportion of the labor force underwent longer periods of general and professional training, which was supplemented at later stages of the occupational career. And a rapidly increasing share of economic positions was contingent upon formal certification, with respect either to educational levels attained, or to specialized skills, or to both. Thus, the trend within the labor force away from entrepreneurial and self-employment to employment status was accompanied by the trends to higher levels of formal and specialized education, professionalization of occupations, and an extension of certification. For our theme, the main bearing of these trends is the increased investment in *human* (as distinct from material) capital, prolongation of the period of education that kept the younger generation out of both economic and household activity, in separate schools. This contributed further to the shift of the transmission of knowledge and experience between generations from the family and household to the nonfamily, nonpersonal institutions.

17. The distinctive characteristics of modern economic growth noted above—rapid changes in production structure, urbanization and vast internal migration (and immigration), the shifts of requirements and conditions of participation in economic activity and the associated increase of emphasis on education and train-

ing, and testable criteria of individual performance—all had profound influences on fertility, family formation, and the life cycle of learning, work, and retirement. These influences were not limited to the urban populations whose proportions in the total were rapidly growing. They extended also to the rural populations that were sending many of their younger generation to the cities and the conditions of whose life were also thoroughly affected by the higher educational and other requirements of modern economic growth. In fact, the declines in rural fertility in a country like the United States were, at least before World War II, relatively as great as those for urban fertility—although the differentials tended to persist.

18. The decline in birth rates was clearly associated with the greatly increased costs of children, resulting partly from the withdrawal of their labor from the family milieu, and partly from the requirement for a longer and more expensive span of education and training. Both of these costs were directly connected with the rearing of the next generation to economic maturity, and with the upward mobility of the parental generation itself. These trends toward greater costliness of children were reinforced by the shift to urban life, and the competitive pressures of a rising standard of consumption, in the cities and in the countryside. The resulting decline in the size of the family was reinforced by the separation of generations. Correspondingly, a trend developed toward the conjugal (or nuclear) family, characterized by "the relative exclusion of a wide range of affinal and blood relatives from its everyday affairs," and effectively limited to parents and their children largely below the adult ages, and free from more extended family ties in the choice of mates, in the process of family formation and in the choice of location.[5] And, too, the life cycle of learning, work, and retirement changed markedly. The age of entry into the labor force in the developed countries rose substantially, associated largely with the prolongation of the period of formal education; and the age of retirement from full-

---

5. The term "conjugal" and the quotation are from William J. Goode, *World Revolution and Family Patterns* (New York: The Free Press, 1963), p. 8. This monograph presents an interesting analysis of the conjugal family as an "ideal type" concept, toward which the evolution of family in modern times tended to converge.

time economic activity dropped sharply, reflecting the more wide-spread employee status combined with the increased obsolescence of human skills and facilitated by institutional provisions for supporting the retired population. Since all these demographic trends can be viewed as responses, in a greater or less degree, to the requirements for effective and productive economic activity under the shifting conditions of modern economic growth, when realized, they contributed significantly to the high growth rates of the developed countries. It is difficult to envisage modern economic growth without the reduced birth rates, the greater investment in human capital represented by education and training, the smaller family, and the concentration of the labor force in the prime ages between the late entry and early retirement.

19. The condensed summary of the interrelations between population trends and modern economic growth must be concluded with a brief reference to four major qualifications. They are reminders of omissions to be kept in mind in evaluating the bearing of the past interrelations on the present and future.

20. First, the coherence between the opportunities and requirements of modern economic growth and the response of the population trends should not be viewed as an easy and smooth process, characterized by close timing and a relatively close relation between the economic and demographic parameters. The movement away from agriculture should not be viewed only as a response of labor to greater opportunities in industry and the cities; it could just as well have been the result of the push from the countryside produced by a shrinking market for agricultural products combined with advanced agricultural technology and institutions that displaced farm labor. The rapid changes in production structure stressed above meant not only greater opportunities in the rapidly growing sectors but also declining opportunities and technological unemployment in the slowly growing sectors; and the adjustment was never a simple and prompt transfer of displaced resources. And, as already indicated, the decline of both death and birth rates lagged for decades behind industrialization in many currently developed countries. In other words, much of modern economic growth took place *before* the modern demographic patterns emerged; also, before the wide spread of literacy and education. The process was long, with leads and lags, and disparities

in adjustment; and like all processes of change in economic and social performance and institutions, it was subject to distortions and changes in pace. Thus, the demographic patterns that developed, did not in their timing, closely conform to those in economic growth. While, in general, birth and death rates are lower in the developed than in the developing countries, *within* the group of developed countries general indexes like per capita product, and birth and death rates, are not closely associated.

21. Second, the duration of the processes the interrelations of which are our theme is partly due to the *gradual* spread, particularly of population trends, among the different social and economic groups within a developed country. The economic and social differentials among birth and death rates could not be considered in our brief summary; but it is clear that the transition to lower birth and death rates, in response to greater opportunities provided by economic growth, could not occur simultaneously and at the same rate for all economic and social groups.[6] Some of the trends in the differential aspects of death and birth rates have significant bearing on changing inequalities in economic position and material welfare. At least the older countries (as distinct from the European offshoots overseas) may have experienced for a while a *widening* of the economic and social differentials in fertility, with possible widening of inequality in size distribution of income. But this topic requires more intensive study than is feasible here; and is mentioned only because of its possible bearing on the prospects in developing countries, once their transition to lower fertility levels begins.

22. Third, modern economic growth spread gradually and began at different dates in the currently developed countries—these dates (rough approximations only) ranging from the late eighteenth century in pioneering England, to the 1840s for several European countries and the United States, to the 1880s in Japan, and to the 1930s for the USSR (after an initial spurt in Russia in the 1890s). The international aspects of modern economic growth could not be covered in this summary. Yet, needless to say, they

---

6. A recent summary is given by Gwendolyn Z. Johnson in "Differential Fertility in European Countries," in Ansley J. Coale, ed., *Demographic and Economic Change in Developed Countries* (Princeton: Princeton University Press, for the National Bureau of Economic Research, 1960), pp. 36–76.

affected population trends—not only through international migration, which was particularly open and responsive, for the European countries of origin, during the nineteenth and early twentieth centuries, but also through the international demonstration effect of the declines in death and birth rates. The innovations in economic and social policies, and later in health technology, made in the pioneer countries, could spread to others, at lesser cost and input than required by the pioneers—just as the economic advance of the pioneer developed countries could be followed, at lesser cost, by other countries that were sufficiently prepared to take advantage of the opportunities. The reduction in birth rates and the shift to the conjugal family, once emerged in the pioneer developed country, could become readily known and even adopted as a desirable model by a growing segment of the population in the follower countries.

23. Fourth and last, the interrelations between economic growth and population trends are, as already indicated, only part of the network of factors determining demographic patterns; and, more relevant here, the connections between economic growth and population trends are not only direct but operate through what, from one standpoint, may be viewed as intermediate variables. Yet each of the latter may have a life and effect of its own, both on population and on economic growth. To illustrate: modern economic growth has been associated with the increasing importance of the national sovereign state, which serves as the arbiter of conflicts generated by rapid economic growth, as the referee of the social and legal innovations stimulated by the latter, and as the regulator of any difficulties stemming from the conflict between private and social interests in a complex market economy. The existence of this effective political and social institution meant that policies relating to both mortality and fertility could be adopted that would not have been possible otherwise. Another illustration: the greater urbanization, the formation of large cities, created a condition of anonymity among the inhabitants that was unknown in the rural and small-town surroundings This condition—a direct result of urbanization, not of economic processes—affected the consumption and living patterns and family formation patterns. Or consider the effects of the power of science and tested knowledge on the diminution of authoritarian religious belief, and hence on

the teachings of religious institutions and their doctrines regarding life and death. In this case, modern economic growth affects ideology indirectly through the demonstration of the power bestowed on man by tested knowledge that accepts no authority except that of observation, experiment, and the canons of scientific inference. In short, both economic growth and modern population trends are parts of the whole modernization process that occurred in the developed countries over the last one and a half to two centuries; and the two have interacted not only directly, but also via other institutional and ideological variables.

Bearing on Current Problems

24. The bearing of the preceding discussion on current problems can be put in general terms. Modern economic growth has provided opportunities for a great reduction in death rates and inducements and requirements for a marked reduction in birth rates; for a small, mobile family unit; and for a great change in the life cycle of education, occupation, and retirement. But with successive innovations and the rapid structural changes underlying the high aggregate rate of modern growth, the response to opportunities and the adjustment to displacement and changing requirements was neither prompt nor smooth, if only because of technological unemployment, and a push toward migration even before the pull became dominant. Differentials in birth rates, death rates, and migration may have widened inequality in the distribution of income before institutional adjustments produced a shift toward equality; and, as exemplified by ecological and other correlates, all the demographic consequences of modern economic growth could not be easily forecast or forestalled if found undesirable. Current social problems, that is, current developments that seem socially undesirable and call for remedial policy action, are largely the results of past growth, in which unforeseen consequences of past desirable attainments have grown to dimensions sufficient to demand attention. Recognition of a current social problem is thus a judgment, in terms of accepted criteria (which may change over time), of undesirable consequences of some past positive achievement. Of course, a current problem that originated in past positive achievement is still a problem calling for action, but relating it to its origin places it in the proper perspec-

tive and within a fairly wide group of similar problems that may have been overcome. And the ways in which the latter have been resolved deserve scrutiny, imitation, or rejection.

25. Consider as an illustration—all that is feasible here—a conspicuous current problem, the high rate of population growth in the less developed countries. That rate puts a heavy burden on economic capacity and makes it increasingly difficult to raise the level of per capita product, to better the internal distribution of income, and to accumulate sufficient reserves to escape any adverse effects of unavoidable fluctuations (in weather and crops) and of other uncertainties. According to recent estimates, in the less developed regions (Asia [excluding Japan], Africa, Latin America [excluding the temperate subgroup], Oceania [excluding Australia and New Zealand]), which in 1750 accounted for two-thirds of world population, crude birth rates between 1750 to 1920 averaged slightly over 40 per 1,000; crude death rates averaged slightly over 36 per 1,000; and the rate of natural increase was barely 4 per 1,000.[7] This rate of natural increase was well below that for the developed regions, which rose from 4 per 1,000 in 1750–1800 to 9 in 1850–1900, and to 13 in 1900–1910. Then, for the three decades 1920–1950, the death rates in the less developed regions declined to about 30 per 1,000, while birth rates remained somewhat above 40, which meant that the rate of natural increase almost tripled to 11 per 1,000, about the same level as for the developed regions in decades free of world wars or "great" depressions. But the striking change came after World War II. The death rate in the less developed regions, which stood at 28 per 1,000 in 1940–1950, dropped to 22 in 1950–60, to 19 in 1960–65, and to 16 in 1965–70, while the crude birthrate moved from 40 per 1,000 in 1940–50 to 43 in 1950–60, to 42 in 1960–65 and to 40.5 in 1965–70. The crude rate of natural increase conse-

---

7. These and other estimates below are from United Nations, *The World Population Situation in 1970* (New York: 1971), a highly useful review of current trends that includes a brief summary of historical antecedents. But the "medium" projection that it presents may already be seen to underestimate the decline in birth rates in the late 1960s in North America and in the USSR, differing in this respect from the projections for the less developed regions. It thus appears that the contrast in the growth rates of population in the near future between the developed and the less developed regions may be even wider than that shown by the projections in this UN report.

quently rose from 12 in 1940–50 to 24 in 1960–65, and to 24.5 in 1965–70. Such a rate of increase, about 2.5 percent per year, was observed in the past only in the few exceptional developed countries (such as the United States before late nineteenth century) that attracted large immigration and could take advantage of an abundance of natural resources; and it was over twice as high as the long-term rates of population growth in the older developed countries of Europe and in Japan.

26. The present medium projections assume that these crude rates of natural increase in the less developed regions will rise from 24.5 per 1,000 in 1965–70 to 25 in 1970–80. While this rise seems slight, even the continuation of the high growth rate for another decade poses a challenging problem. The implications of the projection are even graver when we distinguish between the East Asia region (dominated by Mainland China), which accounted in 1960 for 645 million out of a total of 692, and the others, with a population of 1,315 million in 1960. This distinction is important because of the major differences in social and political structure between Mainland China and other less developed regions and because of the scarcity of basic data and the tenuousness of both current estimates and projections for the former. If we combine the remaining less developed regions (excluding the negligible group in Oceania), the crude birthrate moves from 46 per 1,000 in 1950–60 to 45 in 1960–65, to 44 in 1965–70, and is projected to 42.5 in 1970–80—while the death rate drops over the four periods from 24 to 20 to 17, and is projected to 13.5. The rate of natural increase thus rises from 22.5 to 25.5 to 27.5, and is then projected to the record level of 29 per 1,000 in 1970–80. That such a growth rate of population in the less developed regions, which account for about four-tenths of the world population, constitutes a major problem—if improvement in material welfare is to be attained—can hardly be gainsaid. For both the high birth rates and the low death rates there is ample parallel in the past. But there is no historical parallel for this combination of high birth rates with low death rates, especially for countries that are at the lower levels of current economic performance per head; nor is there a parallel, in the history of modern economic growth, to such rapid declines in death rates (except in the few years of recovery after epidemics).

27. In the light of the preceding discussion, it is obvious that the problem is associated with the rapid decline in the death rates—a positive attainment, made possible in large part by modern economic growth. The high level of technological capacity in production as well as in the medical arts, the ability to establish rapid communication with, and penetration into, the economically less developed world, and the basic philosophy of the value of material welfare and of health, all contributed to this achievement. Although obvious, this comment needs to be made in order to stress that the problem originated in the effective spread of a major *positive* contribution. To be sure, the difficulties could have been avoided by an equally prompt response of birthrates. But the slowness of the adjustment should not blind us to the magnitude of the positive attainment, realized and projected. And it can be argued that such a decline in death is an indispensable prerequisite for modern economic growth; and that it is also a prerequisite for the decline in birth rates, insofar as they are determined by a given size of *surviving* family desired by the parental generation.

28. The second comment stems from our discussion of the connection between modern economic growth and the decline in birthrates in the developed countries. We stressed the changed inducements and requirements of the modern economy that made fewer children, with greater investment in their education and training, and a smaller family, more attractive; and suggested that, in general, economic growth and modernization removed the need for a large family by shifting many of its economic, educational, and protective functions to impersonal business or public enterprise, educational institutions, and the state. These institutional-change corollaries of modern economic growth, components in the general modernization process, took time to evolve, and the decline in birth rates was both delayed and drawn out—particularly in the countries that entered modern economic growth first. The relevant question here for the less developed regions of today is whether the economic, political, and social institutions have been restructured, and the ideological views of society changed, to place emphasis on greater investment in fewer children, to provide political and social stability combined with internal social mobility that would enhance the interest of the parental generation in smaller families.

29. An answer to this question demands more knowledge of the changing social and political institutions of the less developed regions than is at hand. The temptation to give a negative answer is great, but is not fully valid. Modernization has been initiated and substantial reduction in birthrates has been realized in several less developed countries. Yet, to point up the difficulties in establishing political stability, we need only mention the internal conflicts in such major countries of Asia as Pakistan, Indonesia, and the Philippines, and of Sub-Saharan Africa as the Congo, Nigeria, and Ghana, and the spread of military dictatorships in much of Latin American and other less developed regions. The absence of political stability makes it impossible to generate a restructuring of economic and social institutions, which are often likely to sharpen the conflict between traditional and modern interests. The comment is made, despite limitations in our knowledge, in order to emphasize the connection between declines in birthrates and the necessary transformation of economic and social institutions that would *assure* the interest of the parental generation in fewer children and in greater investment in human capital. A social and economic structure that provides no rewards for fewer children, with slight prospect of a better future for them and their parents, would scarcely encourage low birth rates. This is not to minimize the effects of recent improvements in the technology of birth control in response to the recognition of a more acute need for them, nor of relevant changes in public attitudes and governmental policies— all of which may be needed to implement fully the interest in smaller families once it is established. However, far-reaching reductions in birthrates require an economic and social milieu that would not reward reliance on a genetic lottery, i.e., on a large number of surviving children, for lack of assurance that greater investment in fewer numbers would yield appreciable benefits— to the parental and to the younger generation.

30. Third, once birth rates begin to drop in the developing countries, the reduction is likely to be evident first among some groups, usually those in the modern advanced types of professional and modern occupations and those in the upper-income brackets; and will only later spread to the more traditional, and lower-income, occupations. It may, therefore, for a time, have the effect of maintaining, or even widening, the already wide inequali-

ties in income. The pressures on national unity and on tolerance of continuing inequalities, of failure of significant benefit from whatever economic growth takes place, are thus likely to become great —particularly because the spread of economic growth to the less developed regions is accompanied by the spread of modern views on the presumptive power of modern technology to bestow material benefits on all humanity, and the demonstration effects of widespread high standards of consumption elsewhere. This means that, with respect to population, the developing societies must take account not only of the overall difficulty of raising aggregate income per capita when the total rate of population growth is so high, but also of the need to change the economic and social conditions of the large population groups at the lower rungs of the economic ladder to assure their interest in fewer children and smaller families.

31. This suggests the fourth and most general comment on the problem under consideration, in the light of our earlier discussion of interrelations between population growth and modern economic growth in their historical perspective. The adjustment that has to be made to the rapid decline in the death rates in the less developed countries is much greater and more pressing in many important respects than were the similar adjustments of the birth rates in the developed countries in the past. Not only is the current growth rate of population in the less developed regions so much higher than that of the older developed countries in their long-term past. Not only are the economic levels and reserves of the less developed regions so much lower than those of most currently developed countries in their premodern past. Not only may the tolerance of economic deprivation and inequalities have been lowered with the spread of modern economic growth and modern views on the importance of equality of economic opportunity and on assurance of a minimum of material benefit for all groups. There is also a greater awareness of the connections between demographic trends and the conditions of economic advance in the age of modern technology and modern economic growth; and of the role that can be played by a more enlightened policy than the laissez-faire and pronatalist policy which prevailed in the currently developed countries in the past.

32. The above comment should not be interpreted to mean that no economic advance would be possible in the less developed regions of today, without striking reductions in birth rates. After all, despite the high growth rates of population, per capita product of the less developed economies grew over the 1950s and 1960s at a rate of about 1½ percent per year (after all adjustments), which meant a rise over the two decades of about a third.[8] But while this record looks good in comparison with the past, it is far short of that shown by the developed economies over the period. More important, it raises questions as to whether such a gain can be maintained with continuation, and indeed the projected acceleration, in the rate of population growth. Whatever the answer, the historical perspective suggests that a more deliberate population policy might consider not only the spread of knowledge of birth control technology, but also the ways in which the given institutional framework affects incentives on the part of a large proportion of people to shift toward greater investment in human capital and fewer children. This means exploring changes in economic, political, and social institutions that would enhance the interest of an increasing proportion of the population in the modern type of family—given the attainment of death rates low enough to approximate modern levels.

33. As indicated above, the comments on the current problem of high rates of population growth in the less developed countries are illustrative. More intensive consideration was impossible, partly for lack of knowledge and partly for lack of space. In general, inferences from the past for the present and the future can only be suggestive. We could have illustrated the relevance of the historical perspective to the problems of demographic adjustment in the *developed* countries—which are, however, quite different in range and emphasis from those stressed for the current problem for the less developed regions. It was not feasible to do so here. Yet I would like to conclude by stressing the differences in the specific implications of the population adjustment problems between

---

8. Estimates, including the various adjustments, are discussed in my paper, "Problems in Comparing Recent Growth Rates for Developed and Less Developed Countries," *Economic Development and Cultural Change* (vol. 20, no. 2), January 1972, pp. 185–209.

the developed and less developed regions, which are marked—as are those even among some subregions within each of the two groups. This means that the historical perspective would have to be translated into rather different implications for the two groups of countries, or for some subregions within each. Thus, although we are all inhabitants of one planet and members of world humanity, the population problems of the various regions are rather different. This has its favorable aspects, in that we are not all caught in the same bind that constrains many less developed countries, and resources can be transferred. But it also has its unfavorable aspects, in the sense that our interests and concern differ. But regardless of the implications for policy, in order to achieve better understanding, our interpretation of the historical perspective must be geared to the different problems of the several societies and regions. And the very analysis of what we can learn from the past must be refined and tested, if it is to serve as a basis for more intelligent treatment of current population problems.

Rural-Urban Differences in Fertility: An International Comparison

In view of the major shift from rural to urban patterns of living in the process of economic growth, it is of interest to examine the possible differences in fertility between rural and urban populations— particularly for the less developed countries (LDCs). But direct data on birthrates for different population groups in the LDCs are scanty and unreliable; and only the recent censuses (and some sample inquiries) are beginning to yield distributions of rural and urban populations by age and sex. It is these distributions that are the major source for rural-urban fertility differentials, largely through the calculation of the ratios of children below a certain age to the appropriate population base.

This paper is an attempt to summarize the recent data on the topic, largely for the late 1950s and early 1960s. It begins with a summary of the crude fertility ratios in an international cross-section comparison; examines the possible biases in them if they are to be interpreted as indications of rural-urban differences in crude birth rates; and refines the measures by relating children under a

Reprinted from *Proceedings of the American Philosophical Society*, vol. 118, no. 1 (February 1974), pp. 1–29.

certain age not to total population (as in the crude ratios) but to a more appropriate population base. It then summarizes the bearing of these comparisons on our understanding of the interplay between economic growth, urbanization, and the movements of the birth rates and relevant fertility measures.

1. Crude Fertility Ratios

Table 1 provides a summary of the ratios of children under 5 years of age to total population, for rural and urban populations as distinguished in the national sources. The table covers 67 non-Communist countries, and excludes a few for which data are available. Some countries are excluded because they are too small (less than half-million in total population); others because they are untypical of the area (e.g., Uruguay, Trinidad and Tobago, and Guyana in the Latin American region, or South Africa in the Sub-Saharan region); and still others because they could not be easily handled in the summary (e.g., Albania and Israel). In establishing the major regions, we tried to preserve the economic character of each, excluding the single less or more developed country, if the region was largely more or less developed.

In taking group averages we treated each country as a unit, regardless of size—so that the averages are unweighted by population. The implicit assumption is that size of country is not relevant to the rural-urban fertility differentials; and that in this regard a small country is as significant as a large one, however important this difference may be in interpreting the fertility ratios for different parts of the world. Obviously, geometric means of ratios would have been more appropriate than the arithmetic; but the minor improvement did not seem to warrant the extra calculations.

While the ratios are subject to qualifications when viewed as approximations to rural-urban differences in *birth* rates, the major findings are of interest. This preliminary summary would guide us in the exploration of the aspects of the measure that are to be critically examined.

(i) The average urban ratios of children under 5 to total population are lower than the rural in all regions, areas, and groups distinguished in table 1. Interpreted as evidence of lower fertility among urban than among rural populations, the results agree with

TABLE 1

Proportions of Rural—Urban Population, and Children under 5
per 1,000 of Population, Rural and Urban, Major Regions,
Late 1950's and Early 1960's

	No. of coun- tries (1)	% Rural in total popu- lation (2)	Children under 5 per 1,000			No. of coun- tries with ratio above 1 (6)
			Rural (3)	Urban (4)	R/U col. 3/ col. 4 (5)	
1. Subsaharan Africa (ex. South Africa)	13	84.8	179	174	1.03	7
2. North Africa	5	65.8	184	178	1.03	2.5
3. Middle East	3	55.9	194	186	1.04	2
4. Asia	10	81.5	165	147	1.12	9
5. Latin America	17	58.0	182	158	1.15	17
6. LDCs, Europe (non-Comm., incl. Cyprus)	5	59.2	109	101	1.08	4
7. DCs, Europe, non-Comm.	9	38.0	87	79	1.10	8
8. U.S. & Canada	2	30.2	124	116	1.07	2
9. Australia & New Zealand	2	27.0	138.5	103	1.34	2
10. Japan	1	36.5	90	80	1.12	1
11. Eastern Comm. Europe (ex. Albania)	6	59.5	97	81	1.20	6
Area Totals						
12. Africa (ex. South Africa) (lines 1 & 2)	18	79.5	180	175	1.03	9.5
13. Europe (incl. Cyprus, lines 6—7 and 11)	20	49.8	96	85	1.13	18
Non-Communist						
14. LDCs (lines 1—5)	48	70.8	179	164	1.09	37.5
15. DCs (lines 7—10)	14	35.2	100	88	1.14	13

Notes: Unless otherwise indicated, all the underlying data are from the United Nations, *Demographic Yearbook, 1970* (New York, 1971), table 6, pp. 166—407. In a few European countries where a distinction is made between urban and semi-urban, both groups were put under urban.

The countries included in each group with the year to which they refer are:

Subsaharan Africa: Central African Republic (1959—60); Chad (1963—64); Congo, Dem. Republic (African population, 1955—57); Congo, People's Republic (African population, 1960—61); Dahomey (African population, 1961); Gabon (African population, 1960—61); Ghana (1960); Guinea (African population, 1955); Mali (1960—61); Namibia (1960); Nigeria (1963); Togo (1958—60); Zambia (African population, 1963).

North Africa: Algeria (1966); Libya (1964); Morocco (1960); Tunisia (1966); United Arab Republic (1960).

(Notes continued on the following page)

(Table 1 notes continued)
Middle East: Iraq (1965); Jordan (1961); Syria (1960).

Asia: Cambodia (1962); Ceylon (1963); India (1961); Indonesia (1964–65); Iran (1966); South Korea (1960); Sabah and Sarawak (1960); Nepal (1961); Pakistan (1961); Turkey (1960).

Latin America: Costa Rica (1963); Dominican Republic (1960); El Salvador (1961); Guatemala (1964); Honduras (1961); Jamaica (1960); Mexico (1960); Nicaragua (1963); Panama (1960); Puerto Rico (1960); Brazil (1960); Chile (1960); Colombia (1964); Ecuador (1962); Paraguay (1962); Peru (1961); Venezuela (1961). Uruguay was excluded as not belonging to the LDC group; Trinidad and Tobago and Guyana were excluded as two small countries with very high proportions of rural population and high R/U ratios untypical of the larger countries.

LDCs, Europe: Ireland (1961); Greece (1961); Cyprus (1960); Portugal (1960); Spain (1960).

DCs, Europe: Denmark (1960); Finland (1960); France (1962); Netherlands (1959); Norway (1960); Sweden (1960); Switzerland (1960); England and Wales (1961); Scotland (1961).

Other DCs: United States (1960); Canada (1961); Australia (1961); New Zealand (1961); Japan (1960).

Eastern Communist Europe: Bulgaria (average of 1956 and 1969); Czechoslovakia (1961); Hungary (1963); Poland (1960); Romania (average of 1956 and 1966); Yugoslavia (1961).

The ratios in columns 2–4 were calculated for each country; and then averaged for the group (arithmetic means). The entries in column 6 show the number of countries with ratios above 1.0, as in column 5.

---

widely stated observations as to the direction of rural-urban differences in fertility.[1]

(ii) The proportion of surviving children to total population is an approximation to the crude rate of natural increase; and unless we assume that the lower rate for the urban population is com-

---

1. In the United Nations, *The Determinants and Consequences of Population Trends* (New York, 1953), the discussion of rural-urban differences starts with the statement "that urban populations are less fertile than rural is one of the most widely observed and widely discussed phenomena in the field of fertility" (p. 85). In the *Population Bulletin of the United Nations*, no. 7–1963 (New York: 1965), the statement concerning differential fertility in low-fertility countries indicates that, on the basis of the census of 1950, "the child woman ratios (children 5–9 to women 20–49 years old) are significantly higher in rural than in urban areas of each country represented in the table" and "where more refined measures are available, they confirm that fertility is at present higher among rural than among urban residents of low-fertility countries (p. 124). The statement concerning urban-rural differentials in high-fertility countries (i.e., LDCs) is weaker, but uniformly higher fertility is shown for the rural populations of several countries in Asia and Latin America (pp. 129–134).

pensated by much higher survivor rates among the groups aged 5 and over, the rate of natural increase of total urban population is bound to be lower than that of rural population—although, as will be commented upon below, by a moderate margin. If so, rapid urbanization, i.e., marked rise in the *share* of urban in total population, can be produced only by internal migration—from the countryside to the cities; or, in the case of substantial immigration, by a concentration of the latter in urban areas.[2] But this means that when the share of urban population in the total rises substantially, large proportions of urban population must be newcomers, newly arrived immigrants—an inference of considerable interest in relation to some aspects of economic growth of which urbanization is such an integral part.[3]

---

2. This, of course, assumes that the rise in the proportion of urban population is not due to reclassification (of previously rural localities as urban); or at least that the latter is a minor element.

3. Under the simplifying assumptions of a closed population and the same rate of natural increase for urban, rural, and total population, one can derive the relation between the rise in the share of urban population over a period and the proportion in the latter, at the end of the period, of newcomers who in-migrated during the period.

Designate:

S_0, S_1—shares of urban in total population at times 0,1,

T_0, T_1—total population at times 0,1,

r—growth rate (natural increase) of total population.

Then:

urban population at time 1 will be $S_1(T_0)$ $(1 + r)$, whereas the urban population of time 1 that resulted from the natural increase of urban population at time 0 is $S_0 T_0$ $(1 + r)$. The *proportion* of new arrivals in the urban population at time 1, to this total, is then:

$$\frac{S_1 T_0(1 + r) - S_0 T_0(1 + r)}{S_1 T_0(1 + r)} = \frac{S_1 - S_0}{S_1}.$$

In other words, the share of newcomers in urban population equals the proportional change in the share of urban population in the total over the preceding time period, the proportion taken to the share at the *end* of the period. The newcomers component can be quite large when the share of urban population rises rapidly. Thus, in table 4 below the share of urban population in South Asia increased from 15.9 percent in 1950 to 18.2 percent in 1960. Under the simplified assumption above, the implication is that in 1960 in-migrants accounted for $(18.2-15.9)/18.2$, or 13 percent of the 1960 urban population of South Asia.

Of course, if the rate of natural increase of urban populations is *below* that of rural population, a rise in the share of urban in total population implies an even greater proportion of in-migrants than is shown by the equation above.

(iii) The differences between the rural and urban ratios of children under 5 to total population are, while fairly commonly observed, rather narrow—particularly for the LDCs. For the group as a whole (line 14), the difference is about 9 percent; and while the average would be slightly higher if the major regions were weighted by population, the increase would be slight. How narrow a differential that is can be seen by comparing the ratios of the LDCs and DCs (lines 14 and 15). The rural ratios of the LDCs are much larger than those of the DCs—the former exceeding the latter by 79 percent; and the excess of the urban ratios is even greater, amounting to 86 percent. Since any adjustment for infant and young children's mortality, to shift from crude fertility ratios to crude birth rates, will only augment this striking disparity between the LDCs and DCs, observed separately for their rural and urban populations, the *intra*country fertility differentials between rural and urban population, particularly in the LDCs, must be relatively small—compared with the striking *inter*country differentials.

The important implication is that if "rurality" is associated with high fertility and "urbanity" with low fertility, the rural populations of the DCs are far more urban than the urban populations of the LDCs; and the urban populations of the LDCs are far more rural than even the rural populations of the DCs. In other words, rurality and urbanity have different meanings (or consequences), as far as fertility is implied, in the two groups of countries.

(iv) It also follows that in trying to account for the higher overall ratio of children to population (and implicit fertility) in the LDCs than in the DCs, the proportions of rural-urban population are only a minor explanatory component. By weighting the ratios in lines 14 and 15 by the shares of rural and urban population (column 2), we derive an overall ratio for the LDCs of 174.6 per thousand; for the DCs of 92.2—a spread of 82.4 points. Even if we assumed that population in both sets of countries was only rural, the spread would still be 79 points; and if we assumed that population in both sets of countries was only urban, the spread would still be 76 points. In other words, the internal rural-urban differences account for only about 5 percent of the total spread in the crude fertility ratios between the LDCs and DCs.

If fertility is to decline in the process of modernization and economic growth, it must decline sharply among both rural and urban populations. A shift in the rural-urban proportions, while the intra-rural and intraurban fertility rates remain unchanged, will have but a minor effect.

(v) Finally, in several countries, particularly in Africa, the chil-dren-population ratio is *higher* for the urban than the rural popula-tion. Among these are the Democratic Republic of the Congo, the People's Republic of the Congo, Dahomey, Gabon, Mali, and Zambia in Sub-Saharan Africa; Algeria, Libya, and the United Arab Republic in North Africa. The recurrence of this exception suggests that it is not a statistical accident.[4] But further exploration of the African experience must await additional testing and refinement. Here we only note the important exception from a widespread finding.

In testing the findings in table 1, and considering their value as approximations to crude birth rates, we should deal with four prob-lems. First, how meaningful is the distinction between rural and urban population as drawn in the national censuses or samples underlying table 1? Second, how important is the differential trend problem involved in taking a ratio of a cumulated total, like that of children 0 through 4, to represent *annual* ratios of incidence of birth and fertility? Third, what is the possibility of errors in report-ing, particularly of children, and of *differences* in errors of report-ing between rural and urban populations? Finally, how large is the mortality component needed to shift from ratios of children under 5 to total births for the preceding quinquennium, or the crude birth rate?

Obviously, no final and specific adjustments for all these as-pects will be feasible, even with input of time and skill far ex-ceeding those at my disposal. Here, I can only define the problem,

---

4. For the Democratic Republic of the Congo the finding results from a sample study for 1955–1957. In "The Demography of the Democratic Re-public of the Congo," chapter 6 of *The Demography of Tropical Africa,* William Brass and others, eds. (Princeton: Princeton University Press, 1968), Anatole Romaniuk concludes: "Although the urban-rural difference in fertility has not been thoroughly examined in this study, it suffices to men-tion that there is a higher natality among the urban as compared to rural communities. The adjusted birth rate is 44 for rural and 52 for urban areas. This difference is partly attributable to the more favorable age structure of the urban population, partly to a higher proportion of urban married women, particularly in younger age classes" (p. 337).

illustrate its possible magnitude, and speculate on its effect on the conclusions suggested by table 1.

2. The Rural-Urban Division

The rationale for distinguishing urban population is that the implied density of residence—a large number of families in a relatively limited area—is associated with distinctive patterns of living of the population and with a distinctive occupational and industrial structure of the active part of that population. Thus the density of urban residence means some special problems, which often involve political and other service agencies; and it is associated with occupations and productive sectors that, unlike agriculture or fishing or forestry, do not require extensive land areas. The resulting nonagricultural occupations and production sectors imply different sets of social and economic costs of and rewards from children. Hence some significance is assumed to attach to the rural-urban division for fertility differentials.

While the meaning of urbanity as a distinctive pattern of life and a distinctive cast of occupations and production structures is clear, the *identification* of urban units is far from easy. Two criteria, reflected in the national census data, are prevalent. One is *administrative structure,* which has meaning because the presence of a "city" administration indicates the existence of problems in the pattern of living that necessitate a special adjustment in the governmental structure. The other is the *size* of the locality, as measured by total numbers living, with sufficient density, within a limited area. Neither criterion is itself unequivocal. Administrative distinctions can be obsolete, in that they apply to what is no longer an urban locality; or inadequate, in that they respond slowly to the rapid growth of a previously administratively unrecognized community. The size-of-locality criterion requires that the unit be defined, if city boundaries are not administratively fixed. For example, is it justifiable to group a thousand families living fifteen miles away from a thousand other families into one urban locality of two thousand families? Subsidiary criteria—physical proximity of residences, or occupational-production structure of the community—are sometimes employed. Obviously, the basic criteria do not permit firm distinction; and the lower limit of the

TABLE 2

Comparisons of Shares (%) of Rural in Total Population with the
Shares (%) of Agricultural in Total Male Labor Force,
Major Regions and Areas

Region (1)	Share of rural in total population (2)	Share of agricultural in male labor force (3)	Number of countries showing relation of columns 2 and 3 (4)	Area (5)	Share of rural in total population (6)	Share of agricultural in male labor force (7)
1. Subsaharan Africa (13)	84.8	76.8	10	Africa	82	78.8
2. North Afr. (5)	65.8	62.3	4	South Asia	82	71.0
3. Middle East (3)	55.9	50.8	2			
4. Asia (9)	81.2	70.3	9			
5. Latin Amer. (17)	58.0	60.2	14	Latin America (ex. Argentina)	54	57.2
6. LDCs, Europe (5)	59.2	44.4	4			
7. DCs, Europe (8)	39.2	20.0	8	Europe	42	26.8
8. U.S. and Canada (2)	30.2	12.5	2	North America	30	9.4
9. Austr. and N.Z. (2)	27.0	14.7	1			
				Oceania	36	27.1
10. Japan (1)	36.5	35.7	1			
11. East Com. Europe (6)	59.5	42.7	6			
12. LDCs (47)	70.5	66.4	28			
13. DCs (13)	35.7	17.7	12			

Notes: The entries in parentheses in column 1 indicate the number of countries to which the averages in columns 2 and 3 refer.

Columns 1 and 2: From data underlying table 1. Sabah and Sarawak were omitted (from Asia) because labor force data were not available; and England and Wales were combined with Scotland (in line 7) for comparability with labor force data.

Column 3: The underlying data are the share in 1960, of agriculture (and related industries) in total male labor force. The entries are unweighted arithmetic means of the shares for individual countries. For the countries covered see the notes to table 1 and the note above.

The labor force data are from the International Labour Office, *Labour Force Projections, 1965–1985* (Geneva, 1971), Parts I–IV. Table 3 in each Part shows the

(Notes continued on the following page)

(Table 2 notes continued)
distribution of the male labor force among three sectors, one of which is agriculture (including related industries such as fisheries, hunting, and forestry).

Columns 5–6: The underlying data are from United Nations, *Growth of the World's Urban and Rural Population, 1920–2000* (New York, 1969), table 1, p. 12, except that figures for Argentina (from *ibid.*, table 44, pp. 104–105) are subtracted from the totals for Latin America. It should be noted that these areas are continents; and Africa therefore includes South Africa among others and Oceania and North America include, in addition to Australia and New Zealand and United States and Canada, all other territories. East Asia (dominated by Mainland China) is excluded from South Asia. The percentages shown are implicitly weighted by population.

Column 7: The underlying data are from the ILO source cited for column 3.

size of locality treated as urban varies among the countries from a low of 1,000 to a high of 30,000.[5]

Although the distinction between rural and urban populations, as drawn in national censuses, is rough and contains elements of incomparability, it reveals for each country the major difference between the *more* rural, *more* agricultural and the *more* urban, *more* nonagricultural segments of the population (agriculture defined broadly to include related sectors, such as forestry and fisheries). We can, moreover, compare the division based on these census criteria, with those that are suggested by other criteria; and refine the concept of locality size by distinguishing within the urban population cities or towns of different size.

In table 2 we compare the share of rural population in the total, based largely on the census data used in table 1, with the share of agriculture in the total *male* labor force, for the year 1960. We used the agricultural share in male labor force primarily because the treatment of female labor, particularly in the agriculture sector, varies widely among countries. For our purposes it would have been better to have the share of agriculture in the male labor force, *excluding* the very young and unpaid family labor from both numerator and denominator. But the estimates at hand of both the agricultural and total male labor force are fairly inclusive, reaching down to the age of 10.

Columns 1–4 are based on data for individual countries almost identical with those in table 1 (excluding only one less developed,

---

5. For a more detailed discussion see United Nations, *Growth of the World's Urban and Rural Population, 1920–2000* (New York: 1969), pp. 7–10.

and one developed country—both because they were parts of larger national totals; and only the latter were covered in the labor force data). The conclusions are obvious.

(*a*) For the LDCs, the average shares of rural in total population and of agriculture in total male labor force are fairly close. Thus for the 47 LDCs, the averages are 70 and 66 percent, respectively.

(*b*) The two sets of shares tend to differ among the several less developed regions in the same way—with the Latin American and the Middle Eastern regions showing the smallest shares of both.

(*c*) By contrast, in the DCs the shares of rural population are far larger than the shares of agriculture in the male labor force. For the DCs, the average shares are 36 and 18 percent, respectively. This difference is due to the development of suburbs and urban activities in nonurban localities—a trend that has led to the distinction in a country like the United States between rural-farm and rural-nonfarm, with the latter dominating the rural division in recent years.

The comparison in columns 5–7 is for continents, and the average measures are, implicitly, weighted by population. The results are similar to those shown in columns 1–4: the two sets of percentages for the less developed areas are fairly close and the share of rural in total population is much larger than the share of agriculture in male labor force in the developed areas—particularly striking for North America.

One should note that not all the male labor force engaged in agriculture resides in rural localities: in some countries, and among the smaller cities, a substantial part of the urban population (as defined in the census) may follow agricultural or related pursuits. But even if we assume that the whole male labor force in agriculture does reside in rural areas, and that the rural and urban ratios of total population to male labor force are not too different, some of the rural population in Africa, and particularly in Asia, must be engaged in nonagricultural pursuits. In that sense there is not so much difference between these less developed and the developed areas—except that in the latter the nonagricultural components in rural population must be relatively much greater. On the assumption stated above, the nonagricultural component is about one-eighth of rural population in South Asia, about four-tenths in Europe and two-thirds in North America.

One suggestive inference follows: the rural-urban differentials in fertility may understate the agricultural-nonagricultural differentials, i.e., those that would be shown if population were divided between agriculture (and related industries) and the nonagricultural sectors. For the DCs, the difference would largely reflect the admixture of nonagricultural groups within the rural populations. For the LDCs it must reflect an admixture of agricultural population in the small towns and cities classified as urban; and if so, the admixture of nonagricultural population among the rural would be greater than suggested by the comparison of columns 2 and 3 or 6 and 7, of table 2.[6]

Admitting that the lines of division between rural and urban population in the census data blur the agricultural-nonagricultural distinction, we must recognize, however, that rural is far more agricultural than urban and urban far more nonagricultural than rural. And the differences between the rural and urban occupational and production structures should be sufficient to permit the associated fertility differentials to emerge. Nor should we exaggerate the magnitude of the blurring, at least as far as the rural division of the DCs is concerned (in which the disparity between the share of rural in total population and the share of agriculture in male labor force is prominent). In the United States, for which this disparity is among the widest, the number of children under 5 years of age per 1,000 women 20–44 was, in 1950, 766 for rural *farm* and 717 for rural *nonfarm*—a difference of only about 7 percent;[7] and the spread would probably not be much wider (relatively) for the ratio to total population.

The other relevant aspect of the rural-urban division is the distribution of the urban population among communities of different size. This question does not arise with respect to rural population, whose density is assumed to be relatively low throughout. But

---

6. The United Nations report, *The Determinants and Consequences of Population Trends* (New York: 1953), observes: "It has been pointed out that comparisons between the fertility of persons employed in agricultural and non-agricultural occupations often show larger differences than comparisons between residents of town and country" (pp. 85–86). But then it goes on to attribute this largely to the developed countries. "One explanation is that in several highly urbanized countries today, a large proportion of the persons classified as living in the country are inhabitants of city suburbs rather than of areas which are rural in character" (p. 86).

7. See Wilson H. Grabill, Clyde V. Kiser, and Pascal K. Whelpton, *The Fertility of American Women* (New York: 1958), table 32, p. 89.

TABLE 3

Index of Concentration of Urban Population, Major Areas, 1960

	Africa (1)	South Asia (2)	Latin America (ex. Arg.) (3)	Europe (4)	North America (5)	Oceania (6)
1. Urban as per cent of total population	18	18	46	58	70	64
Share in Total Urban Population of Population Living in Urban Localities of Differing Size (%)						
2. Localities of less than 20,000	20.4	24.6	34.1	24.0	16.8	17.0
3. Localities with popul. 20 to 100 thousand	25.8	27.6	21.3	25.4	11.1	15.0
4. Localities with popul. 100 thousand to 0.5 million	25.6	20.6	14.0	17.7	19.7	16.0
5. Localities with popul. 0.5 to 2.5 million	21.6	19.1	14.9	24.0	25.8	52.0
6. Localities with popul. 2.5 million and over	6.6	8.1	15.7	8.9	26.6	0

Assumed Indexes of Relative Fertility for Urban Population
(Fertility for Rural Population = 100)

	Africa	South Asia	Latin America	Europe	North America	Oceania
Assumption 1						
7. Index	86.6	87.1	87.2	86.6	83.3	84.9
8. R/U ratio (derived from line 7)	1.15	1.15	1.15	1.15	1.20	1.18
Assumption 2						
9. Index	84.9	85.3	84.8	84.5	79.3	82.3
10. R/U ratio (derived from line 9)	1.18	1.17	1.18	1.18	1.26	1.22

Line 1: The complements to 100 of the shares of rural population shown in table 2, column 6. They represent the shares of urban population as set in the national censuses.

Lines 2–6: From United Nations, *Growth of the World's Urban and Rural Population, 1920–2000* (New York, 1969), we derived the absolute totals of population in localities of 20 thousand and over, by size of locality classes (table 13, p. 32, with Argentina excluded from Latin America, on the basis of data in tables 42, 43, 44, and 46, pp. 100–105 and 107–113). Having the absolute total urban population for the same areas (from the same source and used for table 2, column 5), we subtracted the total of population living in urban localities of 20,000 and over, to derive the absolute data underlying line 2. The absolutes were then expressed as percentages of total urban population (census definition).

(Notes continued on the following page)

(Table 3 notes continued)

Lines 7 and 9: The relative fertility indexes assumed for the different size of urban localities groups were: in Assumption 1–95, 90, 85, 80, and 75–for groups of increasing size; in Assumption 2–95, 90, 85, 75, and 65. The indexes in lines 7 and 9 are derived by multiplying the percentage shares by the indexes just cited, and dividing the sum by 100. The assumed indexes are illustrative, but were suggested by data on child-women ratios by size of city in India for 1931 and 1941 (in Kingsley Davis, *The Population of India and Pakistan*, Princeton University Press, 1951, table 20, p. 71), in Japan for 1930 (in Irene B. Taeuber, *The Population of Japan*, Princeton University Press, 1958, table 98, p. 248), and in the United States for 1957 (in Clyde V. Kiser, "Differential Fertility in the United States," chart 13, p. 105, for 1957, in *Demographic and Economic Change in Developed Countries*, Princeton University Press for NBER, 1960).

Lines 8 and 10: Derived from lines 7 and 9, dividing 100 by the entry in lines 7 and 9.

---

urban population can reside in small cities of 20 thousand population or in multimillion metropolitan agglomerations. Fertility has been found to vary with the size of city, as selected data from sources cited in table 3 clearly indicate. Hence, we ought to inquire whether urban populations in the various major regions differ significantly in the degree of concentration in large agglomerations or in the degree of dispersion among urban localities of relatively moderate size.

Table 3 provides a rough answer to this question, in terms of the distribution in 1960 for large continental areas. We accept the rural-urban division given in the census data; and use the estimates of urban population for localities of 20,000 or more to derive the urban population in localities below the 20 thousand limit.

For lines 7–10 of the table we use some illustrative assumptions concerning fertility differentials associated with urban localities of different size and relate them to fertility of rural population as base. These assumptions are a substitute for specific knowledge of the fertility or birth rates, for the various countries, for population distributed among urban localities of different size. For lack of such specific data, we use some broad, hopefully realistic, assumptions concerning the association between fertility rates and urban locality size. Applying these assumptions uniformly to all the regions, we can see whether the distribution of urban population by locality-size contributes to the explanation of the findings on the rural-urban differentials in table 1.

Assumption 2 assigns a more sharply depressing effect on relative fertility than assumption 1, for the very large urban agglomerations, i.e., the two groups above the 0.5 million mark; but both assumptions yield roughly similar results.

In general, the indexes of concentration of urban population contribute little to the explanation of inter-area differences in the rural-urban fertility ratios. According to table 3, these ratios should not have differed significantly among the three less developed regions (Africa, South Asia, and Latin America), or between the latter and Europe. But table 1 shows rural-urban ratios that are appreciably lower for Africa than for either Asia or Latin America, or Europe. Again, according to table 3, the widest difference in rural-urban fertility should have been shown for North America, but in table 1 the difference for that area is narrower than that for Europe—and is among the lowest for developed regions. Only in the case of Oceania is there some agreement between the urban concentration indexes in table 3 and the R/U ratios in table 1.

Many more variant assumptions could have been used in table 3, and some might have altered the findings just noted. This would hardly contribute to our knowledge; nor is it necessarily realistic to assume that the function connecting city size and differential fertility (in relation to that of the nonurban population) has similar parameters in countries at different stages of economic development or with different structures of society and family. In the absence of specific data, we can only infer from table 3 that differences in the distribution of urban population by size of urban localities contribute little to the differences observed among the major regions in the magnitude of their rural-urban fertility differentials.

3. The Differential Trends Problem

The number of children under 5 and total population, urban and rural, underlying the ratio summarized in table 1, show fairly marked trends. This is especially true of urban and rural population. In the period immediately preceding 1960, and in practically all the major regions, urban population rose at much higher rates than rural population. Table 4 summarizes the data and the magnitudes of the relevant trends and of the differences between the rural and urban growth rates within each major area.

Disregarding for the moment possible trends in the numerator, i.e., the number of children under 5, and considering only the denominator, one would argue that the ratio should be calculated not to the population in 1960 (i.e., at the end of the period over which the number of children under 5 is cumulated) but to the

TABLE 4

Growth Rates of Rural and Urban Populations from 1950 to 1960,
Major Regions
(absolute totals in millions)

| | Absolute totals | | | | Growth rate per year | | |
| | Rural | | Urban | | Rural popu- lation | Urban popu- lation | Adjustment factor in R/U ratio |
	1950 (1)	1960 (2)	1950 (3)	1960 (4)	(5)	(6)	(7)
1. Africa	190	223	32	50	1.6	4.6	0.931
2. South Asia	586	702	111	156	1.8	3.5	0.961
3. Latin America	96	109	66	103	1.3	4.6	0.924
4. Lines 1−3	872	1,034	209	309	1.7	4.0	0.946
5. Europe	185	178	207	247	−0.4	1.8	0.948
6. North America	60	60	106	139	0	2.7	0.935
7. Oceania	6	6	7	10	0	3.6	0.915
8. Lines 5−7	251	244	320	396	−0.3	2.2	0.941
9. LDCs (as defined in the source)	1,391	1,605	267	409	1.4	4.4	0.932
10. DCs	420	394	438	583	−0.6	2.9	0.916

Notes: The underlying data are from the United Nations, *Growth of the World's Urban and Rural Population, 1920–2000* (New York, 1969), table 1, p. 12.

Lines 9–10: Less developed regions were defined to include East Asia without Japan, South Asia, Latin America without Temperate South America (Argentina, Uruguay, Chile), Africa, and Oceania without Australia and New Zealand. The developed group includes Europe, North America, the Soviet Union, Japan, Temperate South America, Australia, and New Zealand.

Rural and urban populations are distinguished as in the national censuses.

Column 7: The growth rates in columns 5 and 6 are applied backward to a two-and-a-half-year period preceding 1960–yielding revised bases to which to relate numbers of children under five in 1960. Each entry here, the inverse of the ratio of these bases, is the factor by which the R/U ratio in table 1 is to be multiplied, to allow for the differential trend adjustment for the total population base, and disregards any adjustment in the number of children.

middle of the quinquennium represented by the 0–4 age span (i.e., population around the middle of 1957 or 1958). The 1960 population contains sizable components that were added more recently, and cannot therefore be assumed to have contributed to the production of 4- or 3-year-old children. If then we relate the number of children under 5 in 1960 to the smaller population of two and a half years before, the ratios shown in table 1 would all be raised. The important point is that the urban ratios would be raised appreciably more than the rural, because the growth rate of the base population (the denominator) is so much higher.

Since the adjustment would raise the children-population ratio more for the urban than for the rural population, the R/U ratios shown in column 5 of table 1 would be reduced. Column 7 of table 4 shows the proportional reduction, derived from columns 5 and 6 of table 4. The reductions range from 4 to 8.5 percent— and their application to the R/U ratios in table 1 would practically cancel the differentials between the rural and urban ratios, when the R/Us are only slightly above 1 (as they are for Africa and the Middle East); and reduce the R/U ratio for LDCs as a whole to only slightly above 1.0.

But the above procedure implies that the higher rate of growth of total urban population, due, as suggested above, largely to internal migration (or migration from abroad with urban areas as destination), is *not* accompanied by migration of children below the age of 5. If children below 5 do migrate from rural to urban areas, the calculation of the children-population ratio as a gross fertility index should allow not only for the in-migration component of the *denominator* but also for the in-migration component of the *numerator*. Just as the former has to be excluded (and is in table 4 by shifting the population base gain two and a half years), so should the in-migration to urban population of children 0 to 4 be excluded. Our adjustment factor in column 7 of table 4 implies that the population that migrated toward the urban areas, producing a higher upward trend in the growth of urban population, included *no* children who were below 5 years of age in 1960 (or the end of the period).

How plausible is this assumption? One might argue that migratory moves from the countryside to urban localities would be impeded by the presence of infants or tiny children; and that, despite the well-known higher migration propensity of younger people and couples, only those without infants or with children over 5 would be moving. But, as will be suggested below, this conjecture is probably wrong. We need here, as elsewhere, detailed data on rural-urban migration, by age of migrant, particularly ages below 5.

Data for the United States, easily at hand, indicate clearly that "children of preschool age and persons from 18 to 34 years old are the only members of the population who have higher mobility rates than the average of all ages combined. These relatively mobile age groups include both unattached youths and young married couples and their children. Leaving the parental home to take a job or to get married and moving to adjust to the needs of a growing family seem to be key factors in these relatively high mobility rates. Both long-distance and short-distance mobility are affected." Thus for the decade preceding 1957–1958, the average annual mobility rate for long-distance movements (intercounty or interstate), i.e., the proportion of persons who moved during the preceding year, was 9.2 percent for children 1 through 4, compared with a ratio of 6.4 percent for total population. The high mobility groups among older persons were males and females in ages from 18 to 34. The percentage rates for females 20–34, particularly important for our purposes, were: 20–24—14.0 percent; 25–29—10.7 percent; and 30–34—7.2 percent.[8] Similar results are shown for a migration period from 1955 to 1960, yielding migration rates only for the 5–9 age group among children. The rate of non-local movement was also distinctly higher for the 5–9 group than for total population and matched the high rates for the 20–24, 25–29, and 30–34 groups among both males and females.[9]

It may be that in the United States, and perhaps in other developed countries, mobility of couples with children below 5 is higher than in the LDCs, particularly if in the latter the children may remain, at least temporarily, with the extended family in the countryside. To show the quantitative results of an assumption that is at the opposite end of that implied in table 4, we now as-

---

8. The quotation and data are from Henry S. Shyrock Jr., *Population Mobility within the United States,* Community and Family Study Center (University of Chicago, Chicago: 1964), pp. 351–352, and table 11.10, p. 354.

9. See Irene B. Taeuber and Conrad Taeuber, *People of the United States in the 20th Century,* a Census Monograph (U.S. Government Printing Office, Washington, D.C., 1971), table XIV–5, p. 840.

sume that the mobility of children under 5 is as high as that of their parents—and that the migration component among children under 5 in the urban areas can be approximated by comparing the proportions of women aged 20–34 in the urban and rural areas. A higher proportion of women aged 20–34 in urban population than in rural population would suggest higher mobility of women of those ages; and this assumption would imply high mobility for children under 5. In table 5 we assume that the proportional component of in-migrating children under 5 to all children under 5—to be used as an adjustment to the ratios of children under 5 in rural and urban areas—is approximated by the ratio of the proportions of women 20–34 among urban population to the proportions of women 20–34 among the rural population. A far more appropriate base would be provided by migration data or even the growth rates over the period of women aged 20–34 in the urban and rural areas. But even the latter data are not available except for a few developed countries, and are particularly scarce among the LDCs.

Table 5 reveals that the adjustment factor for the in-migration component of children under 5 in urban areas is rather moderate for Africa and Asia, and far more substantial for Latin America and the more developed areas (except Oceania). This difference is due to the very minor differences between the rural and urban shares of females 20–34 in Africa and South Asia—which suggests that on these continents the greater growth in urban population reflects *male,* not female, migration. The suggestion will be confirmed below when we deal with the *refined* fertility ratio differentials between rural and urban population. But since here we associate mobility of children under 5 with the mobility of females (the presumptive mothers) and not with the mobility of males, the adjustment for the migration component in the African and Asian rural-urban ratios is minor. This means that the rather low R/U ratios for these areas in table 1 would not be raised; while the appreciably higher R/U ratios for Latin America and most developed areas in table 1 would be raised further.

This finding concerning the different role of the sexes in the rural-urban migration in Africa and South Asia, compared with Latin America and most developed areas, is confirmed in the discussion of the urban male-female sex ratio in the United Nations

TABLE 5

Proportions of Women, Aged 20–34, in Population, Rural and Urban,
Derived In–Migration Component of Children 0–4 in Urban Population,
and Adjustment Factors to be Applied to the R/U Ratios in table 1,
Major Regions, Late 1950's and Early 1960's

	Number of coun- tries (1)	Proportions, women 20–34 (%) Rural (2)	Proportions, women 20–34 (%) Urban (3)	Ratio col. 3/ col. 2 (4)	Number of coun- tries with ratio above 1 (5)	Adjust- ment factor (6)	R/U (7)	R/U ad- justed (8)
1. Subsaharan Africa	12	13.5	14.6	1.08	11	(1.01)	1.03	1.04
2. North Africa	5	10.8	11.2	1.04	5	(0.97)	1.03	1.00
3. Middle East	3	10.2	10.4	1.02	2	(0.95)	1.04	0.99
4. South Asia	10	11.4	11.5	1.01	4	0.97	1.12	1.09
5. Latin America	17	10.0	12.2	1.22	17	1.13	1.15	1.30
6. LDCs, Europe	5	10.4	12.6	1.21	5	(1.15)	1.08	1.24
7. DCs, Europe	9	8.6	10.4	1.20	9	(1.15)	1.10	1.27
8. North America	2	8.3	10.4	1.25	2	1.17	1.07	1.25
9. Oceania	2	9.2	9.4	1.02	1	0.93	1.34	1.25
10. Japan	1	11.4	13.8	1.21	1	1.16	1.12	1.30
11. Comm. East. Europe	6	10.8	12.7	1.18	6	(1.12)	1.20	1.36
12. Africa	17	12.7	13.6	1.07	16	1.00	1.03	1.03
13. Europe	20	9.7	11.6	1.20	20	1.14	1.13	1.29
14. LDCs	47	11.26	12.43	1.10	39	1.03	1.09	1.12
15. DCs	14	8.86	10.49	1.18	14	1.08	1.14	1.23

Notes: Columns 1–4: The countries are those listed in the notes to table 1 excluding
Zambia from Subsaharan Africa (because of lack of detailed age breaks); and the source
of the data is also given there.

Column 5: Shows the number of countries in which the ratio in col. 4 is above 1.

Column 6: The product of the ratio in column 4 and in table 4, column 7. Since the
latter is given only for major continents, we applied the ratio for Africa in column 7 of
table 4 to the ratios in table 5 for Subsaharan Africa, North Africa, and the Middle East;
the ratio for Europe to the ratios for less developed non-Communist Europe, developed
non-Communist Europe, and Communist Eastern Europe; and the ratio for South Asia
to the ratio for Japan. Because of the disparity in matching areas, the total adjustment
factor in these cases is put in parentheses.

Column 7: From table 1, column 5, and represent the relatives of the rural gross
fertility ratio to the urban.

Column 8: Product of ratios in columns 6 and 7.

document on urbanization. Commenting upon the high sex ratio in urban Africa and Asia, and the low ratio in the urban populations of developed countries, the document presents the possible reasons (quoted here because of their bearing on conditions of migration of children under 5):

> The reasons for this diversity in the distribution of individuals of either sex between town and countryside are complex. Urban conditions may be responsible. Thus, in most of the less developed areas, where the cities may be lacking in suitable residences for families and there are often few employment opportunities for women, the masculinity rate is higher in the urban areas than in the rural areas. In the cities of the more developed areas, two factors are perhaps important. One is the more suitable residential accommodations for wives and children of male workers in cities of the more developed areas. The second is the tendency for office and other service employments to attract female workers to the cities of more developed areas. However, rural conditions may be no less determining, such as the needs for cash income and varied opportunities for men or women to earn them locally, and differences in family roles and responsibilities on the part of young rural men or women.[10]

All one can add is a question as to the conditions in Latin America that, unlike those in Asia and Africa, do induce a much larger migration toward the cities of women than of men.

The combination of the adjustment factors for the migration component among children under 5 in urban communities, with those for the difference in growth rates of total populations, yields net adjustment factors for the R/U ratios of table 1. These, shown in column 6, are applied to the R/U ratios in column 7 to derive the adjusted R/U ratios in column 8. The net adjustment factors accentuate the contrast between the rather low rural-urban differentials in Africa and South Asia, and the fairly sizable differentials in Latin America and in the DCs already suggested in table 1. But even the latter, which range in column 8 around 1.2 to 1.3, are still rather small compared with the international differentials, i.e., those for either the rural or the urban populations between the less and more developed countries.

---

10. See United Nations, *Growth of the World's Population* (New York: 1969), p. 15.

4. Errors of Understatement

Needless to say, the data on number of children under 5, as well as total population, rural and urban, are subject to error; as are all further breakdowns of rural or urban population by sex and age, to be used below. Social and economic data, particularly in the LDCs, are subject to error. The specific bodies of data need to be examined critically and tested whenever possible. Particularly in the case of international comparisons involving a variety of LDCs, findings cannot be much more than suggestive, especially if differences are minor.

The point warrants specific mention here, because the number of children under 5 is commonly understated, usually because of failure to report infants. For the United States, children under 5 years of age were reported in the decennial censuses from the beginning of the nineteenth century, and the check on their enumeration reveals that for the censuses before 1900 (excepting those for 1850, 1870, and 1890, affected by greater-than-usual undercounts), the understatement for white children ranged from 5 to 7 percent, and that for nonwhite children from 10 to 15 percent. More relevant to our discussion is the evidence, available only for 1950, which shows that the undercount was smallest for urban population, and greatest for rural farm.[11] But the question is whether these data for the United States, even if they extend to the beginning of the nineteenth century, are relevant to the current experience of less developed countries (and there is also the problem of differential undercount in the total urban and rural population, or in such relevant components of these as women of child-bearing ages). It can be easily demonstrated that the more urbanized, more developed *countries* would show a relatively smaller understatement of children under 5 than the more rural, less developed countries; and this means that the comparisons in table 1 and others *understate* the wide difference in fertility rates

---

11. See Wilson H. Grabill, Clyde V. Kiser, and Pascal K. Whelpton, *The Fertility of American Women,* a Census Monograph (New York: John Wiley & Sons, 1958), p. 13, for the broad statement; pp. 406–413 of appendix A, for detailed discussion. The estimates for 1950, in table A-8, p. 411, show a percentage undercount for urban white children of only 1 to 2 percent; for rural nonfarm white of 7 to 8 percent; for rural farm white of about 10 percent.

between the LDCs and DCs. But we need to know the differential between the understatement of the urban and rural populations within a given country, developed or less developed, and particularly of the less developed.

Warren C. Robinson has argued in several papers that the non-Western countries have not shown the lower urban than rural fertility rate that has been observed so widely among the Western countries. Having examined the data critically, he concludes, in the specific case of India that there is no basis for assuming that enumerative errors, and particularly net underenumeration, have been "concentrated in rural or urban areas." [12] One could argue that in general, censuses are probably more accurate for cities and urban localities than for the countryside—but this is not necessarily true for cities with large slums populated by recent in-migrants, compared to a countryside well covered by local reporters.

In its *Population Bulletin no. 7–1963* (New York: 1965), dealing largely with worldwide conditions and trends of fertility, the United Nations uses the ratio of children 5–9 years old (to a base comprising women of reproductive ages 20–49). "By relating the number of children aged 5–9 to women 20–49 years of age instead of using a ratio that involves the age group under 5 years, distortion due to differential under-enumeration of infants and very young children is avoided." [13] Although this shift magnifies the problems of adjustment for differential trend bias, and for the mortality component, we followed the example and calculated these ratios for comparison with those of children 0–4 shown in table 1 (table 6).

For a country as a whole and a closed population the number of children 5–9 years old will differ from the number 0–4, for several reasons. *a.* All other conditions being equal, an allowance for mortality over the added years would mean fewer children 5–9 than those 0–4 in the preceding quinquennium. *b.* If the base population grows, the number of children born in one quinquennium should be smaller than the number born in the following quinquennium—again making for fewer children 5–9 than 0–4 years of age. *c.* Since underenumeration is assumed to be much greater

---

12. See his "Urban-Rural Differences in Indian Fertility," *Population Studies* 14, 3 (1961), p. 222.

13. See the report, footnote 8, p. 124.

proportionately for children 0–4 than for those 5–9, all other conditions being equal, the number of older children should be larger than that of the younger group. *d*. A change in the birth rate from the earlier to the later quinquennium may either raise or lower the number of children 5–9, relative to the younger group.

Each of these factors—mortality, trend of the base, underenumeration, and birth rate—may have differential effects on rural and urban children 5–9 compared with children 0–4. In addition we have a fifth factor—the rate of internal migration, which may be different during the later quinquennium from that for the whole decade over which children 5–9 could have moved since their birth. Perhaps the only reasonable assumption concerning the differential effects is that the trend base adjustment, relating in the case of children 5–9 to a seven-and-a-half-year period rather than the two-and-a-half-year period used for children 0–4, is appreciably larger for urban children 5–9 compared with rural children 5–9 than it is for rural-urban differentials for children 0–4. In that case the *unadjusted* ratios of children 5–9 to population should be lower than those for children 0–4 for the *urban* comparison than for the *rural* comparison.

With these brief comments on the possible sources of disparity between children 5–9 and children 0–4 within a closed population for a country as a whole, and the differential impact of the trend in the base, on the rural and urban differences between the two groups of children, we can now examine table 6.

(i) For most regions, the ratios to population of children 5–9 are distinctly lower than the ratios of children 0–4 in table 1. This means that the factors of additional mortality and the use of population at the end of the period as base reduced the number of children 5–9 more than it was raised by lesser underenumeration. And presumably neither the birth rate, if it declined from the earlier to the later quinquennium, nor the migration rate, changed sufficiently to reverse the result.

(ii) But there were some exceptions: in developed Europe (rural population only, line 7), Japan (line 10) and Communist East Europe (line 11), the children 5–9 ratios were higher than children 0–4 ratios. Apparently, in these regions the birth rate *declined* from the earlier to the later quinquennium, in a way in which it did not for the other regions.

TABLE 6

Children, 5–9, per 1,000 of Population, Rural and Urban, Major Regions,
Late 1950's and Early 1960's
(compared with ratios for children 0–4)

	Rural			Urban			R/U Ratios		
	5 to 9 per 1,000 (1)	Rela- tive to 0–4 (2)	No. of coun- tries as in 2 (3)	5 to 9 per 1,000 (4)	Rela- tive to 0–4 (5)	No. of coun- tries as in 5 (6)	Chil- dren 5–9 (col.1/ col.4) (7)	Rela- tion to 0–4 ratio (col.2/ col.5) (8)	No. of coun- tries as in 8 (9)
1. Subsaharan Africa (13)	151	0.84	13	139	0.80	13	1.09	1.05	7.5
2. North Africa (5)	154	0.84	5	146	0.82	5	1.05	1.02	3
3. Middle East (3)	157	0.81	3	146	0.78	3	1.08	1.04	2
4. South Asia (10)	157	0.95	6	141	0.96	6	1.11	0.99	5.5
5. Latin America (17)	163	0.90	17	139	0.88	17	1.17	1.02	10
6. LDCs, Europe (5)	105	0.96	4	88	0.87	5	1.19	1.10	5
7. DCs, Europe (9)	90	1.03	4	77	0.97	7	1.17	1.06	8
8. U.S. and Canada (2)	120.5	0.97	2	103.5	0.89	2	1.16	1.09	2
9. Austr. & New Zealand (2)	124.5	0.90	2	96	0.93	2	1.30	0.97	2
10. Japan	114	1.27	1	89	1.11	1	1.28	1.14	1
11. Comm. East Europe (6)	104	1.07	5.5	90	1.11	4	1.16	0.96	4
12. Africa (18)	152	0.84	18	141	0.81	18	1.07	1.04	10.5
13. Europe (20)	98	1.02	10.5	84	0.99	14	1.17	1.03	15
14. LDCs (48)	157	0.88	44	141	0.86	44	1.11	1.02	27
15. DCs (14)	101	1.01	5	84	0.95	11	1.20	1.05	11

Notes: For the countries included and the basic source for columns 1, 4, and 7, see the notes to table 1.

Columns 1, 4: Arithmetic means of ratios calculated separately for each country.

Columns 2, 5, 7, and 8: Ratios of the averages in columns 1 and 4, of those in columns 2 and 5 and those in table 1, columns 3 and 4.

Columns 3, 6, and 9: Number of countries for which the relative is either below or above 1 –as shown in columns 2, 5, and 8. Equality is counted as a half country.

This can be confirmed for the developed countries, Europe and Latin America, for which acceptable crude birth rates for the two quinquennia, 1950–1954 and 1955–1959 can be secured. The average rates per 1,000 with number of countries for each region shown in parentheses, are: [14]

	1950–1954	1955–1959
LDCs, Europe (5)	22.4	22.3
DCs, Europe (9)	18.6	17.9
Comm. Europe (6)	24.8	21.6
U.S. and Canada (2)	26.1	26.2
Australia and		
New Zealand (2)	24.4	24.4
Japan (1)	23.7	18.2
Latin America (11)	44.6	44.9

The average crude birth rate declined significantly in developed non-Communist Europe, Communist Europe, and Japan—the three regions in table 6 with higher ratios for children 5–9 than for the 0–4 group (see column 2). The absence of such decline explains the shortfall in the ratios for the older children for the LDCs in Europe, the United States and Canada, Australia and New Zealand; and among the less developed regions, Latin America. No reliable birth rates are available for a sufficient number of less developed countries in the other regions.

(iii) As might have been expected, the urban ratios of children 5–9 tend to drop somewhat further below those of children 0–4 than the rural (compare columns 2 and 5). But this difference is neither general, nor is it large when it occurs.

(iv) For our purposes the important comparison is of the R/U ratios in columns 7–9. The differences among regions and groups in the R/U ratios for children 5–9 are quite similar to those shown in table 1. Here also the R/U ratios for Africa and Asia are rather narrow. They are distinctly wider in Latin America, and in the

---

14. The composition of the groups is that given in table 1, except that data were not available for six of the seventeen Latin American countries, included: Dominican Republic; Jamaica; Nicaragua; Puerto Rico; Brazil; and Paraguay.

The source for all but Latin America is the United Nations, *Demographic Yearbook, 1964* (New York: 1965), table 19, pp. 484 ff. Data for Latin America are from the Collver monograph (cited in notes to table 7) table 5, pp. 28–30; table 17, p. 82; and table 20, p. 90.

DCs. For the LDCs and DCs (lines 14 and 15) the R/U ratios in table 6 are 1.11 and 1.20, respectively—in table 1 they were 1.09 and 1.14. And as in table 1, the intracountry rural-urban differentials are much narrower than the intercountry differentials—particularly those for the urban communities.

Thus, in general, if the children 5–9 ratios can be viewed as more reliable indexes of fertility than the children 0–4 ratios, the comparison only confirms the findings for the children 0–4 ratios, the differences being largely explicable in terms of *expected* differences associated with the mortality and trend-base components and the *observed* changes over time in the crude birth rates.

5. The Mortality Component

For the analysis of rural-urban differences in the rate of natural increase, disregarding the internal migration (or immigration) factor, it is the proportional additions through surviving children rather than fertility and births proper that are relevant. But we are also interested in the rural-urban differences in fertility and mortality, because of the distinctive determinants involved and their different responses to modernization and technological change in the process of economic growth. If, having considered the ratios of children 0–4, we can ascertain the rural-urban differences in mortality, it would be possible to shift from the children/ population ratios to the crude birth rates; and, with further refinement in the population base, to standardized birth rates.

Before attempting to establish the mortality rates of children 0–4 for rural and urban populations separately, we do so for countrywide population (table 7). These rates will serve as a check on the representativeness of our sample of countries—since the crude birth rates so derived can be compared with those estimated for the major regions of the world by the United Nations; but even more relevant, they tell us in advance how important the rural-urban differentials in children's mortality can be in shifting from ratios of children to ratios of births. If the overall mortality levels are low, and survival rates high, even substantial *relative* rural-urban differences in mortality will have little effect on the shift from children to birth ratios.

The calculations in table 7 are limited to the groups of countries that enter the total for the LDCs and DCs (omitting the less

TABLE 7

Approximations to Shift from Children 0–4 Ratios to Crude Birth Rates,
Late 1950's and Early 1960's

	Infant mortal-ity (per 1,000 live births) (1)	Ratio to mor-tality to age 5 (2)	Ratio to mor-tality, children 0–4 (3)	Survival ratio, children 0–4 (4)	Children 0–4 per 1,000 (5)	Crude births per 1,000, 5 years (6)
1. DCs, 1955–59 for col. 1 and 3 (14)	24.5	0.80	0.89	0.97	92	95
2. Subsaharan Africa	162	0.60	0.75	0.78	178	228
3. North Africa and Middle East	120	0.60	0.75	0.84	186	222
4. South Asia	120	0.60	0.75	0.84	162	193
5. Latin America, 1955–59 for col. 1 and 3 (11)	93	0.60	0.75	0.88	172	195
6. All LDCs					174	208

Notes: The numbers of countries for which data were used in calculating the averages in column 1 are given in the stubs for lines 1 and 5.

Line 1: The entries in column 1 are averages of infant mortality rates, for each country for 1955-1959, from United Nations, *Demographic Yearbook, 1963* (New York, 1965), table 22, pp. 522*ff.* For list of countries covered see notes to table 1. The ratio in column 2 is from life tables for the United States, which indicate that cumulative death rates to age 5 are barely 10 per cent above those to age 1 (see e.g. U.S. Department of Health, Education and Welfare, Public Health Service, *Life Tables 1959–1961* 1, 3 (May, 1965). Also the Collver monograph, cited for line 5 below, shows for Argentina, for 1955–1959, an infant mortality of 62 and a cumulative death rate to age of 5 of only 71, both per 1,000 (see table 11, p. 66). Column 3 is the ratio of infant mortality to that of children under 5, adding to the former half of the spread between column 2 and 1.0. This is a rough approximation, which balances the lesser mortality in the fourth and fifth years of life by centering the average age at 3.0 rather than at 2.5 years. Column 4 is the survival rate of children under 5, i.e. 1.0 minus [(col. 1:1,000)/col. 3]. Column 5 is from table 1, columns 3 and 4 properly weighted. Column 6 is derived by dividing column 5 by column 4.

Lines 2–4: Column 1 is based on the sources cited in table 8 (which deals with rural-urban differentials in mortality), and several others. The other main sources are: United Nations, *Population Bulletin no. 6, 1962* (with special reference to mortality) (New York, 1963), tables III.16 and III.20, pp. 39 and 45; Gwendolyn Z. Johnson, "Health Conditions in Rural and Urban Areas of Developing Countries," *Population Studies* 17 (March, 1964), tables 1, 5A, 5B, pp. 295, 298–299; A. E. Sarhan, "Mortality Trends in the United Arab Republic," table 1, pp. 359-360, in United Nations, *World Population Conference, 1965*, 2 (New York, 1967); and H. Wiesler, "Mortality in South-East Asia," tables 1 and 2, p. 285 (in the UN volume cited for the Sarhan paper). The ratio in column 2 is that established for the less developed countries in Latin America (see notes to line 5). For the derivation of columns 3, 4, and 5 see the notes to line 1.

(Notes continued on the following page)

(Table 7 notes continued)

Line 5: Arithmetic means for eleven Latin American countries–used in table 1, excluding the Dominican Republic, Jamaica, Nicaragua, Puerto Rico, Brazil, and Paraguay. The data are from Andrew Collver, *Birth Rates in Latin America: New Estimates of Historical Trends and Fluctuations,* Institute of International Studies, University of California, Berkeley, Research Series, no. 7 (Berkeley, 1965), successive tables for individual countries. For the derivation of the rates see chapter 1, particularly his appendix, pp. 15–24. The source gives both infant mortality rates and survival ratios to age 5.

Line 6: Averages of the entries in lines 2–5 weighted by the number of countries covered in table 1 (13 for line 2, 8 for line 3, 10 for line 4, and 17 for line 5).

---

developed countries of Europe and Eastern Communist Europe). For the DCs and Latin America, the data underlying the mortality rates of infants and children under 5 are quite adequate; for Africa and Asia we used data from scattered sources, some of which are cited in table 8, which deals with rural-urban differentials in children's mortality.

The final result appears in column 5, in which the entries represent the ratio of cumulated live births over the 5 years to total population at the *end* of the five-year period. An allowance for the trend bias in the population base, of between 1 and 1.5 percent per year growth for the DCs and varying from over 2 to almost 3 percent per year for the regions within the less developed group, would raise the numbers in column 6 by about 3 percent for the DCs and between 5 and 8 percent for the regions within the less developed group. This would yield a crude birth rate *per year* of about 19.5 per 1,000 for the developed countries (i.e., 95/5 multiplied by 1.03), and between 43.7 and 44.9 per 1,000 for the less developed regions (i.e., 208/5 multiplied by 1.05 to 1.08) with the rates lowest in South Asia and highest in Sub-Saharan Africa. The United Nations estimates of the crude birth rates for 1956–1960, weighted by population (rather than number of countries) for each region (e.g., in *Demographic Yearbook, 1961* [New York: 1962], table 2, p. 120) are 19 for Europe (with many countries) and 25 for North America (with just two countries), 45 in tropical and southern Africa, 47 to 48 in North Africa and Southeast Asia, 42 in Latin America, and 41 in South Asia. Thus the crude birth rates derived from our samples are in conformity with the UN estimates.

Perhaps more important for our purposes are two conclusions suggested by table 7. First, since the mortality rates of children under 5 in the developed countries are about 30 per 1,000 and the survival rates 970 per 1,000, even striking rural-urban differentials in mortality would have little effect on the estimates of rural-urban differences in birth rates derived from ratios of children to population. Thus, even if rural mortality were *twice* that of the urban (or *vice versa*) the difference in survival rates would be between, say, 980 and 960 (corresponding to cumulative mortalities of 20 and 40, respectively)—or barely 2 percent. Only when mortality is very high can the differences between rural and urban fertility as reflected in the ratios of children to population differ markedly from those shown by birth rates.

Second, the difference between the LDCs and the DCs is appreciably wider for crude birth rates than for children/population ratios. The spread of the latter, between 92 and 174, is 82 points; that between the birth rates in column 5 is from 95 to 208, or 113 points—about 40 percent greater. This means that the intracountry rural-urban differentials in birth rates would have to be *wider* than the differentials in the child ratios, in order to contribute even the minor explanatory fraction that was contributed by the latter to the spread between the LDCs and DCs in the ratio of children under 5.

We turn now to the question as to the rural-urban differentials in infant and young children's mortality *within* a country, and their sign and magnitude—particularly for the LDCs where these differences may affect our comparisons significantly. There is no conclusive answer in the literature. Warren C. Robinson, in the paper cited in footnote 12, presents evidence for 1911 to 1950 of higher infant mortality in the large cities than in the countryside of the three large provinces of India: Madras, Bombay, and Bengal (see his paper, table 2, p. 22); and in the paper cited in the notes to table 8 below, he continues to argue for the occurrence of higher urban than rural mortality in the LDCs. On the other hand, Eduardo E. Arriaga (using Mexico to illustrate) argues that mortality is grossly underreported in rural areas of the LDCs because of the difficulties of access; and that a proper correction for the latter factor would show adjusted mortality rates to be higher in the countryside.[15]

---

15. See his "Rural-Urban Mortality in Developing Countries: An Index for Detecting Rural Underregistration, *Demography* 4, 1 (1967), pp. 98–107.

In attempting to arrive at some acceptable conclusion, the following considerations seem important. First, undoubtedly in the past, and perhaps as late as the early twentieth century, children's mortality was higher in the cities than in the countryside even in developed countries. This appears to have been true, at least of the United States, as late as 1910.[16] Second, in the DCs this greater mortality in the cities has been reduced and in recent decades was not higher, a significant change considering the large in-migrations of rural population. Third, in the LDCs mortality rates have declined rapidly within recent decades, and in the course of such declines, the urban-rural differentials may also have changed rapidly. This means that for our purposes, for 1960 or thereabout, it may be misleading to use unadjusted mortality data, even for the preceding decade. Finally, the available data probably understate mortality for both urban and rural populations. But given the state of roads and communications in the rural areas of the LDCs, and the bias toward recording deaths by place of occurrence rather than by place of residence of the deceased (which raises recorded mortality in cities), the chances of a greater understatement in the countryside are rather high.

The mortality data in table 8 illustrate these general statements and carry them forward. By combining them with some general references, we may be able to come to some acceptable conclusions.

Table 8 is *not* based on a complete and exhaustive combing of data for individual countries—a task beyond our resources, and one unlikely to yield much firmer results, considering the scarcity and poor quality of many of the data for the LDCs. But it is a summary of data easily available in the United Nations and the journal literature. With the broad conclusions suggested one can derive implications realistic enough to warrant further exploration of the analytical questions that they raise.

In panel A we have fifteen LDCs for which a comparison can be made between infant mortality for the main city and for the country as a whole in recent years. For Ceylon, the two sources yield conflicting conclusions; for Egypt and Thailand, infant mortality is about the same in the city and in the country as a whole;

---

16. See Irene B. and Conrad Taeuber, *People of the United States in the 20th Century* (Washington, D.C.: 1971), p. 518.

TABLE 8

Infant and Young Children's Mortality, Rural and Urban,
Less Developed Countries

A. Infant Mortality in Major City and Country

Country and Period Covered (1)	Major City (2)	Infant Mortality, per 1,000 Country (3)	Infant Mortality, per 1,000 Major City (4)
1. Madagascar, registration system, 1958	Tananarive City	74	63
2. Egypt, 1950–59	Cairo	166	166
3. Algeria, 1950–59	Algiers	92	98
4. Ceylon, 1950–59	Colombo	74	83
4a. Ceylon, 1959–60	Colombo	58	50
5. India, 1950–59	Bombay	110	122
5a. India (reg.) 1959–60	Bombay, Calcutta, Madras	87	92, 130, 129
6. Philipp. 1950–59	Manila	100	66
7. Thailand, 1950–59	Bangkok	62	62
8. Malay, 1950–59	Singapore	83	58
8a. Malay, 1959–60	Kuala Lumpur	66	51
9. Costa Rica, 1959–60	San Jose	89	44
10. Chile, 1959–60	Santiago, Valparaiso	120	83, 88
11. Colombia, 1950–59	Bogota	110	104
11a. Colombia, 1959–60	Bogota	97	82
12. El Salvador, 1950–60	San Salvador	80	90
12a. El Salvador, 1959–60	San Salvador	78	84
13. Mexico, 1950–59	Mexico City	86	85
14. Panama, 1959–60	Panama City	58	48
15. Venezuela, 1959–60	Caracas	55	53

B. Infant (or Total) Mortality, Rural and Urban, Africa

	Rural (1)	Urban (2)	Total (3)
16. Cent. African Rep. Cent. Oubagui Region, 1959	188	197	190
17. Guinea, 1954–55	200	215	202
17a. Guinea, mortality to age 5, 1954–55	378	346	378
18. Senegal, 1957 La Basse Vallee region	152	172	167
19. Mali, 1957–58	320	246	293

Congo, Democratic Republic, 1955–57 Survey

	Rural (1)	Mixed (2)	Urban (3)	Total (4)
20. Infant mortality, per 1,000	195	142	106	177
21. Mortality to age 5, per 1,000	325	238	178	299

(Continued)

(Table 8 continued)

Taiwan, 292 Townships and Cities Grouped by Density, 1961 Population per Square Mile

		0–299 (1)	300– 999 (2)	1,000– 2,999 (3)	3,000– 9,999 (4)	10,000 and up (5)
22.	Male labor force in agriculture & fishing as % of total	74.4	72.3	64.3	28.5	8.3
23.	Crude death rate per 1,000	8.1	7.3	6.9	6.3	4.5

Thailand, Four Regions, Middle 1960's

		Central (1)	South (2)	North (3)	Northeast (4)
24.	Urban as % of region population	32.3	11.2	6.3	4.0
25.	Standardized death rate	10.3	7.9	12.3	11.6

Bangladesh, Retrospective Study, Two Periods

		1952–56		1957–61	
		Rural (1)	Urban (2)	Rural (3)	Urban (4)
26.	Infant mortality	167	130	150	101

Turkey, 1963 and 1966 Surveys

		Rural (1)	Non-Metro-politan Urban (2)	Metropolitan (3)
27.	Mortality to age of 2, around 1960 (per 1,000)	244	200	128
28.	Infant mortality, around 1966	167	135	114
29.	Expectation of life at birth, around 1966	52.2	57.0	60.3

Notes: Lines 2–4, 5, 6, 7, 8, 11, 12, 13: From Warren C. Robinson, "Urbanization and Fertility: the non-Western Experience," *Milbank Memorial Fund Quart.* 41, 3 (1963): table 2, p. 300. We omitted several countries excluded from our sample in table 1 (Guyana, Argentina, and Uruguay). The ratios shown are infant deaths (below 1 year of age) per 1,000 live births.

Lines 1, 4a, 5a, 8a, 9, 10, 11a, 12a, 14–19: From the Gwendolyn Johnson paper, and the United Nations, *Population Bulletin no. 6* cited in the notes to lines 2–4 of table 7.

Lines 20–21: From Anatole Romaniuk, "The Demography of the Democratic Republic of the Congo," chapter 6 of William Brass and others, *The Demography of Tropical Africa* (Princeton University Press, Princeton, 1968), table 6.36, p. 311.

Lines 22–23: From Andrew Collver, Alden Speare Jr., and Paul K. C. Liu, "Local Variations of Fertility in Taiwan," *Population Studies* 20, 3 (1967): table 4, p. 336.

(Notes continued on the following page)

(Table 8 notes continued)
Lines 24–25: From Sidney Goldstein, "Urbanization in Thailand, 1947–1967," *Demography* 8, 2 (1971): table 6, p. 217.

Line 26: From T. Paul Schultz, "Retrospective Evidence of a Decline in Fertility and Child Mortality in Bangladesh," *Demography* 9, 3 (1972): p. 419.

Lines 27–29: From Frederic C. Shorter, "Information on Fertility, Mortality, and Population Growth in Turkey," *Population Index* 34, 1 (1968): table 3, p. 11. Mr. Shorter observes that the data centering on 1966 are from a sample that refers "to only 71 percent of the population, which excludes areas containing poor rural mortality"; and that "the differentials are probably understated" (p. 11).

---

for nine countries (Costa Rica, Chile, Colombia, Mexico, Panama, Venezuela, Madagascar, Philippines, Malaya), infant mortality is lower in the main city and for three (Algeria, India, and El Salvador), infant mortality in the city is higher. On the balance of this evidence, we should assume a lower mortality in the main city, although the panel is heavily dominated by Latin America. This conclusion is strengthened on the reasonable assumption that the data are more *complete* for the main city. Furthermore, registration of deaths by place of occurrence would inflate the urban mortality ratios.

The conclusions from panel B are also weighted in favor of assuming lower mortality for the urban than for the rural populations. For the 5 African countries, two, the Central African Republic and Senegal, show a higher urban infant mortality (lines 16 and 18); in Guinea mortality to age 5 is greater in rural than in urban areas (although both are quite high, line 17a); and in the Congo the lower mortality in the mixed and urban areas is marked (in table 1 mixed and urban were taken to represent urban). For the four Asian countries (for two of which only total mortality is available), lower urban mortality is clearly indicated.

If one attempts to reach some reasonable conclusions concerning differential rural-urban mortality of children under 5 in the LDCs, the consensus reported for Latin America seems clear. "On the whole, it may be said that in the five countries (Argentina, Brazil, Chile, Panama, and Venezuela, *SK*) for which mortality data have been examined, infant mortality is generally less widespread in the urban than in the total population." [17] A similar

---

17. See Philip M. Hauser, ed., *Urbanization in Latin America,* (Columbia University Press for UNESCO, New York: 1961), "Demographic Aspects of Urbanization in Latin America," by the Population Branch, Bureau of Social Affairs, United Nations, p. 107.

conclusion, referring to the recent spread of control over infectious diseases which reversed the balance in favor of lower mortality in the urban areas, is made in a more recent study.[18]

No such general statement is available for less developed, non-Communist Asia or for Africa. In regard to the former, a United Nations report states that "So far as it is possible to judge by available data, there is apparently no great difference in the rate of natural increase between urban and rural areas in many countries of this region." [19] The implication of this statement combined with the somewhat lower ratio of children under 5 to population in urban than in rural localities (see table 1), is that urban mortality is higher than rural. But this may be only a casual statement.

A general review in Johnson's 1964 paper on health conditions in rural and urban areas of LDCs indicates better health care in the larger cities, a prevalence of lower mortality in urban than in rural areas in Asia and Latin America (disguised by inadequate mortality reporting in the countryside) and varied results for the few countries in Africa.[20] On the whole the consensus in the recent literature is toward lower infant and child mortality in urban than in rural areas in the LDCs.[21]

To assign even approximate parameters to the conclusion just stated is not possible with the present data. But it is possible to make reasonable assumptions (table 9). The first set, by design, assigns the largest probable differential in mortality of children under 5 between the rural and urban populations in the LDCs in favor of the cities. For the DCs equality is assumed, since any realistic differences in mortality rates would have little effect on the shift from child- to birth-ratios. In the second set of assump-

---

18. See Glenn H. Beyer, ed., *The Urban Explosion in Latin America* (Ithaca: Cornell University Press, 1967), "it may be concluded that mortality is lower in urban environments . . . ," p. 85.

19. See ECAFE Secretariat, "The Demographic Situation and Prospective Population Trends in Asia and the Far East," in United Nations, *The Asian Population Conference, 1963* (New York: 1964), p. 82.

20. See Gwendolyn Z. Johnson, "Health Conditions in Rural and Urban Areas of Developing Countries," *Population Studies,* 17 (March 1964): pp. 293–309.

21. Shorter in the paper cited in the notes to lines 27–29 of table 8, writes regarding the findings for Turkey: "The data show a pattern typical of recent experience in developing nations in which the urban population enjoys higher life expectancy than the rural population." See also the summary in the background paper by C. C. Spicer, "Health and Mortality," for the World Population Congress of 1965 (mimeo., pp. 54–56).

TABLE 9
Approximations to Crude Birth Rates, Rural and Urban Populations,
Major Regions, Late 1950's and Early 1960's

	Assumed ratio of rural to urban mortality, children under 5 (1)	Mortality per 1,000, children under 5		Derived births per 1,000, 5-year period		R/U, col. 4/ col. 5 (6)
		Rural (2)	Urban (3)	Rural (4)	Urban (5)	
Assumption 1						
1. Subsaharan Africa	1.5	231	154	233	206	1.13
2. North Africa & Middle East	1.2	170	142	226	211	1.07
3. Asia	1.2	164	137	197	170	1.16
4. Latin America	1.2	128	107	209	177	1.18
5. LDCs		170	132	215	189	1.14
6. DCs	1.0	30	30	103	91	1.13
Assumption 2						
7. Subsaharan Africa	1.25	226	181	231	212	1.09
8. North Africa & Middle East	1.1	166	151	225	213	1.06
9. Asia	1.1	163	148	197	173	1.14
10. Latin America	1.1	124	113	208	178	1.17
11. LDCs		167	145	215	192	1.12
12. DCs	1.0	30	30	103	91	1.13

Notes:

Column 1: For the basis of assumptions see table 8 and discussion in the text.

Columns 2 and 3: Having the ratios in column 1, the shares of rural and urban population and children under 5 per 1,000, respectively, within each region, given in table 1, and the over-all mortality rates estimated in table 7, we derived mortality to age 5 for the rural and urban population separately (from an equation in which x is the mortality for say the urban children and the weights are those of urban and rural children). The rural-urban proportions of children under 5 for lines 2 and 8 were calculated by weighting the two regions in table 1 by the numbers of countries covered.

Columns 4 and 5: Calculated by dividing the ratios of children 0–4 per 1,000 for rural and urban population respectively, from table 1, columns 3 and 4, by the survival ratios (derived from columns 2 and 3, by subtracting the mortality rates, expressed as fractions, from 1.0).

Lines 5 and 11, columns 2–5: Derived from the averages for the four regions, weighted by the number of countries used in table 1 (13 for lines 1 and 7; 8 for lines 2 and 8; 10 for lines 3 and 9; and 17 for lines 4 and 10).

tions the rural-urban differences in children's mortality in the LDCs are cut in half—largely to demonstrate what effects the change has on the R/U ratios for crude birth rates.

Use of the maximum allowance for rural-urban differentials in children's mortality in favor of the cities *widens* the fertility differentials between the rural and urban populations (compare the R/U ratios in table 9, column 6, with those in table 1, column 5). In other words, the rural-urban differentials in number of children 0–4 per 1,000 of population are narrow because in the countryside the higher birth rate is partly offset by the assumed higher mortality. If, on the other hand, we were to assume that children's mortality is higher in the cities than in the countryside, the rural-urban differentials in crude birth rates would be even narrower than the differentials in children to population ratios in table 1.

If the range suggested by the two sets of assumptions in table 9 is at all realistic—and it seems preferable to the assumption of equality of children's mortality in the cities and countryside—some findings observed in table 1 are modified. The R/U ratio of less than 1 in so many cases in Subsaharan Africa, and the generally low R/U ratio for that continent in table 1, are tentatively explained by the rural-urban mortality differentials. As a result, the rural-urban differentials in crude birth rates are about the same for Subsaharan Africa as for South Asia and not very different from those for Latin America (see column 6, lines 1, 3, and 4)—although the ratio for North Africa and the Middle East is still rather low (line 2). The R/U ratio of crude birth rates for the LDCs is similar to that for the DCs, whereas the ratios of children to total population were distinctly lower.

But the other major conclusions of table 1, concerning the limited spread between rural and urban fertility, and its minor contribution to the fertility differentials between LDCs and DCs, remain unchanged when we shift from ratios of children under 5 to crude birth rates. Here, even more than in table 1, both the rural and urban sectors of the LDCs show much higher birth rates than the corresponding sectors of the DCs. Indeed, the crude birth rate for the urban population of the LDCs, at either 189 or 192, is over eight-tenths above that of the *rural* populations of the DCs (103). In discussing the findings of table 1, we emphasized that the rural sector of the DC's (even with allowances for the nonfarm component) is more *urban* than even the urban population of the LDCs—as far as fertility (and associated characteristics of life and behavior) are concerned; and that modernization and economic growth should mean urbanization of both the rural and urban sectors of LDCs. These remarks have even greater relevance with the shift from the ratios of children under 5 to population, to crude birth rates.

6. Allowing for Proportions of Women of Childbearing Ages

Rural-urban differentials in crude birth rates, derived and discussed above, are affected by possible differences in the proportions of women of childbearing ages among the rural and urban populations. These proportions may be associated with internal migration, which is highly selective in its concentration on certain sex and age groups. We should, therefore, consider them, particularly since they shed some light on international differences in the selectivity aspects of internal migration toward the cities.

In columns 1–3 of table 10 we show the average proportions of women aged 15–49 in the rural and urban populations of the major groups of countries. In Africa and Asia, the urban proportion tends to be about the same as, or only slightly higher than, the rural; whereas in Latin America and all other groups, it is significantly greater than the rural. As a result, the average shares for urban and rural population for Asia and Africa combined are 23.6 and 23.5 percent, respectively (line 15, columns 1 and 2), and 15.5 of the 31 countries show lower proportions in the cities; whereas the shares for Latin America are 20.8 and 25.5 percent, more than a fifth higher in the cities (line 5), and the averages for the DCs are 21.5 and 24.7 percent, respectively, an excess of about a seventh (line 16). The results are roughly similar to those for women aged 20–34 in rural and urban populations used in table 5 to derive approximations to internal migration of children under 5. There, too, we found small differences in proportions for Asia and Africa, and much more marked differences for Latin America and the DCs.

The implicit low proportions of women aged 15–49 migrating to the cities in Asia and Africa are associated with implicit high migration proportions of males. For the several groups of coun-

TABLE 10

Shares of Females and Males, Aged 15–49, in Rural and Urban Populations
Major Regions, Late 1950's and Early 1960's (percentages)

	Females			Males			Sex Ratio		
	R (1)	U (2)	No. of coun- tries (3)	R (4)	U (5)	No. of coun- tries (6)	R (col. 4/1) (7)	U (col. 5/2) (8)	Col. 7/8 (9)
1. Subsaharan Africa (13)*	25.9	25.4	8.5	20.6	26.7	11	0.80	1.05	0.76
2. North Africa (5)	21.4	22.0	4	20.6	22.8	5	0.96	1.04	0.92
3. Middle East (3)	20.8	20.8	1 (–)	19.1	22.5	3	0.92	1.08	0.85
4. South Asia (10)	22.6	22.7	5	22.2	26.4	10	0.98	1.16	0.84
5. Latin America (17)	20.8	25.5	17	21.6	21.8	8	1.04	0.85	1.22
6. LDCs, Europe (5)	22.9	26.1	4.5	22.3	24.4	4	0.97	0.93	1.04
7. DCs Europe (9)	21.5	24.7	9	23.3	23.5	5	1.03	0.95	1.14
8. U.S. and Canada (2)	20.8	24.2	2	22.7	23.1	1	1.09	0.95	1.15
9. Australia & New Zealand (2)	20.7	23.4	2	24.6	23.2	2	1.19	0.99	1.20
10. Japan (1)	24.8	28.4	1	22.5	27.4	1	0.91	0.96	0.95
11. Communist Europe (6)	23.6	26.8	6	22.4	26.3	6	0.95	0.98	0.97
12. Africa (18)	24.6	24.4	9.5	20.6	25.6	16	0.84	1.05	0.80
13. Europe (20)	22.5	24.8	19.5	22.8	24.6	15	1.01	0.99	1.02
14. LDCs (48)	22.6	24.2	32.5	21.2	24.2	37	0.94	1.00	0.94
15. Asia and Africa (31)	23.6	23.5	15.5	21.0	25.6	29	0.89	1.09	0.82
16. DCs (14)	21.5	24.7	14	23.3	23.7	7	1.08	0.96	1.12

Notes:
*For Zambia the data are for ages 15–44.

The underlying data are from the source cited for table 1; and the countries included in each group are identical with those used in table 1. The entries in columns 3 and 6 show the number of countries in which the differences between the shares in rural and urban populations are in the same direction as those in columns 1–2 and 4–5, respectively.

tries on these continents, the proportions of *men* aged 15–49 is much greater among the urban than among the rural populations (see lines 1–4, columns 4–6). The average proportions for Asia and Africa combined are 21.0 and 25.6 percent, respectively, a difference of well over a fifth. By contrast, in Latin America and the DCs, where the proportions of women 15–49 in urban were markedly above those in rural populations, the differences of the proportions of men are quite minor. For Latin America these proportions are 21.6 and 21.8 percent, respectively, and for the DCs as a whole they are 23.3 and 23.7 percent, respectively, both insignificant differentials. Obviously in Asia and Africa the internal migration toward the cities is concentrated on men, while that in Latin America and the DCs appears concentrated on women. (Even equal proportions may mean internal migration, given the lower rate of natural increase in the cities.)

As a result of the differences in the propensity of men and women to internal migration in Asia-Africa as compared with Latin America and the DCs, the sex-ratios, i.e., the ratios of men to women, particularly in the active ages of 15–49, are quite different for the rural and urban populations (columns 7–9). In Asia-Africa the sex ratio is low in the countryside, and high in the cities. In Latin America and the DCs, it is high in the countryside and low in the cities. The contrast in this respect between the LDCs and the DCs stressed by the United Nations report on urbanization is true of Asia-Africa, but not of Latin America.

The reasons for these differences between men and women in their propensity to internal migration may be those cited in the United Nations report—poorer residence conditions and fewer employment opportunities for women in the cities of Asia-Africa than in those of Latin America (and the DCs). But other factors are probably the determining ones, since living conditions for rural inmigrants and the potentials of employment opportunities for women may be about the same in Latin America and in Asia-African cities. These other factors may lie in the countryside, in the family structure, and the institutional forces and traditions that may limit the role of women more sharply in Asia-African countries than in Latin America. This topic, however, requires more intensive exploration than can be given to it here.

Knowing the proportions of women in childbearing ages, rural and urban, we can reduce the ratios of children under 5 years to total population to ratios to women of childbearing ages—i.e. to a base that represents childbearing *capacity* (table 11). In columns 1–4 we show the ratios to women 15–49, the latter *unweighted* by differences in childbearing capacity. But the fertility cycle is closely associated with the age of woman, showing low levels for the very

TABLE 11

Children under 5 per 1,000 Women of Childbearing Ages,
Rural and Urban Populations, Major Regions,
Late 1950's and Early 1960's

	Per 1,000 women aged 15–49, unweighted				Per 1,000 women aged 15–49, weighted			
	Rural (1)	Urban (2)	R/U (3)	No. of countries (4)	Rural (5)	Urban (6)	R/U (7)	No. of countries (8)
1. Subsaharan Africa (12)	689	665	1.04	8	905	849	1.06	8
2. North Africa (5)	864	810	1.07	2	1,151	1,077	1.07	4
3. Middle East (3)	939	898	1.05	2	1,258	1,199	1.05	2
4. South Asia (10)	738	653	1.13	9	982	867	1.13	9
5. Latin America (17)	880	621	1.42	17	1,190	837	1.42	17
6. LDCs Europe (5)	481	384	1.25	5	667	523	1.28	5
7. DCs Europe (9)	406	321	1.26	9	578	453	1.28	9
8. U.S. and Canada (2)	599	478	1.25	2	857	669	1.28	2
9. Australia and New Zealand (2)	670	442	1.52	2	928	628	1.48	2
10. Japan (1)	363	282	1.29	1	497	379	1.31	1
11. Communist East Europe (6)	411	302	1.36	6	564	409	1.38	6
12. Africa (17)	741	707	1.05	10	977	916	1.07	12
13. Europe (20)	426	331	1.29	20	596	457	1.30	20
14. LDCs (47)	803	677	1.19	38	1,073	895	1.20	40
15. Asia & Africa (30)	759	708	1.07	21	1,007	928	1.09	23
16. DCs (14)	468	358	1.31	14	662	504	1.31	14

Notes: All entries are from data underlying tables 1 and 10. The number of children per 1,000 women was calculated for each country, and arithmetic means were taken for each group (the number of countries is shown in the stub).

For the countries and dates of coverage see the notes to table 1. The only country omitted here is Zambia, for which the age detail is not available.

In columns 1–4 we use the total number of women aged 15–49. For columns 5–8, women aged 20–34 are weighted by 1, and those aged 15–19 and 35–49 are weighted by ½.

The entries in columns 4 and 8 show the number of countries for which the R/U ratio is above 1, as in columns 3 and 7.

young females, peak fertility in the 20s and early 30s, and a rapid falling off in fertility after the mid-30s. The parameters of this fertility-by-age pattern differ between the high and low birth countries. But to simplify calculations, we assume for columns 5–8 a constant ratio of combined fertility in ages 20–34 double that of combined fertility in ages 15–19 and 35–49. Any significant differences in the age structure *within* the childbearing ages would be revealed by this rough weighting; and, in any case, with the given data, minor differences could not be trusted.[22]

In fact, the differences in R/U ratios between the unweighted and weighted women-population bases are minor; but as might have been expected, the R/U ratios to a weighted base tend to be somewhat higher (columns 7 and 3) for the DCs (except Australia-New Zealand)—suggesting a somewhat greater urban concentration in these countries of the 20–34 age group within the 15–49 year range. But the two sets of ratios agree closely, and while our summary dwells on the ratios in column 7, it applies to column 3 as well.

The R/U ratios in table 11 are quite similar to those in table 1, column 5. The former are somewhat higher than the latter, since the shift in base from total population of women to childbearing ages accentuates somewhat the excess of rural over urban fertility measures. But the moderate spread in Africa and Asia compared with Latin America remains, and the ratio for Latin America, particularly, is magnified by the shift in the base (from 1.15 in table 1 to 1.42 in table 11). The R/U ratios for the DCs are also substantially higher. In short, all the findings of table 1 appear here, but are accentuated.

In table 12, a brief supplement to table 11, we shift the ratios of children 0–4 to women of childbearing ages, weighted, to cumu-

---

22. The ratio used is too favorable to the ages other than twenty to thirty-four, since it is less than ½ to 1, in the low fertility countries and even in Latin America. Thus, in the monograph cited in notes to table 7, in the standardization (for age of women) Collver assumes a fertility schedule of 7, 7, and 6 for ages twenty to twenty-four, twenty-five to twenty-nine, and thirty to thirty-four, respectively (20 in all); of 1 for fifteen to nineteen, of 4 for thirty-five to thirty-nine, of 1 for forty to forty-four, and if we add 1 for forty-five to forty-nine, the total is 7 (see pp. 42–43 of the source). On the other hand, the range may differ for countries where marriages are early, as they are in Africa and Asia, and where the fifteen to nineteen weight may be far greater (see in this connection United Nations, *Interim Report on Conditions and Trends of Fertility in the World, 1960–1965* [New York: 1972], table 9, p. 67; table 15, pp. 75–76; table 19, p. 82; and table 23, p. 88). These tables show relative contributions of women in each age group to gross total fertility, 1960 and 1965, for the DCs (Europe, North America, etc.), Latin American countries, Asian countries, and African countries. For African countries the assumed ratio of 1 to ½ seems valid, as it is for the only large South Asian country shown, viz. Pakistan.

TABLE 12

Approximations to Births (Cumulated over 5 Years) per 1,000 Women
of Childbearing Ages (Weighted), Rural and Urban Populations,
Major Regions, Late 1950's and Early 1960's

	Assumption 1			Assumption 2		
	Rural (1)	Urban (2)	R/U (3)	Rural (4)	Urban (5)	R/U (6)
1. Subsaharan Africa	1,177	1,004	1.17	1,169	1,037	1.13
2. North Africa & Middle East	1,435	1,309	1.10	1,428	1,323	1.08
3. Asia	1,175	1,005	1.17	1,173	1,018	1.15
4. Latin America	1,365	937	1.46	1,358	944	1.44
5. Asia and Africa	1,245	1,086	1.15	1,239	1,107	1.12
6. LDCs	1,291	1,032	1.25	1,282	1,048	1.22
7. DCs	477	363	1.31	477	363	1.31

Notes: Derived from the rural-urban mortality rates for children under 5 (in table 9) and the number of children under 5 per 1,000 women, 15–49 weighted, table 11, columns 5 and 6.

The entries in lines 5 and 6 are averages of lines 1–4, weighting them by the number of countries. For the latter see the notes in table 9, except that only 12 countries are covered for Subsaharan Africa. Weighting by population would result in the averages for Asia dominating and the averages for all the other regions would have little importance.

lative birth rates to the same base—using the two sets of assumptions shown in table 9. The over-all conclusion, on both assumptions, is that the standardized or refined birth rates also show moderate rural-urban differentials in Asia and Africa, the R/U ratio being between 1.13 and 1.17—compared with the ratios for Latin America between 1.45 and 1.47. The latter are wider even than that for the DCs, at 1.31. In short, our findings in table 1 concerning the urban-rural differentials among various LDCs and DCs in ratios of children under 5 to total population are confirmed, and somewhat accentuated, in the birth rates standardized for the proportions of women of childbearing ages (weighted for internal age structure within the 15 to 49 years range).

But the most important confirmation in table 12 is of the limited contribution that *intranational* rural-urban differences in fertility make to the *international* differences in fertility between LDCs and DCs. At this juncture, beyond which we cannot carry the analysis, it may help to recapitulate the evidence for this conclu-

TABLE 13

Contribution of Intra-National Rural-Urban Differences in Fertility to
International Differences in Fertility Between Less Developed and
Developed Countries

A. Proportions and Fertility Rates

	Children under 5 per 1,000 Total Popul.		Crude Birth Rates, 5 Years		5 Year Birth Rates to Women 15–49, Weighted	
	Rural (1)	Urban (2)	Rural (3)	Urban (4)	Rural (5)	Urban (6)
Proportions of Rural and Urban in Relevant Population Bases (%)						
1. LDCs	70.8	29.2	70.8	29.2	69.1	30.9
2. DCs	35.2	64.8	35.2	64.8	31.9	68.1
Fertility Rates						
3. LDCs	179	164	215	189	1,291	1,032
4. DCs	100	88	103	91	477	363

B. Combined Fertility Rates for LDCs and DCs

	Weights of rural and urban as given (1)	Weights of LDCs for both groups (2)	Weights of DCs for both groups (3)
Children under 5 per 1,000 of Total Population			
5. LDCs	174.6	174.6	169.3
6. DCs	92.2	96.5	92.2
7. LDCs/DCs	1.89	1.81	1.84
Crude Birth Rates, 5 Year Total			
8. LDCs	207.4	207.4	198.2
9. DCs	95.2	99.5	95.2
10. LDCs/DCs	2.18	2.08	2.08
5 Year Birth Rates, Women 15–49, Weighted			
11. LDCs	1,211	1,211	1,115
12. DCs	399	442	399
13. LDCs/DCs	3.05	2.74	2.79

Notes:

Panel A: Lines 1–2: Columns 1–4 are from table 1, lines 14 and 15, col. 2; columns 5–6 are calculated from the averages of shares of women aged 20–34 in table 5, and of women aged 15–49 in table 10, weighting the 20–34 group by 1 and the residual within the 15–49 group by ½.

(Notes continued on the following page)

(Table 13 notes continued)

Lines 3 and 4: From table 1, columns 3 and 4, table 9, columns 4 and 5, assumption 1, and table 12, assumption 1.

Panel B: Column 1: The rural-urban ratios given in lines 3 and 4, weighted by the shares given in lines 1 and 2.

Column 2: The rural and urban ratios given in lines 3 and 4, as weighted by the shares for the LDCs given in line 1.

Column 3: The rural and urban ratios given in lines 3 and 4, weighted by the shares for the DCs given in line 2.

---

sion at the successive stages of analysis, from ratios of children under 5 to total population, to birth rates over 5 years per 1,000 women of childbearing ages weighted for age-fertility differentials (table 13).

At the three stages distinguished, the relative spread in fertility differentials between the LDCs and the DCs widens: the ratio of fertility in the former to that in the latter rises from 1.89 for children under 5 per 1,000 of population to 2.18 for crude birth rates, to 3.05 for birth rates to women of childbearing ages. So far as the numbers of children under 5 per 1,000 population are concerned, the contribution to these international spreads of the intra-national urban-rural differentials may be seen by subtracting from the value in column 1, line 7, the average of the values in columns 2 and 3 of line 7, and dividing the difference by the value in column 1, line 7 $(1.89-/1.81 + 1.84/:2)/1.89 = 0.034$ or about 3.5 percent. When crude birth rates are used, the calculation becomes $(2.18-/2.08 + 2.08/:2)/2.18 = 0.046$ or about 5 percent. When the calculation is based on estimated births per 1,000 women 15–49 years of age it becomes $(3.05-/2.74 + 2.79/:2)/3.05 = 0.093$ or about 9 percent. Thus, as we refine the measures, relating them to childbearing capacity, the relative spread in fertility between the LDCs and the DCs becomes wider, and the percentage accounted for by intra-national rural-urban differentials rises; but even at its highest, the latter is below 10 percent.

Finally, one might add that this limited contribution of intra-national urban-rural differences in fertility to the international differences in fertility between the LDCs and DCs would probably not become significantly larger even if city size were covered in the analysis (see evidence on the size of city differences in fertility in table 3 above). Detail on city size might uncover some more narrowly defined rural-urban contrasts in LDCs that are far sharper than the over-all rural-urban comparison; but the contribution of such sharper contrasts to the international rural-urban differences would have to be assigned much smaller weights than those employed for the complete rural and complete urban components in the countrywide total. Considerable interest would attach to comparisons between the very large cities, the smaller cities, etc. with respect to their differential fertility in the LDCs and the DCs; and in some of these narrower comparisons, the contribution of *intra*national differences to *inter*national differences may turn out to be much greater than we found for all rural and all urban differences in table 13. But the validity of our finding would remain, even though such greater detail might pinpoint the loci within the rural and urban components at which this limited contribution of intranational differences to the differences between the LDCs and the DCs emerges.

7. Implications for Trends Over Time

While the intranational rural-urban differentials in fertility are rather moderate, certainly in comparison with the international differences in fertility, they are fairly pervasive; and they tend to show, particularly when we deal with birth rates related to women of childbearing ages, lower fertility among the urban population. Since the share of urban population tends to rise in the course of economic growth, and certainly did over recent decades in most countries, even among the LDCs, the national fertility ratios should have dropped. Yet we know that in most LDCs no such decline occurred in the nationwide fertility ratios, even in the crude or refined birth rates. This means that the rural fertility rate, or the urban fertility rate, or both have risen, and thus compensated for what should have been the depressing effect of the rise in the share of the urban population. And if this occurred, these intraurban or intrarural fertility rises represent trends that cannot be adequately explained within the framework of rural-urban fertility differentials.

Because the rural-urban fertility differentials are widest in Latin America, and because data are available only for Latin America among the less developed regions, we attempt to exploit these data to observe the changes over the decade extending roughly from 1940–1944 to 1950–1954. This period was chosen because rural and urban data on children 5–9 per thousand women aged 20–49 derived from the 1950 census are available in the United

TABLE 14

Data Relating to Urbanization and Fertility in Latin America,
Changes over the Decade Since the Late 1940's or Early 1950's

A. Proportions of Urban in Total Population, and Birth Rates

	Proportion Urban (%) (1)	Crude Birth Rate per 1,000 (2)	Standardized Birth Rates, per 1,000 (3)
Differing Number of Countries			
1. Number of countries	14	11	9
2. 1950, or 1945−49 (for B.R.)	37.4	43.5	42.8
3. 1960 (or 1955−59)	44.4	44.9	46.7
4. Number of countries with change as shown in lines 2−3	14	10	9
Same Countries (7)			
5. 1950, or 1945−49	42.9	42.0	41.8
6. 1960, or 1955−59	50.5	43.8	45.9
7. Number of countries (as in lines 5−6)	7	7	7

B. Children 5−9 per 1,000 Women 20−49 Years of Age and Survival Rates to Age 5

	Children 5−9 per 1,000 Women 20−49		Number of countries as in 1-2 (3)	Survival Rates, Children Under 5, Countrywide	
	About 1950 (1)	1950 and early 1960's (2)		1940-44 (4)	1950-54 (5)
Differing Number of Countries					
8. Number of countries	10	10	−	6	6
9. Rural	898	1,031	9	0.814	0.865
10. Urban	559	707	9	0.814	0.865
11. Number of countries (as in 9−10)	10	10			
Same Countries (6)					
12. Rural	870	1,010	6	0.814	0.865
13. Urban	547	696		0.814	0.865
14. Number of countries (as in 12−13)	6	6			

(Continued)

(Table 14 continued)

C. Approximations to Cumulative Births 5-Year Period, per 1,000 Women Aged 20–49, Rural and Urban (no adjustment for bias in base trend)

	Rural		Urban	
	About 1940–44 (1)	About 1950–54 (2)	About 1940–44 (3)	1950–54 (4)
15. Estimated Rural-Urban proportions in children 0–9	73.6	67.0	26.4	33.0
16. Estimated survival ratio, children under 10, assumption 1	0.786	0.820	0.822	0.850
17. Estimated survival ratio, children under 10, assumption 2	0.791	0.825	0.810	0.841
18. Derived, births per 1,000 women aged 20–49, assumption 1	1,107	1,232	665	819
19. Derived, births per 1,000 women aged 20–49, assumption 2	1,100	1,224	675	828

Notes:
   Panel A Column 1: The underlying data are from United Nations, Demographic Yearbook 1970 (New York, 1971), table 5, pp. 140ff. The fourteen countries included are: Costa Rica, Dominican Republic, El Salvador, Guatemala, Mexico, Nicaragua, Panama, Puerto Rico, Brazil, Chile, Colombia, Ecuador, Paraguay, Venezuela. Honduras was excluded, although the data were available, because the sharp decline in the share of urban (from over 30 in 1950 to 23 per cent in 1960) indicates lack of comparability.
   The seven countries covered in lines 5–6 are: Chile, Colombia, Costa Rica, El Salvador, Mexico, Panama, Venezuela.

   Columns 2 and 3: The basic source is the Collver monograph cited in notes to table 7.
   In addition to the 7 countries just listed, column 2 includes: Ecuador, Guatemala, Honduras, and Peru. The averages in column 3 cover the countries listed for column 2, but exclude Ecuador and Guatemala.

   Panel B
   Column 1: The data are from the United Nations, Population Bulletin no. 7, 1963 (with special reference to fertility) (New York, 1965), table 8.7, p. 133. The ten countries include: Brazil, Chile, Costa Rica, Dominican Republic, Ecuador, El Salvador, Guatemala, Nicaragua, Panama, and Paraguay.
   The six countries covered in lines 12–14 are from the ten above, and exclude the Dominican Republic, Nicaragua, Paraguay, and Brazil.

   Column 2: The entries are derived from the individual country data in the United Nations, Demographic Yearbook 1970 (New York, 1971), table 6.

   Columns 4–5: The underlying data are from the Collver monograph repeatedly cited. The six countries included are: Chile, Costa Rica, Ecuador, El Salvador, Guatemala, Panama.
   The source shows infant mortality and survival rates to age 5. We added to infant mortality, one half of the difference between it and mortality to age 5 (see notes to table 7, col. 3).

(Notes continued on the following page)

(Table 14 notes continued)
Panel C
Line 15: For the six countries (those covered in lines 12–14) the average shares of rural-urban populations were 63.4 and 36.6 per cent about 1950, and 57.9 and 42.1 per cent about 1960 (or early 1960's). But we need the shares for about the period when the births occurred (i.e. mid-1940–1944 and mid-1950–1954, respectively); and we also need the rural-urban shares among women 20–49 years of age, from which we can then approximate the rural-urban distribution of children under 10 (and implicitly births). The balance of backward shift by about 8 years, and of the allowance for higher share of women 20–49 in cities, leaves the shares at 63.5–36.5 in 1950 and 58.0–42.0 in 1960. Weighting these by the ratios in lines 12 and 13, columns 1 and 2, yields the shares now shown.

Lines 16–17: The mortality of children under 10 was set at 1/0.91 of mortality of children under 5 (i.e. about 10 per cent higher). Given the mortality for children under 5 shown implicitly in line 12, columns 4 and 5, we obtain total mortality for children under 10 of 204 per 1,000 for 1940–1944 and 170 in 1950–1954. Having these ratios and the shares of rural-urban groups among children under 10 in line 15, we can derive the rural-urban mortality on assumption 1, 1.2 for rural to 1 for urban (see table 9) or assumption 2, 1.1 for rural to 1 for urban. Subtracting the results from 1,000 and dividing by 1,000 we obtain the survival ratios.

Lines 18–19: The number of children 5–9 per 1,000 women aged 20–49 in lines 12 and 13, columns 1 and 2, divided by the survival ratios in lines 16 and 17, columns 3–4.

Nations source cited in the notes to lines 8–14 of table 14. Since we have comparable data based on the censuses for 1960 (or for some date in the early 1960's), we can observe not only the changes in nationwide fertility rates, but also within the rural and urban populations.

Rather elaborate if rough calculations were necessary; and the detailed notes to table 14 explain the derivation. Here we are interested in the findings and these are summarized briefly.

First, despite the fact that the share of urban population in total increased over the decade (of the 1950s) by 7 percentage points, or between a sixth and a seventh, crude birth rates not only failed to decline, but rose by about 2 percentage points— while birth rates adjusted for women of childbearing ages (properly weighted) rose even more, by 4 percentage points or about a tenth (panel A).

Second, for several countries, we have the number of children 5–9 per 1,000 women aged 20–49, around 1950 and around 1960. These ratios can be adjusted for mortality of children to the age of ten, thus yielding ratios of *births,* in 1940–1944 and 1950–1954 to women of childbearing ages (unweighted)—but uncorrected for the trend bias involved in relating cumulative births to a population about 7½ years later. Any correction for the latter would tend to strengthen the findings. The results of these calculations show that like the observed rise in crude or refined birth rates (in panel A), the estimated birth rates per 1,000 women aged 20–49 for both rural and urban populations also rose.

Third, as the data stand, the *urban* birth rates rose much more than the *rural*. On both assumptions, the rural rate rose about 11 percent and the urban about 23 percent (lines 18 and 19). And the urban ratios of the number of children 5–9 per 1,000 women aged 20–49 also show greater proportional rise. Unless there has been a marked relative *retardation* in the growth of urban population that is at the base of these measures, or an improbably large rise in the survival ratio for urban than for the rural children under 10, the greater rise in the fertility of the urban population over the decade covered in table 14 is genuine.

Such movements, so contrary to what one expects with economic growth and urbanization, have been noted, at least for individual countries.[23] And stability, if not increase, of nationwide birth rates has been found, despite a concurrent rise in the share of urban population in a number of LDCs outside of Latin America. But we are not concerned with thoroughly documenting this point here. The information in the United Nations *Demographic Yearbooks,* although based on approximate estimates, shows a general failure of crude birth rates over the decade of the 1950s to decline in much of Africa and South Asia, while the share of urban population was rising.

It may not be difficult to suggest realistic hypotheses that would explain how a cross-sectional association between lower fertility and urban character of locality could be combined with a rise in both urban and rural fertility ratios—even while the country became increasingly urbanized. A greater influx into the cities of rural in-migrants, constituting a higher proportion of recent in-migrants, could easily raise the fertility rates in the growing cities. A reduction in the share of regions with lower birth rates among rural population, possibly associated with a concentration of migration *out* of the *less* prolific rural regions than others (per-

---

23. See, e.g., John R. Weeks, "Urban and Rural Natural Increase in Chile," *Milbank Memorial Fund Quart.* 48, 1 (1970), pp. 71–89.

haps because of greater proximity to the cities), would result in a higher fertility rate for total rural population—even though fertility by the specific region may show no rise.

Whatever the explanation, sizable movements over time *within* the rural and the urban components of total population—whether upward as they appeared to have been in Latin America and other less developed areas during the decade, or downward as was usually the case in the longer history of the presently developed countries—mean that the rural-urban differentials cannot explain much of the movement *over time*. Here also, the contribution of these differentials as an explanatory variable may be limited.

8. Concluding Comments

The paper deals with an international, cross-sectional comparison of urban and rural fertility measures for a wide variety of countries, the data relating to the late 1950s and early 1960s. The rather lengthy discussion was required because of the several steps needed to pass from the more widely available data on ratios of children under 5 to total population, to the approximations to crude and standardized birth rates.

The few findings can be stated briefly.

First, whether we consider ratios of children under 5 to total population, or the standardized birth rates for women of child-bearing ages, the measures show fairly generally an excess of rural over urban fertility.

Second, this rural-urban difference is quite moderate. It is particularly limited, relatively, for the less developed countries of Africa and South Asia—as contrasted with wider differentials in Latin America and in most of the developed countries. In some African countries, urban fertility appears to be higher than rural; while the rural-urban contrast, in excess of the rural, appears most marked in the standardized birth rates for women of child-bearing ages in Latin America.

Third, while the combination of lower fertility in cities with a shift in population toward the cities should have resulted in a lowering of the total birth rate, there is no evidence of such a decline in total birth rates over the 1950s in the less developed regions. This finding is particularly significant for Latin America, in which urbanization was fairly rapid and the rural-urban differentials in birth rates particularly marked. The implication is that either rural, or urban or both sets of birth rates rose over time—to offset the depressing effect expected from urbanization.

Fourth, because of the narrow range of rural-urban differences in fertility revealed by the data, these *intra*-country differentials contribute little to the explanation of the wide *inter*country differentials in fertility between the less developed and the developed regions of the world. The contribution of these internal rural-urban fertility differentials to accounting for the international differences in fertility is, at its highest, below 10 percent of the international range.

Fifth, there is an interesting difference between South Asia and Africa, on the one hand, and Latin America and developed countries, on the other, in the apparent propensity of migration toward cities of women and men of active ages (15 to 49). In Asia-Africa the cityward migration is much more concentrated on men, as reflected by higher proportions of men of these ages in total urban population than in total rural population and no differences in the proportions of females. In Latin America and the developed countries the cityward migration is much more concentrated on women, as reflected by higher proportions of women of these ages in total urban population than in rural, and no differences in the proportions of males.

The findings raise a number of wider-reaching questions which could not be discussed in the paper and have to be deferred for more intensive analysis in other papers. Three complexes of these questions may be briefly suggested.

The first relates to the experience with trends over time in urban and rural fertility in the course of growth of the presently developed countries. Has it also been true of this historical experience that rural-urban differentials in fertility were moderate —and that the rural-urban shift of the population contributed little to the lowering of the countrywide fertility levels, the latter being largely accounted for by declines within the urban and rural components taken separately? And if so, what is the significance of these findings? Would they apply also if instead of rural-urban differentials we were to deal with fertility differentials by occupation or industrial attachment?

The second group of questions relates to the contrast in sex differences in cityward migration propensity between Asia-Africa, on the one hand, and Latin America-developed countries, on the other. Is there a parallel to it in the historical development of presently developed countries, in a shift over time from a greater migration propensity of the male component of the labor force toward a greater migration propensity of the female component? And if so, what are the determining factors that account for both the differential propensity, and the changes in it over time (or current differences among regions)?

The third group of questions relates to the inferred *rises* within the rural, or urban, fertility rates (or in both) in the currently less developed countries, strongly suggested for the decade of the 1950s—and possibly to be found for the 1960s when the 1970 censuses become fully available. What is the complex of factors underlying such unexpected movements? Has there been a parallel to them in some phase of the growth of the presently developed countries, when the countrywide fertility rate also failed to decline, despite growing urbanization and cross section rural-urban differentials showing lower fertility in the cities?

The paper has raised more questions than it answered. But this was to be expected in a field in which relevant data have emerged only recently, and where the wide variety of demographic and economic experience inhibits easy and clearcut generalizations.

Fertility Differentials between Less Developed and Developed Regions: Components and Implications

1. Introduction

The crude birth rates in the economically less developed countries have been over twice those in the developed countries in the recent decades. Such differentials imply differences in age patterns of birth rates through the life cycles of mothers and fathers; in age at time of marriage, and between husbands and wives in later life; in birth parities; and in the size of households, in so far as they reflect the number of children in them. In turn, all these demographic differences have economic and social connotations, and these provide an indispensable framework for interpreting the persistence of high birth rates in the less developed regions.

The paper presents a brief summary of the easily available recent cross-section data on the demographic components in the international fertility differentials, with emphasis on the comparison of less developed (LDCs) and more developed (DCs) regions among the market economies. This summary, and the accompanying analytical comments, may be familiar to specialists in demography. But the interrelations of these demographic aspects,

Reprinted from *Proceedings of the American Philosophical Society*, vol. 119, no. 5 (October 1975), pp. 363–396.

and their possible connotations, are less familiar to economists; and the recent additions of data on less developed regions, sparsely covered, if at all, in earlier years (most of Africa and much of Asia) make it worth while to assemble the summary measures. No effort was made to go back to the original censuses or mono-graphic studies; and I have relied primarily on the international compilations and special papers of the United Nations. The aim was a broad survey, on the assumption that guidance for a more intensive exploration would be provided by such an approach.

The discussion begins with a review of the age-specific birth rates for women in the successive age classes within the child-bearing span; these, together with number of women in these age classes, absolute and in relation to total population, are used to derive the crude birth rates. We can then establish the contribu-tion of each age class of women to the total crude birth rate of a region. The next section reviews marriage proportions among women, derives age specific marital fertility ratios, and measures the contribution to fertility differences between the LDCs and DCs of the differences in marriage proportions and in intramarital fer-tility. The third section compares the distributions of births by age of mother, and an approximation to the distributions of births by age of father, for the LDCs and the DCs. The fourth section sum-marizes birth by birth order or parity, indicating the greater weight of high parity births in the total fertility of the LDCs; and estab-lishes the association between the incidence of births to parents at more advanced ages and the contribution of high parity births to higher fertility. The fifth, and last, section devoted to statistical evidence deals with the distribution of population among house-holds of different size, stressing the association between higher fertility and the larger average of household, or higher propor-tions of larger households, in the LDCs than in the DCs. In the concluding section an attempt is made to indicate what the find-ings contribute to the explanation of persisting high birth rates in the LDCs.

2. Age-Specific Birth Rates, Women

We begin with a summary of the birth rates of women in the five-year age classes in the childbearing span from 15 through 49 years of age (table 1). Since these are *annual* rates, an entry

TABLE 1

Annual Births per 1,000 Women, by Age of Women, Less Developed
and Developed Regions, Early or Middle 1960's

	Number of countries (1)	Age of Women							Total Fertility (9)
		15-19 (2)	20-24 (3)	25-29 (4)	30-34 (5)	35-39 (6)	40-44 (7)	45-49 (8)	
		A. Market Economies							
		I. Less Developed Regions							
1. East & South-east Asia	9	124	275	280	223	154	64	22	5,710
1a. India-Pakistan	2	158	277	266	209	140	56	24	5,650
1b. Other countries	7	62	268	305	248	179	78	19	5,795
1c. Hong Kong & Singapore	2	48	247	315	237	148	58	8	5,305
2. Middle East	9	113	305	352	290	199	82	17	6,280
3. Sub-Saharan Africa	16	183	295	268	219	153	77	32	6,135
4. Latin America	16	121	296	308	243	181	74	22	6,225
5. Total, LDCs (lines 1–4, weighted)		131	283	289	231	161	69	23	5,935
		II. Developed Regions							
6. Europe	13	32	152	168	106	54	17	1	2,650
7. Overseas offshoots	4	59	221	208	125	64	19	2	3,490
8. Japan	1	4	109	192	83	22	4	0	2,070
9. Total, DCs (lines 6–8, weighted)		38	171	187	110	53	16	1	2,880
		III. Other Market Economies							
10. Europe	4	18	121	186	147	93	36	4	3,025
11. Latin America	3	76	203	185	125	78	31	6	3,520
		B. European Communist Economies							
12. Developed	3	49	177	135	78	38	12	2	2,455
13. Less developed	5	52	173	128	69	34	12	2	2,350
14. Albania	1	56	275	305	256	189	117	58	6,280

(Notes on the following page)

(Notes to Table 1)

Notes:

Entries in columns 2–8 for all countries, except the four listed below, are from United Nations, *Interim Report on Conditions and Trends of Fertility in the World, 1960–1965*, Population Studies, no. 52 (New York, 1972), various Annex tables. We omitted countries with population below a million. In general, we took means of the values for 1960 and 1965; or the values for one of the two years, if its base was more reliable or its coverage more comprehensive. For the Congo (Leopoldville), 1955–1957; Guinea, 1955; India, 1958–1959; and the Philippines, 1950–1955, data are from United Nations, *Population Bulletin no. 7, 1963* (New York. 1965), table 7.1, pp. 102-103.

Unless otherwise indicated, entries for regions that include more than one country are unweighted arithmetic means of the values for the several countries. The weights, when used, are population numbers for 1960 given in United Nations, *Population Estimates by Regions and Countries, 1950–1960*, Working paper ESA/P/WP31, May, 1970.

Line 1: Weighted mean of lines 1*a* and 1*b*, the relative population weights (in the total comprising other East Asia, excluding North Korea; Middle South Asia, and Southeast Asia excluding North Vietnam) being 0.645 for line 1*a* and 0.355 for line 1*b*. Line 1*c* is excluded.

Line 1a: Weighted mean with weights of 0.81 for India and 0.19 for Pakistan.

Line 1b: Includes South Korea, Taiwan, West Malaysia, Thailand, Cambodia, Ceylon, and the Philippines.

Line 2: Represents Southwest Asia and North Africa, and includes Turkey, Iraq, Jordan, Syria, United Arab Republic, Sudan, Libya, Tunisia, and Algeria.

Line 3: Includes Cameroon, Central African Republic, Chad, Congo, Dahomey, Ghana, Guinea, Ivory Coast, Madagascar, Kenya, Mali, Niger, Senegal, Togo, Uganda, and Upper Volta.

Line 4: Includes Mexico, Brazil, Colombia, Peru, Venezuela, Ecuador, Guatemala, Honduras, Nicaragua, Dominican Republic, Chile, Paraguay, El Salvador, Costa Rica, Jamaica, and Panama.

Line 5: Weighted averages of lines 1–4. The weights for line 1 as indicated; for line 2–populations of Southwest Asia and North Africa; for line 3–the sum of populations of West, East, and Central Africa; for line 4 population of Latin America, omitting the Temperate Zone–work out to 63 for line 1, 9 for line 2, and 14 each for lines 3 and 4.

Line 6: Includes Belgium, Denmark, Norway, Sweden, Finland, Netherlands, France, Germany (Federal Republic), Switzerland, Austria, Italy, England and Wales, and Scotland.

Line 7: Includes Canada, United States, Australia, and New Zealand.

Line 9: Weighted averages of lines 6–8. The weights–the population totals for Northern and Western Europe, plus Italy (omitting the rest of Southern Europe); and for the other regions–work out to 46 for Europe, 38 for overseas offshoots, and 16 for Japan.

Line 10: Includes Ireland, Greece, Spain, and Portugal.

Line 11: Includes Argentina, Uruguay, and Puerto Rico.

Line 12: Includes U.S.S.R., Czechoslovakia, and East Germany.

Line 13: Includes Poland, Hungary, Romania, Yugoslavia, and Bulgaria. Excludes Albania shown separately in line 14.

Column 9: Sum of rates for seven age classes, multiplied by five (to allow for the number of years in each class interval). Each entry shows the total number of births over the childbearing span to 1,000 women, aged 15–49, representative of the population reflected in the cross section of 124 in line 1, column 2 means that there were 124 births per year for every 1,000 women 15–49 years old, or 620 births per 1,000 women over the five years covered by that age class.

The regions distinguished are those of most interest in the study of economic growth and levels of living. A more detailed break-down would, of course, be desirable, but the data and resources are not available. In general, the regional rates are unweighted averages of those for individual countries, the presumption being that each country, large or small, represents an item of significant evidence. But we omitted countries with a population of less than a million, because of the possibility of erratic results. Moreover, when large countries showed distinctive patterns (as was the case with India and Pakistan, compared to other countries in East and Southeast Asia) we took weighted averages for them separately. Finally, we weighted regional rates by population in combining them into aggregates for all LDCs and DCs.

Total fertility is the sum of births over the childbearing span to 1,000 women, representative of the population covered in a specific area. Thus, the entry in line 1, column 9, indicates that 1,000 women with the fertility patterns of women in East South-east Asia in the early 1960s bore 5,710 children through their childbearing span, an average of 5.71 births per woman.

Several findings are suggested. To begin with total fertility, birth rates per 1,000 women of childbearing ages were, among the market economies, over twice as high in the LDCs as in the DCs. The few European and Latin American economies that did not clearly fit into either of these two large groups showed fairly low total fertility, closer to that for the DCs than to that for the LDCs. The distinctive, and less expected, finding was that among the European Communist economies, excluding Albania, fertility was low, even relative to the developed countries of Europe; and just as low, or slightly lower, among the less developed Communist economies than among the more developed. Obviously, some as-pects of the social and economic structure of European Communist economies restrict fertility sharply and effectively.

Second, and more relevant to our specific topic is the difference between the LDCs and DCs in the pattern of their age-specific birth rates over the childbearing span. For the LDCs the rates are fairly high not only during the prime ages, from 20 through 29, and the next higher class from 30 through 34, but also during the younger and older ages. Thus, if we view an age-specific birth rate of 100 (500 births in a five-year interval) as an index of substantial childbearing, we find that such engagement extends over five age classes, or 25 years, in the LDCs, and only over three age classes, or 15 years in the DCs (lines 5 and 9).

Indeed, one could argue that it would be difficult, if not impossible, to attain a total fertility as high as that found for the LDCs, i.e. between 5,700 and 6,800, if births were limited to women 20 through 34 years old. With fecundity proportions rising rapidly from about a third of all women aged 17 to a peak of 93 percent at age 22, and then declining slowly beginning at age 23 and through the early 30's, the average proportions of fecund women are 39 percent for age 15–19, 92 percent for age 20–24, 90 percent for age 25–29, and 85 percent for age 30–34.[1] Given these levels, and observing the record for individual countries, we find that a reasonably high age-specific rate would average 350 for the two prime fecundity classes, i.e., 20–24 and 25–29, and about 300 for the 30–34 class—thus yielding total fertility of 5,000, without any births to younger and older women. But this would fall short of the total fertility shown in lines 1–5 by between 12 and 26 percent; yet the assumed total fertility, given an average married proportion below 90 percent (see below) would mean, for the three age classes, an average of almost six births per married woman over the fifteen years. It is unrealistic to assume that an average of one birth every two and a half years, over a span of fifteen years, can be maintained for every married woman in the population. The cumulative total for the three age classes would fall short of the 5,000 total fertility level, and the difference, like that between 5,000 and 6,000 or more, would have to be made up by fairly high birth rates for younger and older women.

Third, if there is an element of necessity about the extended pattern of age-specific birth rates in the LDCs compared with the more concentrated pattern in the DCs, there is still an element of variance or choice. In some countries the additional contribu-

---

1. See Frank Lorimer and others, *Culture and Human Fertility* (Paris: UNESCO, 1954), pp. 52–53; quoted in United Nations, *Population Bulletin, no. 7, 1963* (New York: 1965), p. 101. Section VII of this *Bulletin,* pp. 101–21, has extensive discussion of age patterns of fertility.

Fecundity is the physiological capacity of woman for procreation, and is characterized by a rather narrowly defined span with greatly varying levels within the span.

tion to high total fertility occurs largely among women under 20; in others it occurs among those 35 or older. Thus in India and Pakistan (line 1*a*), and Sub Saharan Africa (line 3), the rate in the 15–19 class is over 150 per thousand, whereas in the other countries in East Southeast Asia (line 1*b*), and to a lesser extent in the Middle East (line 2), the rate for the 15–19 class is relatively low, 62 or 113. And, as one would expect, when the time pattern is extended toward early ages, the specific rates at the later ages tend to be lower than when the time pattern is not extended back of age 20. Thus, for India and Pakistan, and Sub-Saharan Africa, the rates for age 30–34 are 209 and 219 respectively, compared with the much higher rates for other countries in East Southeast Asia and in the Middle East (248 and 290 respectively). When the birth rates are fairly high in the 15–19 class, the rate tends to be at the peak in the 20–24 class, declining somewhat in the 25–29 class; whereas in regions with relatively low rates at the early ages, the peak is reached in the 25–29 class. The differences indicated between the India-Pakistan and Sub-Saharan regions, on the one hand, and the Middle East and East Southeast Asia, reflect different institutional conditions governing age of marriage, particularly of women, and suggest the diversity of age patterns that can be associated with a high level of total fertility.[2]

Finally, it follows that the excess of fertility in the LDCs over that in the DCs may be accounted for by higher birth rates of the former, partly in the young ages (below 20), partly in the prime ages (20–34), and partly in the older ages (35 and over). However, we are interested in a comparison not of total fertility, but

---

2. High total fertility, even higher than that for the less developed countries today, was shown in the past in some of the currently more developed countries—but always with a low birth rate for the younger age class. Thus, in European Russia in 1897, total fertility was as high as 7,060 but the rate for the fifteen to nineteen class was only 30; similar rates for Bulgaria for 1901–1905 were 6,570 and 23; for Serbia and Croatia-Slavonia combined in 1910, 5,595 and 44 (see Robert R. Kuczynski, *The Balance of Births and Deaths 2*: various tables, The Institute of Economics of the Brookings Institution, [New York: 1931]). In the successor states—USSR, Bulgaria, and Yugoslavia—total fertility rates for the mid-1960s, according to United Nations sources, ranged from 2,075 for Bulgaria to 2,695 for Yugoslavia.

If we group the 52 countries covered in lines 1–5 of table 1, i.e., all the less developed, *including* Hong Kong and Singapore, in descending order of the birth rate for the younger age group, fifteen to nineteen, and strike group averages, the following associations are revealed:

of crude birth rates—for it is crude birth rates, in combination with crude death rates, that yield the rate of natural increase, or natural growth of population—with its effects on economic growth and structure. We must, therefore, shift now to the links between total fertility and crude birth rates: the relative size of each age class of women of childbearing ages, and the proportion of *all* women of childbearing ages to total population. Table 2 summarizes the data on both links, shows the resultant aggregate crude birth rates, and measures the contribution to the differences in the crude birth rates made by women in each age class within the childbearing span.

Panel A reveals that the relative magnitude of the age classes among women in the less developed areas declined significantly as we move from the youngest group, 15–19 years of age, to the oldest, 45–49. A simple geometric mean of the relatives of the two youngest and the two oldest classes, for the LDCs as a whole (line 5) yields a rate of rise from the older to the younger groups of 3.3 percent per year (we prefer to think of it as a rise toward the younger, rather than a decline toward the older, age groups). This result is not surprising: the younger groups are larger than the older because they are members of a larger population, i.e., are survivors of a birth cohort that, with population growth, was larger than the one born earlier and now represented by the older classes.

Averages of Age Specific Birth Rates, Countries Grouped in Declining Order of the Rate for the 15–19 Class						
Groups				Changes		
(number of countries in parentheses)	15–19 (1)	20–24 (2)	25–29 (3)	(1–2) (4)	(2–3) (5)	Total Fertility (6)
1. Top (6)	239	309	289	70	−20	6,665
2. II (6)	173	305	285	132	−20	6,455
3. III (7)	147	310	294	163	−16	6,155
4. IV (7)	136	288	298	152	10	6,030
5. V (7)	124	308	339	184	31	6,745
6. VI (7)	105	299	322	194	23	6,435
7. VII (6)	75	265	291	190	26	5,885
8. VIII (6)	45	244	299	191	55	5,250

As the rate for the youngest class declines, the change in the rate from the twenty to twenty-four to the twenty-five to twenty-nine class shifts from a minus to a plus, thus indicating the movement of the peak toward later ages. Even more interesting is the fact that through the sixth of the eight groups, total fertility shows no decline. This is because the decline of more than 100 points in the age-specific rate for the fifteen to nineteen class is offset by the rise in the rates at the later ages.

TABLE 2

Age Distribution of Women within the Childbearing Span, and
Contribution to Crude Birth Rates, Less Developed and
Developed Market Economies, Early or Middle 1960's

A. Number in Successive Age Classes as Relatives of Average Number per Class
Within Childbearing Span

	Age Class of Women							Women 15–49 as % of Total Population
	15-19 (1)	20-24 (2)	25-29 (3)	30-34 (4)	35-39 (5)	40-44 (6)	45-49 (7)	(8)
1. East Southeast Asia	1.45	1.31	1.19	0.98	0.82	0.68	0.57	23.1
2. Middle East	1.47	1.32	1.17	0.99	0.80	0.67	0.57	22.5
3. Sub-Saharan Africa	1.53	1.32	1.13	0.96	0.81	0.68	0.56	23.4
4. Latin America	1.53	1.30	1.11	0.97	0.82	0.69	0.57	22.8
5. LDCs	1.48	1.31	1.17	0.98	0.82	0.68	0.57	23.0
6. Europe	1.02	1.04	0.98	1.02	1.09	0.82	1.02	23.9
7. Overseas offshoots	1.12	0.94	0.93	1.02	1.07	0.99	0.92	23.1
8. Japan	1.28	1.16	1.14	1.04	0.91	0.76	0.71	27.0
9. DCs	1.10	1.03	0.99	1.02	1.05	0.87	0.93	24.1

B. Age Specific Birth Rates, Weighted by Size Relatives of Age Classes

	Age Class of Women							Total Fertility	Implicit Crude Birth Rate
	15-19 (1)	20-24 (2)	25-29 (3)	30-34 (4)	35-39 (5)	40-44 (6)	45-49 (7)	(8)	(9)
10. East Southeast Asia	180	360	333	219	126	44	13	6,375	42.1
11. Middle East	166	403	412	287	159	55	10	7,460	47.9
12. Sub-Saharan Africa	280	389	303	210	124	52	18	6,880	46.0
13. Latin America	185	385	339	236	150	51	13	6,795	44.3
14. LDCs	194	371	338	226	132	47	13	6,605	43.4
15. Europe	33	158	165	108	59	14	1	2,690	18.4
16. Overseas offshoots	66	208	193	128	68	19	2	3,420	22.6
17. Japan	5	126	219	86	20	3	0	2,295	17.7
18. DCs	42	176	185	112	56	14	1	2,930	20.2

(Continued)

(Table 2 continued)

C. Contributions to Crude Birth Rate, by Age of Women

	Age Class of Women							
	15-19 (1)	20-24 (2)	25-29 (3)	30-34 (4)	35-39 (5)	40-44 (6)	45-49 (7)	Total (8)
19. East Southeast Asia	5.9	11.9	11.0	7.2	4.2	1.5	0.4	42.1
20. Middle East	5.3	12.9	13.2	9.2	5.1	1.8	0.4	47.9
21. Sub-Saharan Africa	9.5	13.0	10.1	7.0	4.1	1.7	0.6	46.0
22. Latin America	6.0	12.5	11.1	7.7	4.9	1.7	0.4	44.3
23. LDCs	6.4	12.2	11.1	7.4	4.4	1.5	0.4	43.4
24. Europe	1.1	5.4	5.7	3.7	2.0	0.5	0	18.4
25. Overseas offshoots	2.2	6.9	6.3	4.2	2.3	0.6	0.1	22.6
26. Japan	0.1	4.8	8.6	3.3	0.8	0.1	0	17.7
27. DCs	1.4	6.1	6.4	3.8	1.9	0.5	0.1	20.2

Contribution to Differences in CBR

28. Line 23 minus line 27	5.0	6.1	4.7	3.6	2.5	1.0	0.3	23.2
29. Line 28 as % of Total	22	26	20	16	11	4	1	100

Notes:

Panel A: Calculated from the 1960 population data by age and sex given in the United Nations working paper cited in the notes to table 1. For line 1 we used the sum of Other East Asia, Middle South Asia, and Southeast Asia; for line 2—the sum of Southwest Asia and North Africa; for line 3—the sum of Western, Eastern, and Middle Africa; for line 4—the total for Latin America, minus the subtotal for the Temperate Zone. Line 5 was derived from summation of the four regions as defined above. For line 6 we used the sum for Northern, Western Europe, and Italy; for line 7—the sum for North America and Australia-New Zealand. Line 9 was derived from summation of the three regions as defined.

Panel B: Columns 1–7 were calculated by applying to the age specific rates for the regions, the LDCs, and the DCs (in table 1) the relatives shown in the corresponding columns and lines of this table (in panel A). Column 8 is the sum of rates in columns 1–7, multiplied by five (see notes to column 9 of table 1). Column 9 is obtained by dividing the entries in column 8 by 35 (the number of years within the 15–49 span), and multiplying the result by the proper fraction that all women aged 15–49 form in total population (see column 8 of panel A).

Panel C: The shares of the rates for each age class to the total for women 15–49, in columns 1–7 of lines 10–18, were applied to the total crude birth rate shown for each region, for the LDCs, and for the DCs, in column 9 of panel B.

Furthermore, the older groups would have been smaller, even with the same initial birth cohort, because of the longer cumulation of attrition by death. And it is not difficult to derive the 3.3 percent rate as a combination of a past population growth rate of about 2.5 percent (within some range) and age-specific death rates over the span from 15–19 to 45–49 of say 6 to 8 per 1,000 per year.

Since both past population growth rates, and the death rates within the relevant span, were much lower for the DCs than for the LDCs, one would expect a correspondingly lower rate of rise for the former in the numbers, moving from the older to the younger classes among women. And indeed the rate derived from the geometric means of the two classes at each end is 0.7 (see line 9). The rate is clearly too low, for the usual growth rates for population of the developed regions has been over 1 percent per year, and to this must be added the allowance for the survival rates from ages 15 through 49. Apparently, World War II and the marked fluctuations of birth rates in many developed regions over the last four to five decades have distorted the age pattern, and, in particular, made for somewhat larger relative numbers among the older age groups within the childbearing span. In the sense that the factors involved were transitory, the contrast between the low implicit growth rates within the female population of the DCs and LDCs is exaggerated, although it is in the expected direction.

Obviously, the much greater numbers in the younger groups, with their markedly higher age-specific birth rates, yield a weighted total fertility measure appreciably higher than the unweighted. When we apply, in panel B, the weights derived in panel A, the weighted total fertility measure for the LDCs is 6,606 (line 14, col. 8), compared with the unweighted 5,935 (in line 5, col. 9 of table 1)—a rise of 11 percent. The shift for the DCs is from 2,880 in table 1 to 2,930 in table 2, a rise of only 2 percent.

The only link in shifting from the properly weighted total fertility to the crude birth rate is the proportion of all women of childbearing ages to total population (panel A, col. 8). With higher birth rates and rates of natural increase, and, as before, disregarding the possible effects of international migration, the shares of women aged 15–49 in total population might be somewhat lower for the LDCs than for the DCs. And, indeed, the shares are 23 and 24 percent respectively—but the difference is too slight to offset the differential raising effects on total fertility of the adjustment for the size of the successive age classes within the childbearing span.

With adjusted total fertility, and the share of all women aged 15–49 in total population, we can infer the crude birth rate (panel B, col. 9). For the LDCs, the crude birth rate works out to 43.4 per 1,000; for the DCs to 20.2—a ratio of 2.15, compared with a ratio of unadjusted total fertility in table 1 of 2.06. The inferred birth rates compare well with those given directly in the United Nations sources: for 1960–1964, the weighted average for the LDCs is 42.8 per thousand, for the DCs 19.8—both slightly lower than in table 2, but with the same relative magnitudes.[3] And the regional differentials within the two large groups are about the same, except that here the rate is higher for the Middle East than for Sub-Saharan Africa, and in the United Nations estimates that for Sub-Saharan Africa is higher.

Having the crude birth rates corresponding to the weighted age-specific rates for women, we can calculate the absolute contribution of the births credited to a given age class of women to the aggregate crude birth rate for a given region (panel C). This automatic calculation permits us to observe the age-class origin of the differences in the crude birth rates between any two groups of countries. For our purposes the most interesting is the distribution of the differences in crude birth rates between the LDCs and DCs taken as wholes (lines 28–29).

About six-tenths of the total excess of the crude birth rate of the LDCs over that of the DCs was due to the higher age-specific birth rates in the three prime age classes—those from 20 through 34. Over a fifth was due to the higher birth rates of the young, below 20. About a sixth, 16 percent, was due to the higher

---

3. The underlying population data here are from the *Demographic Yearbook, 1965* (New York: 1966). The total for the LDCs is the weighted average for the four regions; and the rate for each region is the weighted average of the subregions (Other East Asia, Middle South Asia, and Southeast Asia for East Southeast Asia; Southwest Asia and North Africa for the Middle East; the rest of Africa, except South Africa, for the Sub-Saharan region; and Latin America, excluding the Temperate Zone, for Latin America). For the DCs I took Northern and Western Europe, and Italy, to represent Europe; North America, Australia and New Zealand for the overseas offshoots; and Japan. The crude birth rates for 1960–1964 are given in the sources for table 1; and we used the sum of populations in 1960 and 1964 as weights.

birth rates among the older women. Thus the younger and older women combined accounted for almost four-tenths of the differential in the aggregate crude birth rates. To put it differently, if the fertility of younger and older women were the same in the LDCs and DCs, the ratio of the total birth rate of the former to that of the latter would have been 1.7 to 1, not almost 2.2 to 1 as shown in table 2.

Applications of the type just made in table 2, and similar ones measuring the contributions of other characteristics of mothers, fathers, or births, to be made in the sections that follow, are obviously not explanations. They do not indicate the causative factors (decisions by would-be parents, and elements underlying these decisions) that may have been involved in producing the birth rates found. They do, however, *narrow* the locus of the results, and the measures of the different aspects of the parents or of the births may narrow it differently. It is hoped that the causative factors will be more easily perceived, although room will remain for divergent explanatory hypotheses.

3. Married Proportions, Women

A woman, not naturally sterile, can become a mother, no matter what her marital status: whether single, or divorced, or separated, or widowed, she can, provided she is of childbearing age, have children if she finds a mate. In many countries where legal marriage is prevalent, illegitimate births are distinguished. Conversely, a married woman, even if of childbearing age, does not necessarily have children—voluntary control over intramarital fertility having become increasingly prevalent particularly in modern societies. Furthermore, in many countries, stable, nonlegally certified, common law or consensual marriages are widespread; and these have been included here among marriages and the resulting births classified as legitimate.

We deal here with a social institution, not a biological process. Consequently, we confront a diversity of meanings and institutional framework, particularly in international comparisons that span a wide range of societies. Not only is it difficult to establish comparability for analytical relevance, but the data available are subject to greater error reflecting biases in judgment of respondents in terms of preferred marital status. But the institution does have meaning in the fertility process in most societies. The latter involves long-term union between men and women setting up families as lasting units for the major purpose of having children and rearing them toward independence and adequate status in society at their maturity. If we include consensual or common-law marriages as stable unions, as we should, the proportions of total births that are recognized as illegitimate are substantial only in Western societies with a strict legal marriage code and concomitant individual permissiveness. Even so, illegitimate births account for a moderate fraction of total births (ranging up to 15 percent in Sweden).[4] Furthermore, many illegitimate births may, in leading to long-term, legal marriages, become legitimate retroactively, for all intents and purposes.

Marriage, as defined here, implies a long-term commitment to a union, involves family formation, and also, in the dominant proportion of cases, a commitment to children. Therefore, despite statistical difficulties and ambiguities, it must be considered, and its relevant quantitative aspects summarized. Such a summary, for the marriage proportions among women, by age classes, is provided in table 3.

In general, the proportions of *younger* women who are married are higher in the LDCs than in the DCs. This is particularly true of the 15–19 age class: almost half of all women in the LDCs are married, compared with only 6 percent in the DCs. It is also true of the 20–24 age class, in which the proportions are close to 80 percent and about 50 percent, respectively. Only for women 25 or older are the married proportions in the two groups of countries similarly high. And, in fact, for women 35 or older, the married proportions are higher in the DCs than in the LDCs—largely because the incidence of widowhood is less marked, proportionately, in the former.

In addition to this broad, and expected, finding, there are significant differences in the proportions of married women in the younger classes among the several regions within the less devel-

---

4. See e.g., table 21 of United Nations, *Demographic Yearbook, 1969* (New York: 1970), the latest volume emphasizing data on natality. The high proportions of illegitimate births shown for many Latin American countries (and some in Asia) reflect the prevalence of consensual marriages. Since we include consensual with legal marriages, such births must be treated as legitimate.

TABLE 3

Proportions of Married (Including Consensual and Polygamous Marriages),
Women by Age Classes, Less Developed and Developed
Market Economies, 1960's

	Number of countries (1)	Age Classes						
		15-19 (2)	20-24 (3)	25-29 (4)	30-34 (5)	35-39 (6)	40-44 (7)	45-49 (8)
Less Developed								
1. East Southeast Asia, weighted	11	53.2	82.7	91.5	90.9	87.5	79.4	72.0
1a. India–Pakistan, weighted	2	70.3	91.8	94.1	91.5	87.1	77.6	69.8
1b. Other countries	9	22.1	66.0	86.8	89.8	88.1	82.6	75.9
2. Middle East	8	34.9	78.6	89.4	91.4	89.4	84.3	77.2
3. Sub-Saharan Africa	14	54.4	86.8	91.4	91.4	89.3	83.8	75.0
4. Latin America	13	17.5	55.2	73.5	77.7	78.8	75.0	70.0
5. Total, LDCs, weighted		46.7	79.1	88.8	89.2	86.7	79.8	72.7
Developed								
6. Europe	13	5.0	47.7	79.3	85.7	85.8	83.7	80.4
7. Overseas offshoots	4	9.8	60.1	84.6	88.7	88.6	86.8	83.6
8. Japan	1	1.3	31.4	79.7	88.0	87.5	84.9	79.1
9. Total, DCs, weighted		6.2	49.8	81.4	87.2	87.0	85.1	81.4

Notes:
The underlying data are from United Nations, *Demographic Yearbook, 1968,* and *Demographic Yearbook, 1971* (New York, 1969 and 1972, respectively).

Throughout, the share of married women, for a given age class, was to a total excluding those whose marital status was unknown.

For the weights underlying lines 1, 1a, 5, and 9, see notes to table 1.

The following countries were included, with the year of coverage indicated in parentheses: *Line 1a:* India (1951), Pakistan (1961); *line 1b:* Ceylon (1967), Nepal (1961), Indonesia (1964–1965, sample), Khmer (1962), S. Korea (1966), Taiwan (1956), West Malaysia (1957), Philippines (1960), Thailand (1960); *line 2:* Iran (1966), Turkey (1965), Iraq (1965), Jordan (1961), United Arab Republic (1960), Tunisia (1966), Morocco (1960), Algeria (1966); *line 3*: Chad (African population 1963–1964, sample), Central African Republic (1959–1960), Angola (1960), Dahomey (African population, 1961), Congo (Kinshasa) (1955–1957), Guinea (1955), Mali (1960–1961), Kenya (1961), Liberia (1962), Madagascar (1966, sample), Senegal (African population, 1961), Togo (1958–1960), Uganda (1963), Zambia (1969); *line 4:* Costa Rica (1963), Brazil (1970), Guatemala (1964), Honduras (1961), Ecuador (1962), Mexico (1960), El Salvador (1961), Panama (1960), Chile (1970), Colombia (1964), Paraguay (1962), Peru (1961), Venezuela (1961).

For lines 6–8 the coverage is that given in table 1.

(Notes continued on the following page)

(Table 3 notes continued)
For a few countries adjustments had to be made to estimate the proportion for the standard age class (when two were combined, or the lower limit of the youngest class was different from 15 years of age). These adjustments were based on neighboring age classes, or on other countries in the region. The possible errors involved were minor, and it seemed best to include at least the larger countries.

oped group; and a question arises about the statistical limitations of those shown for Latin America. The latter are far below those for any other less developed region; and the higher level of economic development in Latin America would not explain this shortfall, since the proportions are lower even for the older age classes. The possible explanation may be that, with the prevalence of consensual marriages in Latin America, there is a marked tendency (stronger among men, but presumably true also of women) by some partners in consensual marriages to report themselves as single.[5] The married proportions in the 15–19 class are distinctly higher for India-Pakistan and Sub-Saharan Africa than for the other countries in East Southeast Asia, Middle East, and Latin America (the latter even allowing for some understatement). These differences conform roughly to the differences in the age-specific birth rate for the 15–19 class in table 1—which is higher for India-Pakistan and Sub-Saharan Africa than for the others. Such differences in marriage proportions persist in the 20–24 class, although they are much narrower than in the 15–19 class; and they are apparently too slight to be reflected in the age-specific birth rates for the 20–24 class. (Table 1, column 3, lines 1–4, shows no significant differences in birth rates for this age class among the several regions.)

Since in the comparison of the LDCs with the DCs, the differentials in marriage proportions in the younger classes among women are roughly consonant with differences in fertility levels, we related the age-specific birth rates for age classes of all women to the married proportions, deriving age-specific marital fertility rates. These are given in table 4, lines 1 and 2.

Obviously, we introduced an error in relating all births, including illegitimate, in a given age class of women to the married proportions within that age class. The ratios overstate marital fer-

---

5. See discussion of table on marital status (table 7) in United Nations *Demographic Yearbook, 1968* (New York: 1969), pp. 21–22.

TABLE 4

Births per 1,000 Married Women, and Effects of Differences in Marriage Proportions versus Differences in Births per 1,000 Married Women on Differences in Fertility between Less Developed and Developed Market Economies

	Age Classes of Women								
	15-19 (1)	20-24 (2)	15-24 (3)	25-29 (4)	30-34 (5)	35-39 (6)	40-44 (7)	45-49 (8)	Total (9)
Total Births, per 1,000 Married Women									
1. LDCs	281	374	326	325	259	186	86	32	nc
2. DCs	613	344	374	230	126	61	19	1	nc
Effect of Differences in Proportions of Married Women									
3. Assumed identical birth rates per 1,000 married women	350	278		193	124	53	17		nc
4. Married proportions, LDCs (%)		61.9		88.8	89.2	86.7	79.8	72.7	nc
5. Married Proportions, DCs (%)		27.3		81.4	87.2	87.0	85.1	81.4	nc
6. Derived age specific BRs, LDCs		217		247	173	108	42	12	5,080
7. Derived age specific BRs, DCs		96		226	168	108	45	13	3,760
8. Derived BRs, LDCs, weighted by relative size of age class		605		289	170	88	29	7	5,940
9. Derived BRs, DCs, weighted by relative size of age class		204		221	171	113	39	12	3,800
Effect of Differences in Births per 1,000 Married Women									
10. Assumed idential marriage proportions (%)		44.6		85.1	88.2	86.8	82.5	77.0	nc
11. Derived age specific BRs, LDCs		145		277	228	161	71	25	5,310
12. Derived age specific BRs, DCs		167		196	111	53	16	1	3,555
13. Derived BRs, LDCs, weighted by relative size of age class		395		324	223	132	48	14	5,680
14. Derived BRs, DCs, weighted by relative size of age class		356		194	113	56	14	1	3,670

nc—not calculated

(Contined)

(Table 4 continued)

Allocation of Differences in Total Fertility Between LDCs and DCs

	Aggregate Differences (1)	Effects of Differences in Marriage Proportion (2)	Effects of Differences in Births per Married Woman (3)
15. Total fertility, not weighted	3,055	1,320	1,755
16. Total fertility, weighted	3,635	2,140	2,010

Notes:

Lines 1 and 2: For the standard size classes obtained by dividing the age specific birth rates in table 1 (lines 5 and 9) by the marriage proportions (treated as proper fractions) in table 3 (lines 5 and 9). For the 15–24 class (column 3), we derived the joint age specific rate (analogous to that in table 1) by using the weights of the two classes (15–19, and 20–24) as given in the relevant columns and lines of table 2; calculated the joint marriage proportion by using the weights for the two classes again from table 2; and then divided the joint age specific birth rate by the joint marriage proportion.

Line 3: Arithmetic means of the BRs in lines 1 and 2.

Lines 4 and 5: From table 3, lines 5 and 9, with the calculation for the joint class (15–24) as indicated above.

Lines 6 and 7: Birth rates in line 3 multiplied by the married proportions in lines 4 and 5 (treated as proper fractions). Total fertility in column 9 is five times the sum of the class fertilities (with that for 15–24 multiplied by two).

Lines 8 and 9: The weights for the relatives of the size classes are from table 2, lines 5 and 9. These are applied to the derived age specific BRs in lines 6 and 7. Total fertility (column 9) is five times the sum of the entries in columns 3–8 (with that for column 3 multiplied by two).

Line 10: Arithmetic means of the married proportions in lines 4 and 5.

Lines 11 and 12: The BRs given in lines 1 and 2, respectively, multiplied by the assumed marriage proportions (treated as proper fractions) in line 10.

Lines 13 and 14: The age specific birth rates, derived for the age classes in lines 11–12, are weighted by the relative size of these classes, given in table 2, lines 5 and 9.

Lines 15 and 16: Column 1: differences between total fertility of LDCs and DCs, unweighted (from lines 5 and 9, column 9 of table 1); and weighted (from lines 14 and 18, column 8, table 2). Column 2: differences between lines 6 and 7, column 9; and lines 8 and 9, column 9. Column 3: differences between lines 11 and 12, and 13 and 14, column 9.

tility, particularly in the ages in which marriage proportions are low and the ratios of all mothers to married mothers are high. But the exaggeration should affect both the LDCs and the DCs, and its impact is reduced by combining the two young classes—15–19 and 20–24—with due allowance, of course, for the difference in size, total and married.

Because of the striking, and suspect, differences in age specific marital fertility in the two young classes taken separately, we combine them. For the two combined, or up to age 25, the age-specific fertility adjusted for the difference in married proportions is no higher among the LDCs than among the DCs—if anything, it is significantly lower, although some allowance must be made for differential errors in exaggeration (lines 1 and 2). To put it differently, the age-specific fertility in the LDCs up to age 25 (cumulatively) is higher than that in the DCs only in association with the much higher marriage proportions, i.e., the earlier incidence of marriage among the women in the LDCs than in the DCs. Only in the older ages, when the marriage proportions in the LDCs no longer rise, and those in the DCs catch up, do differences in marriage proportions cease to have any effect on the age-specific fertility rates for women, or rather on the differentials between these rates for the LDCs and the DCs.

The finding is hardly surprising. Indeed, it is, in a way, a necessary consequence of the difference in marriage incidence at the younger ages between the LDCs and DCs. If in the DCs marriage proportions at the early ages are low—and they were below 50 percent through the ages of 21–23—those women who did marry were likely to be a group with a high propensity toward having children or high fecundity, or both. The much wider groups of young married women in the LDCs would, therefore, be unlikely to match the marital fertility rates of these early starters among the young women in the DCs. It is the dominant proportion of married women that is the primary cause of the higher marital fertility of the LDCs. And yet the finding is of cardinal importance in interpreting the birth rate differentials between the LDCs and the DCs. To the extent that these differentials in the early ages are so closely associated with differences in marriage proportions, the finding emphasizes the early entry of women into the childbearing family and the early withdrawal of such women from outside activities. Indeed, in many LDCs, a young woman, sheltered in her parental home, moves immediately to marriage, without participating directly in any nondomestic activity through much of her youth and childbearing span. Thus, some light is shed on the structure of the family, particularly with regard to the ages and experiences of wife and husband. We shall find below that this early entry into marriage is not typical of men in the LDCs; and that the age difference between husbands and wives is significantly wider in the LDCs than in the DCs.

Given the age-specific birth rates per 1,000 married women, and the proportions which relate married to all women by age classes, the differences in total fertility between the LDCs and the DCs can be decomposed—into those differences due to marriage proportions (for identical marital fertility ratios) and those due to marital fertility (for identical marriage proportions in the comparable age classes of women). The calculation appears in lines 3–14 of table 4; and the summary of the two sets of effects on unweighted total fertility, or on total fertility weighted as it was in table 2, is shown in lines 15 and 16.

The sum of the two sets of effects does not equal the total, particularly in line 16, because of intercorrelation between marriage proportions and age specific marital fertility. And there are, of course, the limitations already noted on the use of total births in relation to married women. But the rough magnitude of the findings would be little affected by refinements. The general suggestion is that between four-tenths and a half of the difference in total fertility between the LDCs and DCs is due to differences in marriage proportions; and the balance to intramarital fertility differences. These weights should be taken only as a general indication that differences in marriage proportions, among younger women, play a large part, if we assume that early marriage is a *precondition* of the wide age-specific birth rate differences in the ages below 25 and 30. Indeed, it follows automatically from the two findings already noted: (1) that excess of birth rates for the age group below 30, either in table 1 or table 2, would account for about a half of the total fertility differentials; (2) that up to the age between 25 and 30 the higher birth rates of women in the LDCs are completely accounted for by their higher marriage proportions. In this sense, the evidence in the present section is a refinement, a detail in understanding how the much higher age-specific birth rates for the younger women in the LDCs are attained.

4. Married Proportions, Men, and
Distribution of Births by Age of Father

We are concerned here with two questions. The first relates to the ages of married men compared with those of their wives, for the LDCs and the DCs. We shall find that women who marry at an early age marry much older men in the LDCs, and the excess of a husband's age over that of his wife is far wider than in the DCs. Obviously, then, the structure within the family household differs in the two groups of countries. The decision activity of a household composed of an older husband and a younger wife must differ from that of a household in which the ages, and implicitly experience in the outside world, of husband and wife, do not differ as much. The second question concerns the distribution of births by age of father. If, in general, husbands are older relative to their wives in the LDCs than in the DCs, and if, as already observed, childbearing continues to older women (within their childbearing span) in the LDCs than in the DCs, the contribution of older fathers to the crude birth rate must be far greater in the LDCs than in the DCs. And we shall find that a substantial proportion of births in the LDCs can be credited to fathers of 40 years or over. This finding sheds further light on the determinants of the higher birth rates in the LDCs.

Unfortunately, the available data do not directly yield the comparisons and distributions that we seek. Some manipulation and restrictive assumptions must be made before even approximate answers can be reached. Yet the statistical difficulties are of interest in themselves because they reflect substantial international differences in the marriage institutions and differences in the degree of connection of children to their fathers compared with that of children to their mothers.

We begin with the marriage proportions of men, that are to be compared with marriage proportions of women, both for comparable age classes. Our intent is to derive, for comparison with the distribution of married women aged 15–49, a distribution of their husbands by age. In this attempt, we immediately run into difficulties. In the first place, for many less developed countries (but for none of the developed), the reported number of married men is significantly short of the reported number of married women despite the inclusion of the consensually married. The remaining categories are single, widowed, and separated. Yet if reporting is accurate, if polygyny is not practiced, and if differential international migration (in which case shortages of husbands in some countries would be offset by excesses in others) is disregarded, the numbers of all married men and women (albeit of different ages) should be identical.

The explanation is, in good part, that polygyny is practiced in many countries. In fact, for several Sub-Saharan countries, the United Nations *Demographic Yearbooks* report numbers of men with two wives, three wives, and so on; and for several Middle Eastern Moslem countries they report marriages of men already married. The shortage of husbands reported for Latin America, where consensual marriages are common, suggests that some polygynous marriages are also included. The alternative, and contributory assumption, is that even when a consensual marriage is monogamous, there is a greater tendency among men than among women not to report themselves as married.

We must match husbands and wives, for married women in their childbearing ages, and compare the ages of husbands and wives, since they affect decisions regarding children, and in order to derive distributions of births by age of father. For this purpose only monogamous marriages can be handled easily. We have, therefore, excluded from lines 1 and 2 of table 5 all countries in which number of married men fell short of that of married women by more than a few percentage points (there were no opposite pairings). This meant eliminating all Sub-Saharan African countries (except Madagascar, which would not contribute much); and also many Latin American countries. As already indicated this problem did not arise in the case of the DCs. Although illegitimate births and informal departures from monogamy do occur, they are not legally recognized, nor are they recorded in any way within the statistically established marital status categories. The exclusion of polygynous marriages from the LDC estimates probably leads to an understatement of the excess of the age of husband's age over that of all of his *several* wives would presumably be greater than the excess in monogamous pairings. A man usually

TABLE 5

Married Proportions and Age Partition Values for Distributions of Married
Men and Women and of Births by Age of Mother and Father,
Less Developed and Developed Countries, 1960's

A. Married Proportions for Men (and Women, Comparable Coverage)

	Age Classes						
	15-19 (1)	20-24 (2)	25-29 (3)	30-34 (4)	35-39 (5)	40-44 (6)	45-49 (7)
LDCs							
1. Men	11.2	40.9	69.5	85.8	89.7	89.7	89.1
2. Women (comparable coverage)	42.6	75.9	88.7	88.7	86.2	79.1	73.7
DCs							
3. Men	1.1	24.6	65.2	82.5	86.6	88.0	88.2
4. Women (comparable coverage, table 3)	6.2	49.8	81.4	87.2	87.0	85.1	81.4

B. Partition Values for Panel A

	LDCs			DCs		
	1st quarter (1)	Median (2)	3rd quarter (3)	1st quarter (4)	Median (5)	3rd quarter (6)
5. Wives, 15—49, comparable coverage	23.4	29.7	37.6	28.7	35.4	42.2
6. Corresponding married men (husbands, see text)	28.7	36.6	46.9	31.5	38.3	45.5
Age differentials between LDCs and DCs						
7. Wives (line 5)				−5.3	−5.7	−4.6
8. Husbands (line 6)				−2.8	−1.7	1.4
9. Age excess, husbands over wives (line 6 minus line 5)	5.3	6.9	9.3	2.8	2.9	3.3

C. Partition Values, Wives and Mothers (based on Tables 2 and 3)

	LDCs			DCs		
	1st quarter (1)	Median (2)	3rd quarter (3)	1st quarter (4)	Median (5)	3rd quarter (6)
10. Wives, 15—49	23.1	29.5	37.4	28.7	35.4	42.2
11. Mothers, 15—49	21.8	26.4	31.9	23.0	27.0	31.6
Age differentials between LDCs and DCs						
12. Wives (line 10)				−5.6	−5.9	−4.8
13. Mothers (line 11)				−1.2	−0.6	0.3

(Continued)

(Table 5 continued)

14. Lead of age partition
    values, mothers over
    wives (line 11 minus
    line 10) -1.3 -3.1 -5.5 -5.7 -8.4 -10.6

D. Derivation of Age Partition Values, Distribution of Births by Age of Father

	LDCs			DCs		
	1st quarter (1)	Median (2)	3rd quarter (3)	1st quarter (4)	Median (5)	3rd quarter (6)
15. Corrected partition values, married men (line 10 + line 9)	28.4	36.4	46.7	31.5	38.3	45.5
16. Alternative partition values, married men (using median difference only)	30.0	36.4	44.3	31.6	38.6	45.1
17. Partition ages, fathers (line 15 + line 14)	27.1	33.3	41.2	25.8	29.9	34.9
18. Alternative partition ages, fathers (line 16 + line 14)	28.7	33.3	38.7	25.9	29.9	34.5
Age differentials between LDCs and DCs						
19. Line 17				1.3	3.4	6.4
20. Line 18				2.8	3.4	4.3

Notes:

Lines 1–2: The sources of data for individual countries are those cited in the notes to table 3. For reasons given in the text only those countries were used for which the total numbers of married women and men for the given year differed by only a few per cent (well below 10). The following countries were included: for East Southeast Asia (10)— Ceylon, Indonesia, Khmer, S. Korea, Taiwan, India, West Malaysia, Pakistan, Philippines, and Thailand—with the usual weighting within the region; for the Middle East (8)—Iran, Turkey, Iraq, Algeria, Libya, Tunisia, Morocco, and UAR; for Sub-Saharan Africa—none; for Latin America (11)—Brazil, Chile, Mexico, Colombia, Costa Rica, Guatemala, Honduras, Panama, Paraguay, Peru, and Venezuela. The usual weighting by total population in 1960 was followed in combining the three major regions covered.

Lines 3–4: Coverage is that given in the notes to tables 1 and 3, from the same sources.

Line 5: The product of the proportions married within the successive age classes, 15–49 (in lines 2 and 4 above) and the relative weight of each age class (from table 2, lines 5 and 9) is the distribution of married women, 15–49, by five-year age classes. The use of class weights of all LDCs, from table 2, is justified because the relative weights of the age classes in the omitted region (Sub-Saharan Africa) are quite close to those of the LDCs as a whole (see table 2, lines 3 and 5). From the distributions we derive, by linear interpolation, the three age partition values shown.

Line 6: The basic assumption here is that younger husbands are matched with younger wives. Knowing the distribution of married men and of married women, for the

(Notes continued on the following page)

(Table 5 notes continued)
same countries and years, we can then calculate the partition age of husbands *corresponding* to the partition age of wives. The weights for age classes among men used in the calculation were the same as those for age classes among women. The close similarity of the two is shown in the distributions for large regions in the UN Working Paper cited in the notes to panel A of table 2.

Line 10: The underlying proportions of married women within each age class are from table 3, lines 5 and 9. The relative weights are from table 2, lines 5 and 9; and the procedure is the same as that for line 5 above.

Line 11: Table 2, lines 23 and 27 show the contribution of each age class within the total of all women 15–49 to the crude birth rate (or to total births), for the LDCs and DCs, respectively. From these two distributions we derive, again by linear interpolation, the age partition values. Since we are assuming that all births are by married women, the distributions of births by age of mother and by age of married mother are identical.

Line 16: Instead of matching the youngest husbands to the youngest wives (as was done for line 6 above), which yields a widening excess of age of husband over age of wife as the age of wives increases, here we assume a constant age differential between husbands and wives and set it at the differential at the median partition value. An element of matching younger husbands to younger wives still remains, but only in the sense that for all wives, 15–49, the younger group of husbands (in equal number) is selected among the total of married men. But there is no selectivity *within* the age span of wives 15–49.

---

acquires his second or third wife as he grows older and his economic status improves. Moreover, he usually selects much younger second and third mates.

But we have to go beyond the married proportions for men and women separately, toward some approximation to the relative ages of wives and their husbands. For this purpose the age distribution of married men must be linked to that of married women. No problem would arise if data were available on the cross-classification of married couples by ages of husband and wife; or if data on the ages of brides and grooms at time of marriage were available, cross-classified, for an adequate sample of countries. But neither body of data is provided in the international compilations of demographic information; and a search in the records of individual countries was not practicable here. Hence we attempted an approximation by the use of some plausible assumptions (panel B).

The distributions of married women, 15–49, by age class, can be derived from marriage proportions and the data in table 2 on the relative size of each age class; and the quartiles and medians in line 5 can then be estimated directly. These estimates show that the quartile and median ages of married women (within the childbearing span) in the LDCs are about five years below those in the DCs (line 7). But we would like a similar set of partition values for the married men, who can be viewed as husbands of the married women aged 15–49, since these men are the most involved in decisions on the production of the next generation. The *corresponding* partition values for married men (husbands) in line 6 are derived on the assumption that younger married men should be matched with younger married women—perhaps the most plausible of alternative simple assumptions. Using this principle in matching and having the age distribution of married men, we assign a number equal to that of the first quartile of the distribution of married women—to establish the age partition value that separates this number from all other, older married men; and continue up the age scale for married women, and correspondingly, married men.

Three related conclusions emerge. First, whereas married women age 15–49, were about 5 years younger in the LDCs than in the DCs, the husbands of these women in the LDCs were only slightly younger at the median than the husbands in the DCs (less than 2 years); and at the third quartile of the distribution they were distinctly older (lines 7 and 8). Second, the age excess of husbands over wives (the latter aged 15–49) was much wider in the LDCs than in the DCs: at the median about 7 years for the former and about 3 years for the latter (line 9). Third, the age excess of husbands over wives in the LDCs rises markedly from the younger to the older ages of wives (still within the 15–49 span)—from 5.3 at the first quartile to 9.3 at the third; whereas the age excess of husbands in the DCs increases only slightly—from 2.8 at the first quartile to 3.3 at the third (line 9).

These conclusions are subject to two qualifications: the limited coverage of the LDCs and, particularly, the assumption underlying the "matching" of husbands and wives. It is this assumption, applied *within* the age distribution of married women, that produces the steep rise in excess of age of husband for the LDCs. On the other hand, the omission of Sub-Saharan Africa may have resulted in understating the age excess of husband over wife in the LDCs. Consequently, the general order of magnitudes is likely to stand. To put it briefly, the age excess of husbands over wives is probably significantly wider in the LDCs than in the DCs, particularly at the older ages; the average ages of husbands of wives aged 15–49 are not too different in the LDCs and the DCs; and the wives are distinctly younger in the former than in the latter.[6] The contrast in ages of wives and husbands in the LDCs and those in the DCs is of interest in itself. It suggests a difference in the structure of the household, at least as far as the parental generation is concerned. But it also is an indirect indication of the distribution of births by age of father, from which we can infer the contribution of older fathers to the difference in crude birth rates between the LDCs and the DCs. Panels C and D of table 5 show the results of an attempt to link the age distributions of married men and women with the distributions of births by ages of fathers and mothers. The underlying assumption is that births are related to married men and women, and illegitimate births are disregarded. However, the latter are clearly definable, and of some limited importance, only in the DCs.

---

6. Some confirmation of the findings is suggested by the rather meager data on age distributions of brides and grooms in the LDCs (compared with the DCs). For five countries in the Middle East and six countries in Latin America we have the median ages of brides and grooms and those of married men and women (consensual marriages excluded)—both groups covered only through age classes fifteen to forty-nine. In the tabulation below we compare these with similar data for twelve countries in the DC group.

Median Ages of Brides and Married Women, and of Bridegrooms and Married Men, LDCs and DCs, 1960s
(for brides and wives below 50)

	Median age, bride (1)	Corresponding age, groom (2)	Difference (2–1) (3)	Median age, wife (4)	Corresponding age, husband (5)	Difference (5–4) (6)
1. Middle East, 5 countries	20.3	26.3	6.0	31.1	39.2	8.1
2. Latin America, 6 countries	22.0	26.2	4.2	32.1	37.2	5.1
3. ME and LA	21.2	26.2	5.1	31.6	38.2	6.6
4. Developed countries	22.7	25.4	2.7	35.3	38.2	2.9

Notes:
Underlying data are from United Nations, *Demographic Yearbook, 1968* (New York: 1969), table 27 (for age at marriage) and table 7 (for distribution by age and marital status).

In panel C we link the distribution of married women with that of married mothers (unmarried mothers having been excluded by assumption). For the LDCs the distribution of married women underlying the partition values shown in line 10, columns 1–3, is from tables 2 and 3, and includes all regions—much more complete coverage than that in line 5—which explains the slight difference between the two sets of partition values in lines 5 and 10. This minor discrepancy suggests that the limitation of coverage for the LDCs in panels A and B was not of great consequence. Panel C indicates, as one would expect, that the population of current mothers is distinctly younger than the population of current wives, aged 15–49, reflecting the higher age specific birth rates for the younger age classes, particularly those under 35 (line 14). Since the concentration of childbearing within the prime age classes, 20–34 among the married women is greater in the DCs than in the LDCs, and since married women are, on the average, older in the DCs, the lead of age partition values of mothers over wives is far

---

In general, the year of marriage was assumed to lie between three and five years before the year for which marital status was reported.

Countries covered in the Middle East are Iraq, Jordan, United Arab Republic, Tunisia, and Algeria; for Latin America—Mexico, Colombia, Peru, Guatemala, Chile and Venezuela. The consensual category was omitted and the two regions were weighted equally.

The DCs covered are the eight largest countries in Europe, all overseas offshoots except New Zealand, and Japan. The weights for the three regions were those used in the text tables. In deriving the age partition values for men corresponding to the median age of bride (wife), we matched younger grooms (husbands) with younger brides (wives). For *medians* this implies no *internal* matching within the age distribution, since the full range of the younger grooms (husbands) is assumed to correspond to the total fifteen to forty-nine range of brides (wives).

Both the excess of age of husband over wife and the excess of age of groom over that of bride are wider in the LDCs than in the DCs. Moreover, the spread is somewhat wider for ages of wives and husbands than for ages of brides and grooms in the LDCs (from 5.1 to 6.6 years), not true of DCs (where it changes from 2.7 to 2.9 years). The wife-husband population is, of course, older than the bride-groom—and the widening of the excess of ages of husband over wife, compared with groom over bride, suggests the tendency observed in table 5, for the excess of the age of husband over wife to rise as the wife grows older—particularly notable in the LDCs, but rather minor in the DCs.

Needless to say, because countries in East Southeast Asia (particularly India, Pakistan, and Indonesia) and in Sub-Saharan Africa are omitted, the median age for the bride among the LDCs in the tabulation just shown is too high. Hence, the difference between the LDCs and the DCs in the median age of brides in lines 3 and 4, col. 2 is underestimated.

wider in the DCs than in the LDCs—over 8 years compared with 3 years at the median respectively (see line 14 again).

In panel D we apply the differentials in the age partition values between wives and mothers to the estimated age partition values of husbands, to derive the age partition values for fathers. The assumption underlying this calculation is that the age excess of husband over wife, for a given age class of the latter, is identical with that of father over mother within the given age class of wife. However, if, e.g. wives age 20–24 have husbands who are 25–29 (i.e. five years older), the current mothers among these wives (say a quarter of them) may have husbands who are *more* or *less* than five years older. Unfortunately, we have no basis for adjusting the age differential between husband and wife to that between father and mother. In any case, the adjustment is not likely to be *substantial.* Moreover, the distribution of births by age of father in lines 17 and 18 will be checked by alternative sets of data in following tables.

Line 17 allows for internal "matching," whereas for line 18 we assumed a constant excess of age of husband within the range of married women 15–49—an assumption somewhat less realistic than that used in other panels, but one that reduces the effect of the matching assumption. Still, the differences between the two lines are so slight that they suggest the same conclusion.

The conclusion is that fathers of about 40 or over contribute a quarter of all births in the LDCs. Thus, in the latter, with the crude birth rate at 43.4 per 1,000, a component of 10.85 is to be credited to these fathers. In the DCs, the age partition value for fathers at the third quartile is below 35 years; and it seems reasonable in the light of other evidence to suggest that fathers aged 40 and over can be credited with about one-tenth of all births. With a crude birth rate of 20.2, the contribution of the older fathers in the DCs is then 2.02. The difference between the contributions of older fathers in the LDCs and DCs is then 10.85 minus 2.02, or 8.83, out of a total difference in the crude birth rates of 23.2 points, or well over a third. This finding differs markedly from that for mothers. Mothers aged 40 or more account for only 1.3 out of 23.2 points of total difference; and even women aged 35 and over contribute only a seventh of the total difference in crude birth rates between LDCs and the DCs (see table 2, line 28).

TABLE 6

Distributions of Births by Age of Mothern and of Father,
Selected Groups of Countries,
Late 1950's and Mid-1960's (percentages)

A. Distribution of Births

| | Age Classes of Mothers and Fathers | | | | | | |
	Below 20 (1)	20-24 (2)	25-29 (3)	30-34 (4)	35-39 (5)	40-44 (6)	45 & over (7)	Total (8)
Less Developed Countries								
Taiwan & Philippines								
1. Mothers	5.8	26.1	29.1	20.7	12.8	4.7	0.8	100
2. Fathers	1.1	14.4	27.0	24.3	17.2	9.8	6.2	100
3. Line 2 − line 1	−4.7	−11.7	−2.1	3.6	4.4	5.1	5.4	37.0
Middle East (3 countries)								
4. Mothers	8.3	21.8	26.0	21.4	14.6	6.1	1.8	100
5. Fathers	0.4	7.1	19.0	22.5	20.0	13.5	17.5	100
6. Line 5 − line 4	−7.9	−14.7	−7.0	1.1	5.4	7.4	15.7	59.2
Latin America (6 countries)								
7. Mothers	14.3	29.4	24.2	16.6	11.0	3.7	0.8	100
8. Fathers	2.3	18.6	24.6	21.0	15.0	9.3	9.2	100
9. Line 8 − line 7	−12.0	−10.8	0.4	4.4	4.0	5.6	8.4	45.6
Average of ME and LA (equal weights)								
10. Mothers	11.3	25.6	25.1	19.0	12.8	4.9	1.3	100
11. Fathers	1.3	12.9	21.8	21.8	17.5	11.4	13.3	100
12. Line 11 − line 10	−10.0	−12.7	−3.3	2.8	4.7	6.5	12.0	52.0
Developed Countries								
Europe (10 countries)								
13. Mothers	4.9	26.3	31.3	21.9	11.7	3.5	0.4	100
14. Fathers	0.7	13.8	30.7	26.2	15.9	7.8	4.9	100
15. Line 14 − line 13	−4.2	−12.5	−0.6	4.3	4.2	4.3	4.5	34.6
Overseas Offshoots (3 countries)								
16. Mothers	8.9	31.5	29.4	17.8	9.4	2.8	0.2	100
17. Fathers	1.6	18.3	30.5	24.3	14.7	6.9	3.7	100
18. Line 17 − line 16	−7.3	−13.2	1.1	6.5	5.3	4.1	3.5	41.0

(Continued)

(Table 6 continued)

A. Distribution of Births –Developed Countries (continued)

	Age Classes of Mothers and Fathers							
	Below 20 (1)	20-24 (2)	25-29 (3)	30-34 (4)	35-39 (5)	40-44 (6)	45 & over (7)	Total (8)
Japan								
19. Mothers	1.2	27.2	43.3	20.2	6.6	1.4	0.1	100
20. Fathers	0	7.5	39.4	33.1	12.4	5.1	2.5	100
21. Line 20 – line 19	-1.2	-19.7	-3.9	12.9	5.8	3.7	2.4	49.6
All Developed (weighted average)								
22. Mothers	5.8	28.4	32.5	20.1	10.0.	2.9	0.3	100
23. Fathers	0.9	14.5	32.0	26.6	14.9	7.0	4.1	100
24. Line 23 – line 22	-4.9	-13.9	-0.5	6.5	4.9	4.1	3.8	38.6

B. Age Partition Values in the Distribution of Births, Mothers and Fathers

	Taiwan & Philip. (1)	Middle East (2)	Latin Am. (3)	LA & ME (4)	Europe (5)	Ov. off. (6)	Japan (7)	DCs (8)
Mothers								
25. 1st quartile	23.7	23.8	21.8	22.7	23.8	22.6	24.3	23.4
26. Median	28.1	28.8	26.3	27.6	28.0	26.6	27.5	27.4
27. 3rd quartile	33.4	34.4	32.1	33.4	32.9	31.5	30.8	32.1
Fathers								
28. 1st quartile	26.6	29.6	25.8	27.5	26.7	25.8	27.2	26.5
29. Median	31.5	35.2	31.1	33.2	30.9	29.9	30.5	30.5
30. 3rd quartile	37.4	42.2	37.8	39.9	36.1	35.1	34.2	35.3
Excess of Age of Fathers								
31. 1st quartile	2.9	5.8	4.0	4.8	2.9	3.2	2.9	3.1
32. Median	3.4	6.4	4.8	5.6	2.9	3.3	3.0	3.1
33. 3rd quartile	4.0	7.8	5.7	6.5	3.2	3.6	3.4	3.2

Notes:
The distributions of births by age of mothers and of fathers for identical countries for the same year. Column 8 of lines 3, 6, 9 . . . 24, is the sum of columns 1–7, signs disregarded.

The data for the LDCs are largely from United Nations, *Demographic Yearbook, 1969* (New York, 1970), tables 14 and 19. Taiwan is the one country for an earlier year, 1958, from *Demographic Yearbook, 1959* (New York, 1959), tables 11 and 13.

Lines 1–2: Includes the Philippines (1964) and Taiwan (1958).

Lines 4–5: Includes Algeria (1965), Tunisia (1965), and the United Arab Republic `966).

(Notes continued on the following page)

(Table 6 notes continued)

Lines 7–8: Includes Puerto Rico (1963), Peru (1963), Chile (1963), Guatemala (1963), and Costa Rica and Panama, combined (1963). Many Latin American countries also reporting had to be omitted because in the distribution by age of father, the unallocated births were more than 20 per cent of the total.

Lines 13–14: Because of inadequate coverage of Europe in later years, we had to use data on legitimate births for 1957 or 1958, given in the *Demographic Yearbook, 1959.* The only country included for a recent year (total births, 1963) was England and Wales.

The following countries were included: Austria (1958), Belgium (1958), Denmark (1957), Finland (1958), France (1958), Germany (Federal Republic, 1955), Netherlands (1958), Norway (1957), Sweden (1957), and England and Wales (1963).

Lines 16–17: Includes Canada (1958), United States (1955), and Australia (1963).

Lines 19–20: For 1957.

Lines 22–23: The weights used are population for 1960 (see notes to table 1).

Lines 25–30: Derived by linear interpolation from the percentage distributions in panel A.

The contribution of older fathers can be checked with an alternative set of data, also incomplete, but in other ways. For eleven less developed countries we have for recent years distributions of births by age of father, which can be compared with distributions by age of mother. Similar data are available for all developed countries, but for the 1950s, not the 1960s; and for legitimate births only. The evidence is summarized in table 6.

Regrettably, we have no data for the populous Asian countries, like India and Pakistan, or for Sub-Saharan Africa, both regions with high specific birth rates in the younger age classes of women. We use Middle East and Latin America, weighted equally (since the structure of the former is closer to the missing regions), to represent the LDCs. This approach, while understating the excess of ages of fathers over those of mothers, may nevertheless yield a good approximation of the share of older fathers in total births.

The share of fathers aged 40 and over in the distribution of births by age of fathers for the average of ME and LA, is about a quarter (line 11). This finding checks with that indicated by the age partition values established in table 5. By contrast, the share of fathers 40 or older in total births in the DCs is about 11 percent, which also checks with the finding based on table 5 (line 23).

In comparing directly the shares in total births of fathers and mothers of identical age classes (lines 3, 6, and so on of panel A), or in comparing the age partition values derived from the distributions of births by ages of fathers and mothers, we are implicitly matching younger fathers and mothers. Since this plausible assumption is used also in connection with table 5, we can compare the differentials in age partition values between mothers and fathers, with those obtained in comparing wives and husbands in table 5. There the age excess of husbands over wives, for the LDCs, was 5.3 years at the first quartile, 6.9 years at the median, and 9.3 years at the third quartile; for the DCs it was 2.8, 2.9, 3.3 years respectively (see table 5, line 9). In table 6, the age excess of fathers over mothers, for the average of the Middle East and Latin America, is 4.8 years at the first quartile, 5.6 years at the median, and 6.5 years at the third quartile; while the corresponding differentials for the DCs are 3.1, 3.1, 3.2 years (lines 31–33, columns 4 and 8). For the DCs the differentials between the age partition values of husbands and wives are about the same as between those of fathers and mothers, although the average ages of wives and husbands differ from those of mothers and fathers. For the LDCs the age excess of fathers over mothers in table 6 is narrower than that of husbands over wives in table 5, but the difference may be due partially to inadequate coverage in table 5. Yet table 6 confirms, for fathers and mothers, the finding for husbands and wives in table 5: the age excess of men is much wider in the LDCs than in the DCs, and it increases more significantly in the former as the age of wife or mother rises.

On the basis of table 6, and the assumption that the average for the Middle East and Latin America represents the LDCs, we derive the distributions of births by the quinquennial age classes of fathers, as we did for mothers in table 2. We then calculate the contributions of each age class to the differences in crude birth rates between the LDCs and DCs (table 7).

The finding here confirms the inference from table 5 that the contribution of fathers aged forty and over is so much greater in the LDCs than in the DCs that it accounts for one-third of the total difference between the crude birth rates of the two groups of countries. In table 2 we found that *young* mothers, those below the age of 20, contributed more than a fifth of the total difference between the crude birth rates of the LDCs and the DCs (see table 2, line 29). Assuming little overlapping between husbands 40 and over and wives below the age of 20, one could say that if the

TABLE 7

Distribution of Births by Age of Father, Less Developed and
Developed Market Economies, 1950's and 1960's

| | Age of Mother or Father | | | | | | |
	Below 20 (1)	20-24 (2)	25-29 (3)	30-34 (4)	35-39 (5)	40-44 (6)	45 & over (7)	Total (8)
% Shares of Births by Age of Mother (lines 1—4)								
1. Middle East	11.1	27.0	27.6	19.2	10.7	3.7	0.7	100
2. Latin America	13.6	28.3	24.9	17.4	11.0	3.8	1.0	100
3. ME and LA (equal weights)	12.4	27.6	26.3	18.3	10.8	3.7	0.9	100
4. LDCs	14.6	28.1	25.6	17.1	10.0	3.6	1.0	100
5. Differences in % shares of births, age of father minus age of mother, ME and LA	−10.0	−12.7	−3.3	2.8	4.7	6.5	12.0	0
6. Derived % shares of births by age of father (line 4 + line 5), LDCs	4.6	15.4	22.3	19.9	14.7	10.1	13.0	100
7. % Shares of births age of mother, DCs	7.2	30.0	31.6	19.1	9.5	2.4	0.2	100
8. Differences in % share of births, age of father minus age of mother, DCs	−4.9	−13.9	−0.5	6.5	4.9	4.1	3.8	0
9. Derived % shares of births by age of father, DCs (line 7 + line 8)	2.3	16.1	31.1	25.6	14.4	6.5	4.0	100
Contributions to Differences in Crude Birth Rates, Age Classes of Fathers								
10. LDCs	2.0	6.7	9.7	8.6	6.4	4.4	5.6	43.4
11. DCs	0.5	3.2	6.3	5.2	2.9	1.3	0.8	20.2
12. Contributions to differences	1.5	3.5	3.4	3.4	3.5	3.1	4.8	23.2
13. % Distribution of line 12	7	15	15	15	15	13	20	100

(Notes on the following page)

(Table 7 notes)
Notes:
   Lines 1, 2, and 4: Calculated from table 2, lines 20, 22, and 23.
   Line 5: From table 6, line 12.
   Line 7: From table 2, line 27.
   Line 8: From table 6, line 24.
   Lines 10–13: Shares in lines 6 and 9 applied to total crude birth rates for the LDCs (43.4 per 1,000) and the DCs (20.2). See also table 2, panel C.

---

age-specific birth rates for women below age 20 and for men 40 or more were the same in the LDCs and the DCs, the difference in the crude birth rates between the two groups of countries would be cut by more than half; and the crude birth rate for the LDCs would be somewhat over 30 per 1,000 (compared with about 20 for the DCs), instead of over 43 per 1,000 as shown now.

5. Distribution of Births by Parity

Parity refers to the birth order in the childbearing sequence for a given mother—first birth, second, third, and so on. It suggests the number of children presumed to be living when the given birth occurs—although these statistics could be estimated directly if data were available on numbers of surviving children cross-classified with the occurrence of the next birth. Parity data also shed some light on the age of parents, since, obviously, high parities, i.e., high orders of birth, are connected with advanced ages of mother and, particularly, of father. The two connections—between parity and older siblings, and between parity and age of parents—set the lines for the discussion here of the summary data.

In table 8 we show the distribution of births by birth order for the LDCs and the DCs. The coverage for the LDCs omits Sub-Saharan Africa for which the data are not available, and is quite limited for other regions. But for the three subregions shown, the distributions are quite similar: the share of the high parity births (i.e., the fifth and higher order) is 37 percent for East Southeast Asia, 33 percent for the Middle East, and 35 percent for Latin America. There is somewhat greater variation among the developed countries: the share of the same high parities is less than 10 percent for Europe, only 2 percent for Japan, and 16 percent for the overseas countries. But each of these, and their average, about 11 percent, are distinctly below the shares of high parities

TABLE 8
Distribution of Births by Birth Order, Less Developed and
Developed Market Economies, Early 1960's

	Number of Countries (1)	Shares of Births in Increasing Order (Parity)							
		1 (2)	2 (3)	3 (4)	4 (5)	5 (6)	6 & 7 (7)	8+ (8)	Total (9)
Less Developed									
1. East Southeast Asia	4	18.4	16.9	14.9	13.0	10.9	14.9	11.0	100
2. Middle East	2	17.2	19.7	16.1	13.9	11.0	14.0	8.1	100
3. Latin America	12	21.6	16.7	14.5	12.0	9.6	13.2	12.4	100
4. Total LDCs, weighted		18.8	17.1	15.0	12.9	10.7	14.6	10.9	100
Developed									
5. Europe	13	36.5	29.4	16.4	8.3	4.2	3.5	1.7	100
6. Overseas offshoots	4	28.9	24.8	18.5	11.7	6.6	6.0	3.5	100
7. Japan	1	47.5	35.7	11.8	3.0	1.1	0.7	0.2	100
8. Total DCs, weighted		35.4	28.7	16.5	8.7	4.6	4.0	2.1	100
Contributions to Crude Birth Rates									
9. LDCs		8.2	7.4	6.5	5.6	4.7	6.3	4.7	43.4
10. DCs		7.2	5.8	3.3	1.7	0.9	0.9	0.4	20.2
11. Line 9 minus line 10		1.0	1.6	3.2	3.9	3.8	5.4	4.3	23.2
12. % Distribution of line 11		4	7	14	17	16	23	19	100

Notes:

Lines 1–3 and 5–7: The underlying data are from United Nations, *Demographic Yearbook, 1969* (New York, 1970), table 17, supplemented for one or two countries in the *Demographic Yearbook, 1965* (New York, 1966), table 16.

The data refer primarily to 1963, but another year was taken if data for 1963 were missing or their coverage was incomplete. No adequate data were available for Sub-Saharan Africa.

Percentages were taken to totals excluding the unallocated, except for Mexico where the unallocated were combined in the source with the top parity group (but the effect on column 8 is negligible). For Sweden, the shares of the two top parity groups had to be estimated from the averages for the other twelve countries in the region.

Line 1: Includes Pakistan, West Malaysia, Philippines, and Thailand. The data for India, relating to a limited sample of urban communities could not be used; therefore, we took an unweighted mean of entries for the four countries.

Line 2: Includes Tunisia and the United Arab Republic.

(Notes continued on the following page)

(Table 8 notes continued)

Line 3: Includes Costa Rica, Dominican Republic, El Salvador, Guatemala, Jamaica, Mexico, Panama, Chile, Colombia, Ecuador, Peru, and Venezuela.

Lines 4 and 8: The weighting was the same as that in tables 1 and 2.

Lines 5–6: The coverage is the same as that in table 1.

Lines 9–10: The percentage shares in lines 4 and 8 were applied to the crude birth rates for the LDCs and DCs (43.4 and 20.2 respectively, see table 2).

Lines 11–12: Calculated similarly to lines 28–29 of table 2.

---

for the LDCs. The finding is not surprising since we found in table 1 that complete fertility averaged about 6 children for the LDCs and less than 3 children for the DCs—and thus clearly implied much greater proportions of births of high parities in the LDCs than in the DCs.

Nor is it surprising that the high parity births account for much of the excess of the crude birth rate in the LDCs over that in the DCs. Births of the fifth and higher orders contribute close to six-tenths of the total difference in the crude birth rates between the LDCs and the DCs (line 12). Thus, if the proportions of high parity births to total population were the same for the LDCs as for the DCs the crude birth rates would differ by only four-tenths, i.e., would be somewhat below 30 per 1,000 in the LDCs, instead of the 43.4 per 1,000 for the late 1960s.

But we are more concerned here with the connection between births of high parity and the presumed number of older surviving siblings. For the latter we require data on mortality for the younger ages, which are even scarcer for the LDCs than those on births by parity. But we can approximate the necessary coefficients for Latin America, the only subregion among the LDCs for which the coverage in table 8 is adequate.

Estimates of survival of children to age 5 are available for a number of Latin American countries.[7] For 1955–1959 (the latest quinquennium shown), the number of survivors at age 5 (from an initial cohort of 1,000) varies from a high of 929 for Argentina to a low of 787 for Guatemala. The arithmetic mean number of

---

7. See O. Andrew Collver, *Birth Rates in Latin America: New Estimates of Historical Trends and Fluctuations*. Research Series no. 7, Institute of Studies, University of California (Berkeley: 1965). The estimates are taken from tables 11, 16, 19, 22, 28, 31, 34, 37, 40, 44, 47, and 50, pp. 66, 81, 89, 99, 116, 121, 127, 135, 144, 154, 160, and 169.

survivors for 11 countries (excluding Argentina, but comprising Chile, Colombia, Costa Rica, Ecuador, El Salvador, Guatemala, Honduras, Mexico, Panama, Peru, and Venezuela) is 849. But we also need estimates of survivors to ages from 10 to 20. We know from the standard sources that age specific death rates between age 5 and the late teens are extremely low. We have, therefore, assumed a relevant survivor estimate to high parity ages of 800 to 825 for Latin America or a cumulative mortality of 175 to 200 per 1,000. For the DCs we have assumed 925 to 940 survivors, or a cumulative mortality of 60 to 75 per 1,000 (a sizable error in this estimate will have little effect on our comparison).

The comparison of the birth parity grouping for Latin America, with that for all the DCs is given in the following tabulation:

	Contribution to CBR Low Parities (1–4)			Contribution to CBR High Parities (5+)		
	Total	Survival rate	Adjusted (1 × 2)	Total	Survival rate	Adjusted (4 × 5)
	(1)	(2)	(3)	(4)	(5)	(6)
1. Latin America	28.7	0.825	23.68	15.6	0.80	12.48
2. DCs	18.0	0.940	16.92	2.2	0.925	2.04
3. Excess, Latin America over DCs	10.7		6.76	13.4		10.44

Note: The contribution for Latin America was calculated by multiplying the shares of parity groups in total births (line 3, table 8) by the total crude birth rate of 44.3 per 1,000 (for the latter see table 2, line 13).

The data show that by the time the average mother in Latin America gives birth to her fifth child, she must have over three surviving children. Moreover, the contribution even of mothers with birth parity below 5, in terms of surviving children, 23.7 per 1,000, exceeds not only the total surviving birth rate (18.96) but also the total crude birth rate (20.2) for the DCs. Yet the contributions to the crude birth rate in Latin America continued beyond the fourth birth order—with the survivors of these high births exceeding those in the DCs by over 10 points and accounting for about six-tenths of the total difference in the proportion of surviving births (to about age 20) between Latin America and

TABLE 9

Shares in Total Births of High Parity Births to Older Mothers,
Selected LDCs and DCs; and Contribution to Differences in
Birth Rates, Selected Countries

A. Shares in Total Births of High Parity Births (5th and over)
to Older Mothers (%)

	Age of Mothers				
	30-34 (1)	35-39 (2)	40 and over (3)	30 and over (4)	All ages (5)
Less Developed					
1. Philippines, 1963	10.7	9.0	3.7	23.4	35.4
2. Thailand, 1964	11.0	10.3	5.5	26.8	32.9
3. United Arab Republic, 1966	7.2	9.4	5.7	22.3	25.9
4. Guatemala, 1963	10.3	8.5	3.8	22.6	33.1
5. Colombia, 1964	11.0	9.6	3.9	24.5	30.3
6. Average, lines 1-5	10.0	9.4	4.5	23.9	31.5
Developed					
7. France, 1963	7.0	4.4	1.9	13.3	14.2
8. Germany, Federal Republic, 1964	2.3	2.1	1.1	5.5	6.6
9. USA, 1964	5.7	4.0	1.3	11.0	17.4
10. Japan, 1963	0.7	0.8	0.3	1.8	2.4
11. Average, lines 7-10	3.9	2.8	1.2	7.9	10.15

B. Contribution to Differences in Birth Rates

	Shares of High Parity Births (%)		Contributions to CBR	
	Mothers, aged 30+ (1)	Mothers, aged 35+ (2)	Mothers, aged 30+ (3)	Mothers, aged 35+ (4)
12. LDCs	27.5	15.9	11.9	6.90
13. DCs	8.3	4.2	1.7	0.85

Notes:

Panel A: The data are from United Nations, *Demographic Yearbook, 1969* (New York, 1970), table 17. We chose the major countries in the regions for which data were available, to secure a rough approximation. Because of the limited coverage of the less developed regions, other than Latin America, even inclusion of all reporting countries could not yield adequate representation.

Panel B, columns 1 and 2: First we derived the ratios of the shares of high parity births for the older mothers to the shares of high parity births for mothers of all ages

(Notes continued on the following page)

(Table 9 notes continued)
(i.e. the ratio of column 4 to column 5, in lines 6 and 11 for column 1 or of the sums of columns 2 and 3 to column 5 in lines 6 and 11, for column 2). These worked out to 0.76 and 0.44 for the LDCs and 0.78 and 0.39 for the DCs. We then applied these to the total shares of higher parities in table 8 (i.e. 36.2 per cent for LDCs and 10.7 per cent for the DCs), to secure the entries in lines 12 and 13.

Panel B, columns 3 and 4: The shares in columns 1–2 were multiplied by the total CBR for the LDCs (43.4) and for the DCs (20.2), respectively. The calculation thus parallels that in panel C of table 2, except that here it is limited to a comparison of higher parity births to older mothers, not of all births to all mothers.

---

the DCs. In short, in the LDCs, the high fertility and high birth parities persist *despite* the substantial number of surviving children within the families that continue to grow. The mortality rates may be somewhat higher in the other LDC regions than in Latin America, but the conclusion is likely to stand.

We return now to the connection between high parities and the advanced age of parents. The relevant data provide cross-classifications of births by parity and age of mother alone, and for only a few countries, particularly among the less developed. Hence we present the data for a few individual countries, and do not attempt to derive comprehensive average (table 9). However, the general order of magnitudes suggested would probably be confirmed by more abundant data if they were available.

Needless to say, the role of the older mothers in high parity births is substantial. Thus the average for the five selected less developed countries shows that of 31.5 percent, the share of high parity births in the total, over four-tenths was contributed by mothers 35 years of age or older. Interestingly, in the DCs also, the contribution of mothers that old to the high parity births was also about four-tenths, although the latter accounted for only about 10 percent of total births. Given the excess in the age of father over mother, discussed in the preceding section, we may assume that mothers 35 years old or more are to be matched with fathers well over 40; and mothers 30 years old or more imply fathers 35 or more.

Panel B of table 9 provides an illustrative calculation of the contribution of high parity births to older parents to the total differential (23.2 points) in the crude birth rates between the LDCs and DCs. The high parity births to mothers aged 35 or more (and implicitly to fathers well over 40) account for over 6 points, or over a quarter of the total difference in the CBRs between the LDCs and the DCs. The high parity births to mothers aged 30 and over (and implicitly to fathers 35 and older) account for 10.2 points, or almost half of the differential in the crude birth rates.

We have emphasized the large contribution of high parities, associated with sizable numbers of surviving siblings and with the advanced age of parents, to the excess of crude birth rates in the LDCs over the DCs. The reason for this is that these findings must be recognized in dealing with the persistence of the high birth rates in the LDCs. We must, in analyzing the latter, explain not only the connection between the higher fertility and the earlier marriage and younger parents, i.e., at the low parities, but also the relation of high parities to older parents. Why does a family with a mother whose fecundity is declining, and with a father who approaches or passes beyond the age of forty, continue to have high parity births? Why do such families contribute between a quarter and a half of the total birth rate differential between the LDCs and the DCs?

6. Distribution by Size of Household

The family, a group related by blood-ties and usually residing together, is the unit in society primarily responsible for rearing children to the age of maturity, when they can leave the parental home and assume the responsibilities of adult life. Given the higher fertility, predominantly intramarital, in the LDCs, the average family should be larger in these countries than in the DCs, if only because more surviving children are brought up within the family fold.

But the family is a complex concept that does not lend itself easily to statistical observation; in the larger meaning, relevant to pooling of economic assets and income for coverage of consumer expenditures and accumulation, a family should include not only the nuclear unit of parents and their children residing together but also others. The available statistics do not refer to the family but to the household—a group of individuals sharing quarters (including single-person households) "who make common provision for food and other essentials of living. The persons in the group may pool their incomes and have a common budget to a greater or lesser extent; they may be related or unrelated persons, or a combination of both." [8] A household can then be wider than a family, since it may include members not related by blood-ties, or narrower since it may exclude closely related members living elsewhere. Still, it is a fairly useful approximation to what may be called the cohabiting family unit, in that households with members not related by blood-ties (e.g., domestic servants, hired workers for a family business, boarders, and the like) constitute limited proportions of all households. Being largely family households, they are relevant to tracing the effects of differential fertility on the number of children within the unit. More important for our purpose—consideration of the possible effects of numbers of children on the economic position of the closely relevant family unit —the household is the unit most often employed in studies of the distribution of income by size.

Table 10 summarizes the data on distribution of households and population by size of household, with emphasis on comparison between the LDCs and DCs. The difficulties with the definition of a household, particularly in cases of unrelated individuals living communally in lodging houses, dormitories, and the like—in addition to those involved in establishing fully the sharing of quarters by a family household with nonrelated members—yield statistical divergences from the true situation (illustrations can be found in the source in footnote 8). In table 10 these difficulties appear to affect particularly the averages for Sub-Saharan Africa, which suffers also from inadequate country coverage. For these reasons, we excluded Sub-Saharan Africa from the average for all LDCs—although the broad differences between the LDCs and the DCs would not have been much affected by its inclusion.

The larger size of household, and particularly the larger proportion of households and population in the larger units in the LDCs than in the DCs, is clear. Households of seven persons or more are 28 percent of all households in the LDCs (line 5) and they account for close to a half of total population (line 14), whereas the corresponding proportions in the DCs are less than 6 and less than 14 percent respectively (lines 9 and 18). By contrast, one-person households in the LDCs are only 6 percent of

---

8. The quotation is from p. 6 of the United Nations manual on *Methods of Projecting Households and Families,* referred to as the main source for table 10 below. A useful, if summary, discussion of the concepts of family and household is found on pp. 5–12.

TABLE 10

Distribution of Households and Population by Size of Household,
LDCs and DCs, Early and Late 1960's (percentages)

	1 (1)	2 (2)	3–4 (3)	5–6 (4)	7–8 (5)	9+ (6)
A. Distribution of Households						
1. East Southeast Asia (8)	5.7	8.8	29.7	28.2	17.8	9.8
2. Middle East (9)	6.0	10.8	28.6	29.3	15.7	9.6
3. Sub-Saharan Africa (8)	11.4	48.1		20.1	20.4	
4. Latin America (15)	7.4	10.5	27.1	24.9	16.5	13.6
5. LDCs (ex. line 3)	6.0	9.3	29.1	27.8	17.4	10.4
6. Europe (13)	16.9	26.1	37.9	14.5	4.6	
7. Overseas offshoots (4)	10.9	24.7	37.1	19.8	7.5	
8. Japan (1970)	13.1	15.0	44.0	22.3	5.6	
9. DCs	14.0	23.8	38.6	17.8	5.8	
B. Distribution of Population (Same Countries as in Panel A)						
10. East Southeast Asia	1.1	3.6	20.6	29.7	25.6	19.4
11. Middle East	1.2	4.2	19.7	31.4	23.9	19.6
12. Sub-Saharan Africa	2.7	31.7		24.2	41.4	
13. Latin America	1.5	4.1	19.0	26.0	23.0	26.4
14. LDCs (ex. line 12)	1.2	3.7	20.3	29.3	25.0	20.5
15. Europe	5.4	16.8	41.9	24.4	11.5	
16. Overseas offshoots	3.1	13.9	36.5	29.7	16.8	
17. Japan	3.6	8.3	43.4	33.1	11.6	
18. DCs	4.2	14.3	40.1	27.8	13.6	

Notes:
The major source is the United Nations, *Methods of Projecting Households and Families*, Manual VIII in the series of manuals on methods of estimating population (New York, 1973), table 3, pp. 12–15, which distinguishes the following size classes of households: 1, 2–4, 5–6, 7 and over. To obtain greater detail, we used data from somewhat fewer countries for each region (except Sub-Saharan Africa) taken from the *Demographic Yearbooks* (particularly those for 1962 and 1963, and 1971). From these we derived allocation ratios for the 2–4 and 7+ groups; and applied them to the total shares for these two size groups.

Lines 1 and 10: Include Cambodia, Ceylon, South Korea, Federation of Malaya, Philippines, Thailand, India (allocated within the wider size groups by ratios for Ceylon), and Pakistan. The usual weighting was employed for this region.

Lines 2 and 11: Include Turkey, Iran, Iraq, Syria, Jordan, Libya, Tunisia, Morocco, and the United Arab Republic.

Lines 3 and 12: Include several smaller countries for better coverage: Lesotho, Dahomey, Gabon, Kenya, Mali, Sierra Leone, Liberia, and Zambia. Cameroon was excluded because of the exceptional showing for the 1-person group.

(Notes continued on the following page)

(Table 10 notes continued)
Lines 4 and 13: Include Costa Rica, Dominican Republic, El Salvador, Honduras, Jamaica, Mexico, Nicaragua, Panama, Brazil, Colombia, Chile, Ecuador, Paraguay, Peru, and Venezuela.
Lines 6–9 and 15–18: Coverage is as complete as in table 1. We took the 1970 data for Japan (rather than those for earlier years) to give greater weight to the recent experience (with the rapid changes in Japan's birth rate and family structure).

the total and they account for about 1 percent of total population, while the corresponding proportions for the DCs are 14 and 4 percent respectively.

The arithmetic mean size of household is clearly greater in the LDCs than in the DCs. This mean is easily calculated by dividing the percentage shares of one-person households in the total of households by the share of one-person households in total population (or, with the necessary adjustment, by relating the proportions of two-person households in households and in population). The resultant averages are 5.0 persons per household in the LDCs and 3.33 persons per household in the DCs. This difference, while substantial, may appear to be too narrow, considering that total fertility in the LDCs is over twice as high as that in the DCs (see table 1). However, the average size of household is a weighted arithmetic mean, in which the younger (and smaller) households have a greater weight in the LDCs than in the DCs (see table 2 for relative weights of women in the successive age groups within the childbearing span). If we use the weights in table 2 for women aged 15 to 49 and assume that the size of household corresponding to these ages, grows in the LDCs from 3 for the 15–19 age group of women by one person for each successive quinquennium reaching 9 persons in the age group 45–49, the weighted average size of household works out to somewhat over 5.5. The addition of single-person households (6 percent of households, but only 1.2 percent of population) would reduce the arithmetic mean to 5.3; and if we reasonably assume that households with women aged 50 years and over are, on the whole, smaller, the average of 5.0 obtained from table 10 is consistent with the assumption that during the childbearing cycle the average woman in the LDCs may have over 7 births (accounting for the top size of 9 persons). A similar calculation for the DCs, using a progression in size of household from 2 persons for women 15–19 years old, to 3 for the 20–24 age bracket, to 4 for the 25–29 age bracket, and to 4.5

for the remaining age brackets through 45–49, would yield a weighted arithmetic mean of 3.8, which with inclusion of one-person households (14 percent of households and 4.2 percent of population), would be reduced to 3.4—and be consistent with the 3.33 mean derived from table 10, with allowance for the remaining households with women aged 50 years and over. The consistency then is with the assumption that women in the DCs bear 2.5 children (or somewhat more)—less than half of the number assumed in the calculation for the LDCs.

The interest in the conjectural calculations just presented is less in the consistency between the difference in mean size of households in the LDCs and the DCs and the difference in their fertility, than in the emphasis on the fact that the range in the size of households within each group of countries is a reflection of the stages in the life cycle of a family. A new family begins with two members, grows as children are born and have to be maintained within the family for a prolonged period to maturity; then contracts as the parents and children grow older and the children leave to form a new and separate household. The average size of the household is a somewhat artificial measure that is a weighted combination of units of widely divergent magnitudes. It must therefore be remembered that differences in size of household reflect, in large part, differences in the stage in the life cycle of growth and contraction of the various family units.

Two further observations are relevant to the findings in table 10. First, it can be demonstrated that much of the difference between the 5.0 person average household in the LDCs and the 3.33 person average household in the DCs is due to the different proportions of children in total population. In 1960 in the LDCs (excluding Sub-Saharan Africa) the proportion of children under 15 to total population was 42.8 percent; of persons under 20 years of age—52.5 percent.[9] The similar proportions for the DCs (Western and Northern Europe and Italy, North America, Australia and New Zealand and Japan) were 27.8 and 33.3 percent respectively. If we apply these percentages to the mean size of household we find that of the total discrepancy of 1.67 persons, children under 15 accounted for 1.22 persons (or over three-quarters of the dif-

9. The data are from the United Nations working paper, *Population Estimates by Regions and Countries, 1950–1960*, ESA/P/WP. 31, May 1970.

ference) and those under 20 years of age accounted for 1.44 persons (or 86 percent of the difference). The calculation implies, realistically, that few children under 15 or persons under 20 live outside the family unit.

The second observation involves data relating size of household and income per *person;* and is associated with the finding (still to be tested) that if we group households by size, and then divide household income by number of persons, per person income declines fairly consistently as we move up the scale in size of household.[10] If this negative association, however mitigated by reduction of number of persons to equivalent consuming units, is accepted, the significantly wider range in size of households in the LDCs than in the DCs is of further interest. Thus if we assume that the smaller the household, the higher the per person income, and array population in descending order of per person income, using the data in table 10 for all LDCs and DCs, we can interpolate the shares of the top 20 and lowest 50 percent of population. We find that the average size of households for these two partition groups are 2.17 and 7.90 in the LDCs, and 1.70 and 5.38 for the DCs—the ratios being 3.64 and 3.15, respectively. Again, if the relation between per person income and size of household is negative, the figures suggest that per person income differentials due to differences in size of household tend to be greater in the LDCs than in the DCs.

Of course, the relation just suggested may not be that simple; and the function connecting size of household and income per person may not be the same for the LDCs and the DCs. But we make the observation here to point at the line of connection between higher fertility in the LDCs, larger average household,

10. For illustrative data for the United States see my paper, "Income-Related Differences in Natural Increase: Bearing on Growth and Distribution of Income," in Paul A. David and Melvin W. Reder, eds., *Nations and Households in Economic Growth,* Essays in Honor of Moses Abramovitz (New York: 1974), tables 1 and 2, pp. 130 and 133.[1] Evidence for Taiwan and the Philippines indicates that this negative association between size of household and income per person is found also in the LDCs.

This, and related, topics are discussed at greater length in my paper, "Demographic Components in Size-Distributions of Income," prepared for a conference on Income Distribution, Employment, and Economic Development in Southeast Asia, held in Tokyo in late December 1974, under the auspices of the Japan Economic Research Center (Tokyo) and the Council of Asian Manpower Studies (Manila).

wider range of size of household, and hence possible greater effects on differences in per person income associated with households of differing size. Thus, the higher levels of fertility in the LDCs may affect not only over-all levels and growth rates in per capita product, compared with the DCs, but also the *internal* distribution of income by size *within* the LDCs, compared with the DCs, associated with the wider differentials in size of household in the former.

The last observation is also relevant to much of the writing on size distribution of income in recent years. It is almost entirely based on data on household income, with some information on size of household, but with classifications of households by per household rather than per person (or per consuming unit) income. Needless to say, cross-section differences in distributions of households by size, and changes in these distributions over time, would affect these customary measures; and the latter alone could easily be misleading if we are concerned with income per person (or per consuming unit) rather than with income per household. One should also note that the emphasis on effects of fertility on size of household during the successive phases of the life cycle of the household only strengthens the conviction that adequate analysis of income inequalities within a country must take account of the demographic components that affect the size of household, and determine the life cycle of a household—with its parameters different for the LDCs and the DCs, and with its possible changes over time within each.

7. Concluding Comments

In concluding this paper, it may be useful to list the findings bearing on the demographic corollaries of the much higher birth rates (over 43 per 1,000) in the less developed market economies (LDCs), compared with those (about 20 per 1,000) in the developed (DCs). These findings are based largely on international comparisons for the 1960s for the market economies—excluding the Communist countries.

1. The age-specific fertility rates for women are, for each age group within the childbearing span, consistently and significantly higher in the LDCs than in the DCs. Women in the LDCs begin bearing children at earlier ages, and continue to bear them through

later ages, than women in the DCs. The proportions of younger women within the childbearing span are also somewhat higher in the LDCs than in the DCs—a factor only partly offset by the lower proportion of all women of childbearing ages within the total population of the LDCs. The higher fertility of the very young women (under 20 years of age) and the older women (35 years or more) in the LDCs accounts for almost four-tenths of the total difference in crude birth rates between the two groups of countries.

2. The higher age-specific fertility rates of women below age 25 in the LDCs is associated with a significantly higher proportion married in these young age classes—both as compared with the DCs. Indeed, intramarital fertility rates for women 15–24 are somewhat *lower* for the LDCs than for the DCs. The early marriages of women in some of the major LDC regions (particularly the populous countries in Asia, and in Sub-Saharan Africa) suggest a direct transition of a young woman from the parental household to the household of her husband. In the DCs, on the other hand, young women spend several years on education and work outside the parental household before marriage.

3. The differential in the age of married men between the LDCs and the DCs is far narrower. This is true both at time of marriage and within the married state. The bridegroom or husband is between 5 and 8 or 9 years older than the bride or wife in the LDCs, as compared with 2 to 3 years older in the DCs. The composition of the parental couple (even setting aside some incidence of polygyny in the LDCs), with regard to the disparity in age and experience between husband and wife, is clearly different in the LDCs from that in the DCs—with implications for decisions concerning births and children.

4. Given the extension of childbearing to the more advanced ages of women, and the substantial age excess of husbands over wives in the LDCs, it follows that older fathers account for a larger proportion of births in the LDCs than in the DCs. The estimates suggest that fathers 40 years or older account for almost a quarter of all births in the LDCs, but for only about a tenth in the DCs; and that a third of the total excess of crude birth rates of the LDCs over those of the DCs is due to births associated with older fathers. Thus, much of the difference in birth rates between the two groups of countries is due to higher fertility of younger women and to the excess of births associated with older

men in the LDCs, the greater motherhood of younger women, and the greater fatherhood of older men.

5. The higher parity births (fifth or higher order) account for almost four-tenths of all births in the LDCs, for less than one-tenth in the DCs. This difference in the contribution of higher parity births accounts for almost six-tenths of the total difference in crude birth rates between the LDCs and the DCs; and a substantial proportion is due to high parity births to *older* parents (women 35 years or older; men 40 years or older). Thus much of the higher fertility in the LDCs is due to high parity births, incurred despite the presence within the household of well over three children, on the average, and despite the more advanced age of parents, particularly the father.

6. Given the larger number of children within the household in the LDCs—and they can be only within the family household, one of whose main functions is to raise children to maturity and independence—we would expect that in the LDCs the average household would be substantially larger and the proportion of the total population within fairly large households much greater. Indeed, the household in the LDCs averages about 5 persons, compared with 3.3 in the DCs; and the proportion of population in households of 7 or more persons is close to one-half of the total population in the LDCs, and less than a seventh in the DCs. These results which are consistent with the assumption that fertility rates in the LDCs are over twice as high as those in the DCs, raise intriguing questions concerning the impact of differences in size of households on the measures of inequality in the size distribution of income among households or among persons.

Before we turn to the possible implications of these demographic corollaries of birth rates for the factors that might explain the persistence of high birth rates in the LDCs, one other finding, not explicitly considered so far, ought to be noted. The high fertility rates in the LDCs observed for the 1960s and persisting into the early 1970s, have been maintained despite the fact that in most of the less developed regions, death rates, in general, and infant mortality rates, in particular, have declined substantially over the last three to four decades. Given the assumption that the desired number of children was limited and below total capacity, fewer births should have been needed to achieve a limited total surviving children target. In many of these regions other processes of modernization have spread, either since the 1920s or 1930s, or at least since shortly after World War II. Such modernization should have brought about a modernization of the demographic patterns, particularly lower birth rates and smaller family units.

It would take us too far afield to document this observation in detail. But in view of the relevance of the death rates, and their sharp decline in recent decades in the LDCs, we present a brief summary of the world-wide data easily available, and we supplement it with data for individual countries in Latin America, a less developed region the records for which are relatively good, and the political independence of which goes back a century and a half so that recent decades are not disturbed by major political changes like those that have affected most other less developed countries after World War II (table 11).

We eliminated Mainland China from the aggregates for the LDCs because it is difficult to establish the soundness of the basis of the China estimates for recent years. Three findings can be briefly stated. First, for all LDCs, except China, with the sharp decline in the crude death rates of almost a half (from 30.8 to 16.0), the crude birth rates remained about the same. Infant mortality also declined, perhaps as much as four-tenths. Second, for the ten Latin American countries in panel B, both the cumulative death rates to age 5 and crude death rates for total population declined sharply from 1920–1929 to 1950–1959 (and could be shown to have declined more from 1920–1924 to 1954–1959)—the average decline in the former being about four-tenths and that in the latter somewhat greater proportionately (lines 20 and 21, columns 1–4). Over the same period, crude birth rates barely changed; and when standardized for age structure of women within childbearing ages actually rose (lines 20–21, columns 5–8). Finally, panel C shows that the decline in the death rates in Latin America continued in the recent two decades, and the crude birth rates too began to decline, but slowly. In fact, the total absolute drop in birth rates over the last fifteen years was somewhat less than that in death rates (leading to a slight rise in the rate of natural increase). For many of the populous less developed countries in Asia and North Africa (less so for Sub-Saharan Africa) similar rapidly declining death rates and constant or slightly rising

TABLE 11

Trends in Birth Rates and Death Rates, Less Developed Regions and Countries

A. Crude Vital Rates (per 1,000), LDCs and DCs, 1936—38 and 1970—75

	DCs (1)	LDCs (2)	China (3)	Other LDCs (4)
1936—1938				
1. Birth rates	24.1	42.5	42.5	42.5
2. Death rates	15.5	31.6	32.5	30.8
3. Infant mortality rates	106	230	na	na
1970—1975				
4. Birth rates	17.2	37.5	26.9	42.0
5. Death rates	9.2	14.3	10.3	16.0
6. Infant mortality rates (1965—1969)	27	140	na	na
Change, 1936—1938 to 1970—1975				
7. Birth rates	-6.9	-5.0	-15.6	-0.5
8. Death rates	-6.3	-17.3	-22.3	-14.8
9. Infant mortality rates (to 1965— 1969)	-79	-90	na	na

B. Vital Rates (per 1,000), 10 Countries in Latin America, 1920—1929 (I) and 1950—1959 (II)

	Cumulative death rates to age 5		Crude death rates		Crude birth rates		Standardized birth rates	
	I	II	I	II	I	II	I	II
10. Chile	388.0	145.0	28.85	13.10	43.0	37.3	40.65	37.15
11. Colombia	256.5	192.5	23.05	17.20	44.75	44.55	42.6	44.8
12. Costa Rica	184.5	115.5	23.4	9.9	45.55	45.15	46.0	47.45
13. Ecuador	295.0	197.5	28.55	16.65	48.4	46.45	na	na
14. El Salvador	340.5	197.5	33.45	18.85	46.85	47.9	44.6*	48.35
15. Guatemala	278.5	224.0	33.15	21.7	48.75	49.95	na	na
16. Honduras	210.0	131.5	23.1	13.7	44.2	46.0	43.6*	49.2
17. Mexico	291.0	147.0	27.55	13.05	44.8	45.4	40.45	47.6
18. Panama	172.5	88.0	16.95	9.1	39.5	39.5	37.7*	42.1
19. Venezuela	242.5	121.0	25.3	11.55	42.15	44.25	na	na

Averages (Unweighted Arithmetic Means)

20. 7 countries (except lines 13, 15, & 19)	256.0	145.3	25.3	13.7	44.1	43.7	42.2	45.2
21. All 10 countries	260.8	156.0	26.4	14.6	44.8	44.6	na	na

(Continued)

(Table 11 continued)

C. Crude Vital Rates, Latin America (ex. Temperate Zone), 1950–1955 to 1965–1970

	Death Rates				Birth Rates			
	1950– 1955 (1)	1955– 1960 (2)	1960– 1965 (3)	1965– 1970 (4)	1950– 1955 (5)	1955– 1960 (6)	1960– 1965 (7)	1965– 1970 (8)
22. Caribbean	15	13	12	11	38	38	37	35
23. Middle America	16	13	11	10	46	45	44	43
24. Tropical South America	15	13	11	10	45	43	40	39
25. Total weighted	15.2	13.1	11.1	10.0	44.4	42.9	40.7	39.5

na–not available
*–the standard birth rate was calculated from the crude for 1920–1929, using ratios of crude to standardized for 1930–1939 or 1925–1929.

Notes

Lines 1–2: Data from United Nations, *World Population Trends, 1920–1947* (New York, December 1949), table 2, p. 10. We took the mid-value of the range shown. DCs comprise North America, Japan, Europe, and Oceania (but exclude Temperate South America, a minor omission here and a minor inclusion under LDCs as compared with line 3 or lines 4–6). All other countries are included in the LDCs. China is identified with the region in the source designated "Remaining Far East" (after exclusion of Japan). The population weights used to combine the rates are from table 1, p. 3 of the source.

Lines 3 and 6: From the United Nations Background paper prepared for the 1974 World Population Conference, entitled *Demographic Trends in the World and Its Major Regions, 1950–1970* (New York, April 16, 1974), table 6, p. 15.

Lines 4 and 5: From United Nations, *World Population Prospects, 1970–2000, As Assessed in 1973*, mimeographed, ESA/P/WP.53 (New York, March 1975), table 2.1, pp. 25–26 (birth and death rates) and table 1.1, pp. 12–14 (population totals, used as weights in distinguishing between China and other LDCs). The estimates (under "medium" variant) shown for 1970–1975 are partly projections, but are obviously close to the recent data and are the best estimates for the current quinquennium.

Lines 10 to 21: Calculated from the successive country tables in O. Andrew Collver, *Birth Rates in Latin America: New Estimates of Historical Trends and Fluctuations*, no. 7 in Research Series of Institute of International Studies, University of California, Berkeley, 1965. The source shows quinquennial averages, which we converted to initial and terminal decadal averages. The standardization of birth rates in columns 7 and 8 is for the ages of women within the childbearing span (see pp. 42–47 of source for the weighting).

Lines 22 to 25: Calculated from the source cited for lines 3 and 6 above. The death rates are derived by subtracting rates of natural increase (table 7, p. 17) from birth rates (table 5, p. 13). The weighting in line 25 is by population in 1950 for the first quinquennium, average of 1950 and 1960 for the second quinquennium; 1960 population for the third; and the average of 1960 and 1970 for the fourth quinquennium. The population totals are given in table 2, p. 2, of the source.

birth rates could be found—although for a somewhat shorter period than that covered for Latin America.

There have been other important modernization trends in the LDCs over the recent decades when the high birth rates persisted. We cite the evidence for Latin America to illustrate rather than claim thorough confirmation. The proportion of population in "urban agglomerations"—urban communities larger than small towns of up to 20,000 inhabitants—in the three subregions of Latin America (excluding the Temperate Zone) rose from 10.8 percent in 1920, to 20.9 percent in 1950, and to 29.2 percent in 1960.[11] This trend must have continued through the 1960s. With urban defined differently (and using the national definitions) the percentage of urban to total population for all of Latin America rose from 40.9 in 1950 to 56.7 in 1970.[12] *Per capita* gross domestic product (in constant prices) must also have been rising at a significant rate since the mid-1920s. Approximate estimates indicate an average rise between 1925 and 1950 of about 1.7 percent per year; between 1950 and 1970 of close to 2.6 percent per year; and for the full 45-year period from 1925 to 1970, 2.1 percent per year—suggesting that the level in 1970 was over 2.5 times that in the initial year.[13] One may assume that other aspects of the social structure were also modernized in Latin America (e.g., higher literacy and level of education, improved health, greater levels of consumption). However, the fact that birth rates failed to decline means that modernization was partial, and may have failed to affect some other aspects of the social and economic structure. Finally, one should note that in two other less developed regions the rough indexes of aggregate product per capita rose substantially: from 1950 to 1970 in East and Southeast Asia (ex-

11. See United Nations, *Growth of the World's Urban and Rural Population, 1920–2000* (New York: 1969), table 47, p. 115, and table 48, p. 116.

12. See the United Nations background paper prepared for the 1974 World Population Conference, cited for table 11, lines 3 and 6, table 14, p. 30.

13. The estimates for 1925–1950 are from Alexander Ganz, "Problems and Uses of National Wealth Estimates in Latin America," in Raymond Goldsmith and Christopher Saunders, eds., *Income and Wealth Series No. VIII* (Bowes and Bowes, London: 1969), table III, p. 226. The estimates for 1950–1960 and 1960–1970 are from table 6B of United Nations, *Yearbook of National Accounts Statistics, 1969:* vol. II, *International Tables* (New York: 1970), and *Yearbook of National Accounts Statistics, 1972,* vol. III, *International Tables,* (New York: 1974).

cluding Japan) and from 1960 to 1970 in Africa (excluding South Africa).[14]

We come now to the question: why have the much higher birth rates in the LDCs persisted through decades of declining death rates and rising urbanization and per capita income? Only conjectures are possible. The summary findings above, relating to the demographic components of these high fertility levels are only suggestive of a deliberate process. And the extensive literature, bearing largely on fertility differentials and trends in the economically developed countries, is also only suggestive, particularly with respect to the transition theory. The latter outlines a paradigm of a shift from the traditional or preindustrial to the modern demographic patterns; and thus implicitly indicates the factors underlying the "traditionally" high fertility rates in the current LDCs.[15] But, as has been indicated, one must allow for the different fertility and mortality levels, and the different historical conditions of the current LDCs compared with the vital rates and historical conditions of the presently developed countries in their preindustrial periods in the eighteenth or nineteenth century. The literature on demographic experience of the LDCs is quite limited, if only because statistical data have become available only recently (and are still deficient) and the accumulation of analytical results has just begun.[16] Nor is it feasible here to comb the limited but

---

14. The source for 1950–60 is the United Nations *Yearbook, 1969* and for 1960–70, the *Yearbook, 1972*, both cited in footnote 13. For East and Southeast Asia the annual growth rate for 1950–1970 in gross domestic product per capita was somewhat over 2 percent, yielding a cumulative rise of 50 percent over the two decades; that for Africa for 1960–1970 was only slightly lower. It must be noted, however, that these are aggregates, and make no allowance for divergences among countries or for income inequalities within countries.

15. For an illuminating summary of the transition theory and the modifications in it in the light of current research see A. J. Coale, "The Demographic Transition Reconsidered," a paper presented at the Liege 1973 International Population Conference of the International Union for Scientific Study of Population, pp. 53–72.

16. In the 1953 United Nations volume, *The Determinants and Consequences of Population Trends* (New York: 1953), which was a valuable compilation of findings of studies on the relations between population changes and economic and social conditions, the summary of chapter V noted that statistical data on fertility are lacking, particularly for "most under-developed countries" (p. 96, par. 141) and in referring to factors that account for high fertility ("in the neighborhood of 40 per thousand," p. 97, par. 145) notes "factors such as the nearly universal marriage of women at

still vast literature. The attempt is rather to present a few broad reflections, induced partly by the evidence summarized, partly by the readily available literature on demographic and economic patterns. These, we hope, will be of interest as at least indications of possible directions of further research.

It might help to group the factors that could serve to explain the higher fertility rates in the LDCs under three broad heads: the technology of birth control; the possibly lower costs of larger numbers of children in the LDCs; the possibly higher returns from larger numbers of children in the LDCs. These three groups are not mutually exclusive, and each comprises a wide range of subvariables. But one can secure at least an impression of the relative magnitudes of their contributions to the demographic pattern to be explained, and a notion of the identity of some of the subvariables.

As the quotation in footnote 16 indicates, even in the LDCs fertility is controlled. In all of them some institutions and customs keep fertility below the biological potential. This is a matter of some importance, since it suggests that modernization may destroy or weaken these institutions and customs *before* the new restraining factors associated with modernization become fully operative. But the technology of birth control referred to above is clearly the modern technology, that is far more readily available in the eco-

---

young ages and the absence of the use of birth control measures." But the summary also notes that even these LDCs have "institutions and customs which reduce fertility substantially below the biological potential."

The revised edition of the volume, United Nations, *The Determinants and Consequences of Population Trends: New Summary of Findings on Interaction of Demographic, Economic and Social Factors, vol. I* (New York: 1973), contains in chapter IV a much richer discussion of fertility levels and trends in the high fertility (i.e., LDC) countries; and a wider exploration of the cultural, economic and social factors behind them. But the discussion comments on the difficulties of applying the past experience of the presently developed countries to the current LDCs (see paragraph 134, p. 96); and, in trying to explain why there has been little response of the birth rates in the LDCs to much higher levels of income and lower levels of death rates, still emphasizes the "threshold" hypothesis. The latter assumes that modernization and economic growth must reach some relatively high levels before effects on birth rates may be expected. But as I suggested in another connection, the hypothesis is but another name for the puzzle—rather than a substantive explanation that would specify factors that prevent sizable rises in income and declines in death rates from having an effect; see the comments in my paper, "Economic Aspects of Fertility Trends in the Less-Developed Countries," in S. J. Behrman, Leslie Corsa, Jr., and Ronald Freedman, eds., *Fertility and Family Planning: A World View* (Ann Arbor: University of Michigan Press, 1969, pp. 157–159).

nomically developed countries. In the DCs generally the population is richer and more literate, the transport and communication systems are better, and government has a more permissive or favorable attitude. The implication is that the modern, effective, technology of birth control is *not* available to the population of the LDCs, because of high economic costs of delivery, or the indifferent or negative attitude of the government, or both; and that much of the high birth rate is due to *unwanted* births, unwanted by the parents who could have avoided them, given more effective control technology.

There is little question that *some* group in every large population, whether in a developed or less developed country, would have, with better application of better birth control technology, avoided some births that were unwanted. However, "unwanted" is a term subject to many ambiguities in application in quantitative research (unwanted as to timing, or forever, unwanted under what conditions, and the like). Nevertheless, more effective technology and at lower costs would have, in any population, *some* net curbing effect on births—almost by definition of effectiveness and cost. But how significant is such a factor, in explaining the wide differentials in fertility between the LDCs and the DCs?

Several weighty arguments can be adduced to suggest that it is of limited importance. To begin with, age at time of marriage, particularly of women, is clearly an important variable which can be modified, as it has been in the past history of several European and related societies, and thereby affect fertility significantly. This, however, is a change in human and institutional practices, and is little influenced by birth control technology more directly relevant to intramarital fertility. Furthermore, intramarital fertility has varied markedly among the current DCs in their preindustrial phase, when birth control was far less advanced that it is today. These variations find some parallels today among the less developed countries. The two factors just mentioned yielded crude birth rates in the late eighteenth century that ranged from 31 per 1,000 in Norway and Denmark to 38 per 1,000 in Finland, to 55 per 1,000 in the United States.[17]

If the spread in crude birth rates could be so wide with late

---

17. For a convenient summary of these vital rates see Simon Kuznets, *Modern Economic Growth* (New Haven: Yale University Press, 1966), table 2.3, pp. 42–44.

eighteenth-century birth control technology, one wonders why the current technology within the LDCs has been so inadequate. More important, one may ask why, if more children were seen to lead to economic misery, have the families in the LDCs not manifested a sufficiently strong demand for effective birth control means, a demand that would overcome the indifference of government and the obstacles connected with high costs. After all, other products and aspects of modern technology—ranging from those that reduced death rates so rapidly to popular products like radio sets and Coca Cola—have spread widely and been accepted. If the argument is that established views and ideas, which persist despite changing events, did not encompass the need for modern birth control technology, then the identifiable factor is not the absence of such technology, but the lack of demand for it. Why, then, have the high fertility levels continued to be wanted—presumably by dominant proportions of the population, if not by the small group who really desired fewer children but were inhibited by difficulties in securing effective tools?

In turning now to costs of, and returns from, children, we note first that these costs and returns can be economic, social, or psychological. Then we may also ask what units weigh these costs and returns—giving not only explicit, overt consideration to these minuses and pluses, but also intuitive responses that nevertheless reflect balances. Is it the parental pair, the larger family of which the pair is a member, the larger blood-related collective (tribe, caste, etc.), or even a still larger aggregate that sets the norms to which the parental pair may refer? In the discussion here, we emphasize the economic and related social costs; and given the structure of LDCs, one must bear in mind the possible reference of decisions regarding the number of children to norms established by a much wider, if still blood-related, group than the nuclear, or even the extended, family.

Under the largely rural, family business conditions in the LDCs, direct and indirect costs of a child are far lower than for the competitive, nuclear family of an economically developed country. In the latter much reliance is placed on the individual earning (or social) power of the father, which would be adversely affected by the economic and other burdens of many children. In a developed economy, substantial earnings and other opportunities for the wife and would-be mother would be foregone, if her time and energy were to be absorbed in childbearing and childrearing. Furthermore, in the developed societies a much greater investment must be made in the rearing of children, so that the direct inputs (as distinct from indirect costs) per child are much higher than in the LDCs. In the latter, only a small investment is needed to rear a child to maturity as an effective economic agent under the conditions of the country and the family.

There is little question that the *absolute* costs of children, direct or indirect, are far lower in the LDCs than in the DCs. One related point may be added. Because of the closer ties of family in a less developed country to a larger, blood-related aggregate, any unusual costs of the specific family, particularly in connection with children, may be covered, partly at least, by its associates within the tribe, caste, or similar type of group.

Yet one must consider absolute costs in relation to the total income of the family unit involved. Are the direct and indirect costs of a child in the family of a less developed country clearly lower *relative* to the total income of the family than the greater costs of a child in a family in a developed country relative to its larger income? If the potential income of the latter is X dollars, and it is reduced to X-C by the direct and indirect costs of a prospective child, and if the potential income of the former is X/K dollars and it is reduced to $(X/K)-(C/L)$, is L necessarily less than K (K and L being larger than one)? Even if the proportional burden of the monetary magnitude of the costs of a child are the same in the LDCs and DCs, with the generally lower income in the former, the welfare burden would still be greater.

But costs are not independent of returns. They would be independent only if we fixed the latter by assumption. And one may argue that returns are a major factor in any explanation of the persistence of high fertility rates in the LDCs. This judgment reflects the general notion that societies, and groups within them, are responsive to differential cost and return opportunities. Although a long persisting framework of such opportunities clothes the largely rational responses in social norms and ideological garments, once the framework of costs and returns has changed for families or for groups of families, the adjustment should be relatively rapid. If the response, in fact, deviates significantly from the rational content, and if the lag, in fact, is long, one must attempt to establish, in a testable fashion, both the factors that underlie the deviation and the mechanism that generates the lag. Broad references to peculiarities of human nature, or to the existence of a lag, are merely descriptions of the puzzle, rather than explanations.[18]

If then we consider the returns from children, the implication is that the families in the LDCs view children as a source of wealth, the latter defined broadly as economic or social power. Either in weighing costs against returns, or in adherence to social norms still justified in their eyes, the families invest in children because they view them as a source of economic or social gain. This view may be held also by the blood-related collectives larger than the family household or extended family, even reaching into the large politically sovereign aggregates. But in our discussion we shall be concerned primarily with the family.

Three aspects of the investment in children may be distinguished. One is the economic, labor pool aspect, the desire for more children because under the rural or small family business conditions of the LDCs they provide a supply of labor at the disposal of the family that, after some years, provides economic savings and advance far greater than any that could be generated by the same family unit with fewer offspring. A crude calculation, based on reasonably low mortality rates and economical ways of raising the younger generation, might show that the *net* contribution of an additional child starting work in his teens and continuing to the early or mid-twenties would be quite substantial—if the child is male, and even if he leaves his family upon marriage.[19]

---

18. This applies also to the "threshold" hypothesis referred to in footnote 16, and criticized in my earlier paper cited in that footnote.

In that paper, I argued that in explaining the high birth rates in the LDCs a rather limited weight should be assigned to the "purely economic factors" (pp. 160–164). The seeming inconsistency between the position taken then and the discussion here is due largely to the narrow definition of the term "economic factors" in the earlier paper.

19. See the discussion in Mahmood Mamdani, *The Myth of Population Control: Family, Caste, and Class in an Indian Village* (New York: Monthly Review Press, 1972). This short book is based largely on interviews with members of different castes in a Punjab village that was the focus of an earlier long-term study and prolonged field effort at education in family planning and birth control. One cannot judge the validity of the results even in terms of the given village, let alone their relevance to a wider field of population experience and motivation among the LDCs. But the book is useful in quoting the reasons adduced by various occupational groups for having more children, particularly sons.

Nor should one overlook the possible contribution of an additional daughter, not only from work within the family, but also in many countries from the bride price or the benefit from the connections with the husband's family.

The second aspect of investment in children might be designated the genetic pool aspect. It is relevant to those less developed countries in which, because of the inequality within the economic and social structure, investment in greater personal equipment and further education of few children is no assurance of upward social mobility. In these societies mobility is blocked by monopolization of economic and social power by a limited number of families. Under such conditions, advance for the offspring of the lowly is a matter of success based on personal characteristics and endowments, on a kind of genetic lottery that may turn up a dictatorial corporal or general, or a successful athlete (or their female consorts), so prevalent in many LDCs. A rational calculation would encourage a family in such circumstances to have as many children as can survive in passable health to maturity—on the chance that one may be so endowed genetically as to raise himself or herself, and thus also the family, above the low initial level. One should note that both the genetic pool and the labor pool aspects of returns from children apply also to the lower economic groups within the developed countries—particularly if these groups are socially discriminated against.

The third, and widest reaching aspect, of the investment in children is that of security. The latter involves not merely, and not foremost, economic security of parents who, in their old age, have to rely on the help of children, reliance needed in the absence of social provisions for such security in most LDCs.[20] The scope of the security aspect is much broader, encompassing the protection against natural and social calamities, which is *not* provided by government or other organs of society (not blood-related)—and must be supplied by the family, or larger, blood-re-

---

20. See the analysis in papers by David M. Heer and Dean O. Smith which use simulation techniques to derive the number of births required if, given the mortality levels prevailing in the LDCs, a parental couple wishes to assure a high probability that at least one son will survive to the father's old age. The papers are "Mortality Level, Desired Family Size, and Population Increase," *Demography* 5, 1 (1968): pp. 104–121, and "Mortality Level, Desired Family Size and Population Increase: Further Variations on a Basic Model," *Demography* 6, 2 (May 1969): pp. 141–150.

lated collectives. The pressure toward large families has been associated with the weakness and unreliability of governmental structure in many preindustrial societies, and the need to rely on the family in a weakly organized community that fails to provide adequate protection to the individual member as an individual. Even today, in many LDCs, the need to rely heavily on the family, the tribe, or some blood-tie subgroup different from the national community as a whole, is fairly apparent. So long as the conditions persist, an adequate increase in numbers of those related by protective blood-ties will be a goal, justified even despite possible short-term disadvantages.[21]

To digress from discussion of the family, one should note the decentralization of authority and the intensification of nationalist ties in the world in recent decades; and the prevalence within many national states, particularly LDCs, of regional and ethnic divergences, only exacerbated by uneven pressures of modern economic growth. In these conditions, despite the Malthus argument that the *quality* of population is important, the *quantity* of population has become charged with political significance, and has turned into a tool in international and intranational contests and potential conflicts. The continuing controversy in Nigeria concerning reliability of the regional population totals in the several censuses is one illustration of the value ascribed to numbers. And the recent stand by Brazil (at the 1974 Bucharest World Population Conference) on its own population-growth aims is another illustration that, in the international power game, numbers are not a sign of weakness but of strength. This is not to deny the desire of Brazil to spread a larger population over its wide open spaces; but it does reflect a point of view, shared by the governments of many other LDCs, large and small, that see advantages in large numbers. These advantages may be envisioned as wider domestic markets and a larger labor force for exploiting unutilized re-

---

21. This argument applies, in particular, in cases of natural calamities and breakdowns of civil authority in internal conflicts. The vulnerability of LDCs to such disasters, combined with the weakness of central authority, is obvious. While natural and social calamities may raise the death rate temporarily, the sustaining long-term effects making for higher birth rates probably more than compensate in the aftermath.

For a suggestive analysis of the key role of the family as a major resource in a recent calamity see Robert W. Kates and others, "The Human Impact of the Managua Earthquake," *Science* 182 (December 7, 1973): pp. 981–990.

sources, or as a larger protective reserve in a world still beset by international tensions, armed conflicts, and possibly enormous dangers associated with some aspects of modern technology. In any case, the LDCs, in particular, tend to see in larger population a source of strength that they may lack, relative to the DCs, in technology and material capital.

In short, while there may be some validity to the statement that LDCs are poor because they are prolific, it may be said that they are prolific because they are poor. To put it more precisely, they are prolific because under their economic and social conditions large proportions of the population see their economic and social interests in more children as a supply of family labor, as a pool for a genetic lottery, and as a matter of economic and social security in a weakly organized, nonprotecting, society. Furthermore, while the private interests of the parental generation may be in conflict with the long-term economic interests of the national community, there is some agreement between the two when we relate families to larger blood-tie groups within the nation and consider the family and the nation in terms of external security interests in a divided and dangerously tense world.

It is hardly necessary to emphasize the speculative character of the comments just made. Yet they are suggested by, and are consistent with, the implications of much of the statistical evidence summarized.[22] The conjectures would be more useful if some attention were given to components of change *within* countries. Thus, it may be that the declining death rates and rising income per capita had different impacts on different groups within the LDCs. It may be that the fertility of some modernizing groups declined, but that of other groups increased, with greater health and nutrition and relaxation of traditional restraints. In that case, the persistence of high aggregate fertility rates would be the result of a balance of conflicting trends within the population, promising a decline as the relative weights of the groups shift. But it was not feasible to pursue these hints here; and in any case, there would be serious data problems in the way.

Nor is it feasible here to discuss the policy implications of the

---

22. Many of the arguments are identical with those used in the *transition* theory to explain "traditional" high birth rates (see the long summary quotation from Notestein in the Coale paper cited in footnote 15).

situation suggested by the double statement that LDCs are poor because they are prolific and prolific because they are poor—except to indicate that in many similar situations in the past innovative breakthroughs brought about changes in economic and social institutions and led to the emergence and spread of groups pioneering in new and modern directions.

Finally, one must stress that the above comments constitute judgments on the importance of various groups of factors that might explain the persisting high birth rates in the LDCs—for which I have no quantitative weights derived from tested evidence. They should, therefore, be viewed as tentative and rough, although plausibly inferred from the demographic patterns summarized.

Demographic Aspects of the Distribution of Income among Families: Recent Trends in the United States

Distribution of income among families is the dominant component of the size distribution of income among a country's population. As of March 1969, the family distribution accounted for 184 million persons out of a total population of the United States of 203 million—the rest being unattached persons and the institutional population.[1] And if families are defined, as they are in the basic source used here, as "a group of two or more persons related by blood, marriage, or adoption, and residing together" (see S-II, p. 6), they are the units that make most decisions relating to search for employment and for other sources of income and on the disposition of income received—and are thus the relevant recipient unit in the analysis of the size distribution of income. But this means that differences and changes in the structure of family units have direct bearing upon the income distribution.

This paper deals with changes in a few demographic charac-

A later, slightly different version of this paper appeared in Willy Selle-kaerts, ed., *Econometrics and Economic Theory: Essays in Honour of Jan Tinbergen* (London: Macmillan, 1974), pp. 223–245.

1. For the total number of persons in families see U.S. Bureau of the Census, *Current Population Reports, Series P-60, no. 66* (Washington: 1969), table 13, p. 35 (referred to below as S-II). For total population of the United States (average of that on March 1 and April 1, 1969) see *Statistical Abstract of the United States, 1969* (Washington: 1969), table 2, p. 5.

teristics of family units, and their bearing on the distribution of money income among families in the United States since 1947. To this end we used the results of an annual current survey of family income. While deficient in the exclusion of nonmoney income (the two important types are farm products retained for own consumption, and income from owner-occupied dwellings), and while short in its coverage of money income, the survey provides a great deal of information on the demographic and labor force characteristics of family heads and of some of the members of the families.[2] For our purpose, that of illustrating the increasing importance within the family income distribution of certain distinctive demographic groups among the families, the data—despite their shortcomings—are adequate.

1. The Three Selected Family Subgroups

Three groups among families distinguished by the age and sex of their head are of particular interest here: those with a relatively

----

2. The total money income of the family, as defined in the data, is the sum of money wages and salaries, net income from self-employment, and income other than earnings—summed for all income recipients in the family. The amounts cover gross income before deductions for personal taxes, social security, and the like. Income other than earnings includes not only the usual property incomes (dividends, interest, net rental income, royalties, income from trusts and estates) but also public assistance and welfare payments, unemployment compensation, government pensions and veterans' payments, private pensions, annuities, alimony, regular contributions from persons not living in the household, and a variety of transfers. The only receipts remotely resembling income that are excluded are gifts and tax refunds, as well as receipts and gains from sale of property (unless the person is engaged in the business, in which case it is recorded under net income from self-employment).

"It is estimated that the income surveys conducted by the Bureau of the Census during the past few years obtained about 87 percent of the comparable total money income aggregates and about 95 percent of the comparable money wage or salary aggregates included in the personal income series prepared by the Office of Business Economics" (S-II, p. 10). For a similar comparison with the national income accounts series on personal income see also S-I (identified in note to lines 12–13 of table 1), p. 41, which shows somewhat higher percentages of coverage.

A reader interested in a more detailed appraisal of the data will find a discussion in the basic sources S-I and S-II referred to in the notes to the tables; and also in Joint Committee Print, 88th Congress, 2nd Session, *The Distribution of Personal Income* (prepared for the Subcommittee on Economic Statistics of the Joint Economic Committee, [Washington: 1965]), in particular chapter III, section B, pp. 58–72.

young head; those with a relatively old head; and those with a female head. Given the data, the more specific definitions are:
families with all heads under the age of 25 (listed in the data as
14 through 24); families with all heads aged 65 and over; families
with female heads aged 25 through 64. This leaves a residual
fourth category—families with male heads aged 25 through 64.
Table 1 summarizes the characteristics of these family subgroups
that are easily derived from the data—and they suggest why this
particular classification is of bearing on the income distribution
among families (and hence total size distribution of income).

By definition, a family can have only one head. And while the
source defines as head "the person regarded as the head by the
members of the family" (S-II, p. 7), it is clear that the term relates to the person whose contribution to family income is major,
whatever weight he or she carries in decisions on uses of income.
One should also note that "women are not classified as heads if
their husbands are resident members of the family at the time of
survey" (*ibid.*, p. 7); and that married couples related to the head
of the family and living within the family are included in the
head's family and not treated as separate units. It is the implied
importance of the characteristics of the head as the main source
of family income that warrants the grouping distinguished in table
1. Some of the associated characteristics may now be noted.

First, the three groups, with young heads, old heads, and female heads aged 25–64, accounted together for well over a quarter
of the total number of families in 1968. As expected, the income
per family for each of these three groups was clearly below the
countrywide average—by proportions ranging from about 33 percent for the group with the young heads to over 40 percent for
the families with female heads (of all ages). Obviously, the position of the young head at the very beginning of the life cycle of
earnings and of the old head past the phase of full engagement,
and the distinctive disadvantage of the female head as an income
provider (in a family without a male head) result in lower family
income levels; and contribute significantly to income inequality
among families in the customary size distribution.

Second, one should note the large proportion of Negroes in the
group with female heads—about a quarter compared with the
countrywide ratio of Negro heads in the total of only 9 percent
(lines 4–5), pointing to the greater prevalence of "broken" family

TABLE 1

Selected Demographic Characteristics of Families, United States,
1968 (unless otherwise indicated)

		Age and Sex of Head				
	Total (1)	All, age below 25 (2)	All, age 65+ (3)	Female, age 25–64 (4)	Male, age 25–64 (5)	All, Female (6)
Numbers and Income						
1. Number of families (total in million) and percentage share	50.51	6.6	14.0	7.9	71.5	10.8
2. Families with female heads, % of those in line 1	10.8	9.6	16.1	100	0	100
3. Money income per family, arithmetic mean, thousand $	9.67	6.43	6.21	5.63	11.08	5.55
Race (% shares of all families)						
4. White	90.0	88.5	92.1	72.1	91.6	74.5
5. Negro	9.0	11.1	7.4	26.6	7.5	24.4
Size-of-Family Groups (% shares)						
6. 2 persons	34.4	45.8	77.5	37.7	24.6	45.7
7. 3 persons	20.8	33.7	14.4	24.5	20.8	22.7
8. 4 and more persons	44.8	20.5	8.1	37.8	54.6	31.6
9. Average number of persons per family	3.64	3.05	2.40	3.45	3.96	3.24
10. Money income per person, thousand $, line 3/line 9	2.66	2.11	2.59	1.63	2.80	1.72
Proportion with Own Children under 18						
11. % of families	55.8	57.5	3.3	64.8	65.0	52.8
Shares of Families by Age and Sex of Head, Nonfarm and Farm (1962–64, totals in column 1 in millions)						
12. Nonfarm	44.29	6.0	13.9	na	na	10.6
13. Farm	3.13	2.7	19.6	na	na	5.7

(Continued)

(Table 1 continued)

Labor Force Participation Ratios (%), Male Only

	1950 (1)	1960 (2)	1960 (3)	1965 (4)
14. Aged 20–24	81.9	86.1	88.9	86.2
15. Aged 65 and over	41.4	30.5	32.2	26.9

Notes:

Lines 1–3: Calculated from Bureau of the Census, *Current Population Reports, Series P-60, no. 66,* "Income in 1968 of Families and Persons in the United States" (Washington: 1969) (referred to below as S-II), table 15, pp. 42–43.

Lines 4–5: Calculated from S-II, table 12, pp. 30–34. The shares do not add to 100, because of the contribution of other nonwhite races.

Lines 6–9: Calculated from S-II, table 13, p. 35. The average number for families with 4 or more persons, as derived from this table in the source, is 5.2. This average was applied to the entries in line 8 (and 2 and 3 to the entries in lines 6 and 7, respectively) to calculate the average in line 9. Lines 6–8 are from S-II, table 15, pp. 42–43.

Line 11: Calculated from S-II, table 16, pp. 44–45.

Lines 12–13: Calculated from Bureau of the Census, *Technical Paper no. 17, Trends in the Income of Families and Persons in the United States, 1947–1964,* by Mary F. Henson (Washington, 1967, referred to below as S-I), tables 2 and 3, pp. 51–62. The shares were calculated from arithmetic means of the numbers of families for the three years, 1962 through 1964.

Lines 14–15, columns 1–2: From Bureau of the Census, *Historical Statistics of the United States* (Washington: 1960), Series D-15, D-16, and D-19, census data, p. 71, and *Historical Statistics of the United States, Continuation to 1962 and Revisions* (Washington: 1965), p. 13. The ratios relate to the United States excluding Hawaii and Alaska.

Lines 14–15, columns 3–4: From Bureau of the Census, *Statistical Abstract of The United States, 1969* (Washington: 1969), table 308, p. 212. Includes Hawaii and Alaska.

units among Negroes than among the whites. It also contributes to reducing the per family income among families with female heads, although the average income even among the families with white female heads is still distinctly below the countrywide average (the arithmetic mean income for families with white female heads aged 25 through 64 is $6.42 thousand in 1968; for families with white female heads, all ages, $6.09 thousand; see S-II, table 12, pp. 28–34).

Third, while the three groups are subaverage with respect to income per family, two of the groups are also characterized by a smaller size of family (lines 6–11). The families with young heads average somewhat over 3 persons per family, about two-tenths below the countrywide average family; and for families with heads over 65 years of age, the average number is only 2.4 persons. Only the families with female heads, while still of somewhat smaller size, are fairly close to the average. There are similar differentials in the proportion of families with own children under 18, particularly distinctive for the families with heads over 65 years of age (line 11). While it is not fully justifiable to divide the average income per family by the average number of persons in the family, if only because not all persons are of the same weight as consuming units, the results in line 10 suggest that the three groups distinguished are still characterized by lower than average income per person—although the shortfall from the countrywide average is quite small for the families with heads aged 65 and over.

Fourth, the distinction between farm and nonfarm (lines 12–13) reveals that the families with young or female heads are far less common among the farm than among the nonfarm families. On the other hand, the proportion of families with head aged 65 and over is distinctly higher among the farm than among the nonfarm families (close to 20 as compared with 14 percent). And yet even here the greater weight given to this group with subaverage income is reduced in importance by the finding that for farm families, the per family income for families with heads aged 65 and over was (in 1962–64) as high as 77 percent of the per family income for all farm families; whereas the average income of the same group among the nonfarm families was less than 70 percent of that for all nonfarm families (for 1959–61 the corresponding relatives were 85 percent for the farm families and less than 70 percent for the nonfarm group; see S-I, table 25, pp. 182–87).

Fifth, the extent of participation in the labor force must clearly differ between male and female heads of families; and among males, between the young and the very old heads, on the one hand, and those aged 25 through 64 on the other. The differences can be illustrated, however, only for male heads; and even for the latter, the labor force participation rates shown in lines 14–15 cannot be applied directly to male heads of families, since not all males within a given age class can be presumed to be heads of families. However, if we assume that almost all male heads of families in the young group are in the ages of 20 through 24, the ratio of heads among the latter for 1968 is roughly 41 percent;

whereas the ratio of family heads aged 65 and over to all males aged 65 and over is roughly 73 percent.[3] These figures suggest that the high labor force participation rates among all males aged 20–24, between 80 and 90 percent, would tend to be true also of the young male heads of families; and that the relatively low labor force participation rates among all males aged 65 and over, between 40 and 27 percent, and rapidly declining, would tend to be true also of the old heads of families.

2. Trends in Shares of Selected Family Groups Within Ordinal Divisions of the Family Distribution by Money Income

(a) THE FINDINGS. Given the three selected subaverage income family groups and their associated characteristics noted for 1968, the question of most interest here is as to the changing importance of these groups within the total family distribution (and hence within the total size-of-income distribution); and the possible effects of any trends in the shares of these groups upon changes in income inequality as shown by the size distribution of money income among all families.

Table 2 summarizes the data on the shares of the three subgroups within the ordinal divisions in the distribution of all families by money income, for some two decades extending from 1947 to 1968. We also added data on the shares, within ordinal divisions, of family heads who were not members of the labor force; and of the average number of persons per family—because of the close association between these characteristics, the low levels of labor force participation among the family heads aged 65 and over and among female heads of families, and the relatively small size of families among those with very young heads or heads aged 65 and over.

The first major finding suggested by table 2 is that over the

---

3. The percentages are derived by comparing the absolute numbers of male heads aged below twenty-five in 1968 with the absolute numbers of all males aged twenty to twenty-four in the same year; and of male heads aged sixty-five and over with all males aged sixty-five and over in 1968. The data on male heads of families by age are from S-II, table 15, pp. 42–43; those on all males by age for mid-1968 are from the *Statistical Abstract of the United States, 1969* (Washington: 1969), table 8, p. 10.

TABLE 2

Changes in Selected Aspects of Family Structure, Within Ordinal Groups in the Distribution by Family Money Income, United States, 1947—68

	Lowest Fifth (1)	Second Fifth (2)	Middle Fifth (3)	Fourth Fifth (4)	Top 80 to 95% (5)	Top 5% (6)	All Fam- ilies (7)	Income per family, relative to income of all families (8)
	\multicolumn{6}{c}{Ordinal Groups}							
Families, Head Aged Below 25, % Shares								
1. 1947—52	6.2	8.1	5.7	4.0	1.9	0.3	5.1	0.725
2. 1953—58	6.5	8.3	5.5	3.4	1.7	0.3	5.0	0.717
3. 1959—61	7.8	8.9	5.7	3.5	1.4	0.3	5.4	0.672
4. 1962—64	8.9	9.2	6.4	3.6	1.2	0.2	5.8	0.657
5. 1968	10.4	10.4	7.1	3.8	1.3	0.1	6.6	0.665
Families, Head Aged 65+, % Shares								
6. 1947—52	27.7	11.8	7.1	6.1	7.0	10.5	12.1	0.748
7. 1953—58	31.2	13.5	7.3	5.7	6.6	8.9	13.0	0.698
8. 1959—61	32.4	15.3	7.4	6.1	5.8	10.0	13.6	0.700
9. 1962—64	34.1	16.2	7.9	6.2	6.4	9.7	14.3	0.694
10. 1968	35.2	15.8	8.1	5.6	5.4	5.9	14.0	0.644
Families, Female Heads Aged 25—64 (Lines 11—14 Estimated)								
11. 1947—52	14.2	7.2	5.3	4.1	4.9	3.4	7.1	0.694
12. 1953—58	15.5	7.6	5.0	3.8	3.8	2.8	7.1	0.642
13. 1959—61	16.6	8.2	4.9	3.6	2.9	1.9	7.2	0.592
14. 1962—64	17.4	8.5	5.0	3.4	3.1	2.7	7.5	0.596
15. 1968	19.6	9.4	4.7	3.5	2.5	1.8	7.9	0.574
Total of the Three-Family Groups Above								
16. 1947—52	48.1	27.1	18.1	14.2	13.8	14.2	24.2	0.726
17. 1953—58	53.2	29.4	17.8	12.9	12.1	12.0	25.1	0.686
18. 1959—61	56.8	32.4	18.0	13.2	10.1	12.2	26.2	0.665
19. 1962—64	60.4	33.9	19.3	13.2	10.7	12.6	27.6	0.660
20. 1968	65.2	35.6	19.9	12.9	9.3	7.8	28.5	0.629
Families, Head not in Labor Force (including members of Armed Forces, living on post or with their families off post)								
21. 1947—51	31.4	13.6	8.2	7.0	7.3	5.9	13.4	0.661
22. 1953—58	40.2	16.8	9.1	6.6	6.6	6.3	15.8	0.615
23. 1959—61	43.8	20.0	9.6	6.8	6.6	7.0	17.4	0.609
24. 1962—64	46.7	21.2	9.9	7.2	6.8	6.9	18.4	0.603
25. 1968	50.4	21.2	10.8	6.9	5.8	5.3	19.0	0.577

(Continued)

(Table 2 continued)

	Ordinal Groups						All Families (7)	Income per family, relative to income of all families (8)
	Lowest Fifth (1)	Second Fifth (2)	Middle Fifth (3)	Fourth Fifth (4)	Top 80 to 95% (5)	Top 5% (6)		

Average Number of Persons per Family
(Column 8 shows sum of absolute deviations, signs disregarded, of the average within each ordinal group, the groups properly weighted, from the average for all families)

26. 1947−52	3.27	3.55	3.63	3.66	3.86	4.08	3.60	0.157
27. 1955−58	3.36	3.67	3.83	3.82	3.83	4.01	3.71	0.157
28. 1969−61	3.30	3.67	3.87	3.87	3.89	4.00	3.73	0.192
29. 1962−64	3.30	3.69	3.91	3.98	3.94	4.07	3.77	0.220
30. 1968	3.16	3.55	3.77	3.94	4.01	4.07	3.69	0.267

Persons per Family, 1947−52 and 1968, Estimated from the 1968 Averages
for the Four Family Subgroups
(Table 1, line 9, columns 2−5 and Percentage Shares of the Subgroups in
Lines 1, 5, 6, 10, 11, 15, Above) (Column headings as for lines 26−30)

31. 1947−52	3.40	3.67	3.77	3.81	3.81	3.78	3.69	0.125
32. 1968	3.21	3.57	3.75	3.82	3.85	3.86	3.64	0.201

Notes

Lines 1−4, 6−9, and 21−24, columns 1−7: Taken directly or calculated from S-I (see notes to table 1), tables A and C, pp. 3−14, and 20−31. These tables contain annual series, 1947 through 1964, showing the percentage shares of family groups distinguished by age of head, or by sex of head, or by nonparticipation of head in labor force (except 1952), totals and within each ordinal group. The entries here are arithmetic means of these shares for the periods shown in the stub. The shares for the top 80−95 percent group were derived from those shown for the top fifth and the top 5 percent.

Lines 11−14, columns 1−7: S-I does not provide a breakdown of families with female heads by age of head. We use the relation for 1968 of female heads, aged 25−64, to female heads of all ages, within each ordinal group, to approximate the entries in lines 11−14, columns 1−6 (the ratios for 1968 of female heads, aged 25−64 to all female heads, were 0.7 within the lowest and second fifth; and roughly 0.8 within the other ordinal groups). The combined percentage share in column 7 was then derived from the percentage shares within the ordinal groups properly weighted (to allow for the difference in weight between columns 1−4 and 5 and 6).

Lines 1−4, 6−9, 11−14, 16−19, and 21−24, column 8: Taken directly or calculated from S-I, tables 24, 25, and 29, pp. 176−87 and 200−204. These tables show the annual arithmetic mean income per family for groups of families distinguished either by age of head, or sex of head, or the head's nonparticipation in the labor force. These average incomes, in current prices, were then averaged for the periods indicated in the stub (logarithmic means), and converted to ratios of the average income per family for all families.

For families with female heads aged 25−64 we assumed an average income per family identical with that of all families with female heads (the only relevant average available). This assumption seemed justified since for 1968 the two average incomes were less than 2 percent apart (see table 1, line 3, column 4 compared with column 6).

(Notes continued on the following page)

(Table 2 notes continued)

Lines 16–20, column 8: Calculated from lines 1–15, column 8, by weighting the income relative for each of the three groups by the shares in the total of all families shown in column 7 (and dividing by the sum of these shares shown in column 7, lines 16–20).

Lines 5, 10, 15, and 25: Taken directly or calculated from S-II. The entries in columns 7 and 8 were taken directly from the relevant tables. For shares *within* ordinal groups (columns 1–6), not shown for 1968 in the manner in which they were given in table C of S-I for the earlier years, estimates had to be made. These were based on the distributions of families by eighteen detailed family money income brackets, shown for all families, and for families distinguished by age, sex, and labor force status of the head (table 15, pp. 42–43, for age and sex of head groups; and table 23, p. 59, for families with head not in labor force). From these frequency distributions by eighteen income brackets, the shares of the selected age, sex, and labor force status of head subgroups were calculated, *corresponding* to the ordinal groups within the total family income distribution (by arithmetic interpolation, to preserve the additivity of the percentage shares to 100).

Lines 26–29, columns 1–7: Calculated from S-I, tables A and C. These tables show the percentage shares of families with 2, 3, and up to 7 and over persons, within each ordinal group and for all families, annually, for 1947 through 1952, and 1955 through 1964. Arithmetic means of these shares, for the ordinal groups and for the total of all families, were calculated for the periods shown in the stub; and the average number of persons was computed, setting the average for the group of 7 persons and over at 9 persons (this estimate corresponds to the average shown for that group in 1968; see S-II, table 13, p. 35). With this calculation made for columns 1–6, column 7 was derived as a weighted mean of the averages in columns 1–6.

Line 30, columns 1–6: Here, as in the case of all estimates for 1968, the shares within the ordinal groups had to be calculated from the tables showing the distribution by eighteen income brackets and the grouping of families by size corresponding to each income bracket (table 13, p. 35 in S-II). The average in column 7 was derived as a weighted mean of the averages obtained for the six ordinal groups in columns 1–6. For all families, the mean, 3.69, is slightly larger than that shown in the source (3.64), but we retained it for consistency with the means within the ordinal groups.

Lines 26–30, column 8: A sum of absolute deviations of the averages within the ordinal groups (columns 1–6) from the average for the distribution of all families in column 7, the deviations weighted to allow for the lower weight of the ordinal groups in columns 5 and 6. The summation is, of course, disregarding the signs of the deviations.

Lines 31–32: The averages in columns 1–6 were obtained by weighting the averages for the four subgroups (young, old, female heads, and male heads aged 25–64) in line 9 of table 1 (for 1968) by the percentage shares of these four groups in this table—for 1947–52 and 1968. The over-all average in column 7 is derived from the averages in columns 1–6, appropriately weighted. The average deviation in column 8 is calculated in the same manner as that in lines 26–30.

two-decade period, covering most of the post–World War II years, the shares of the three selected family subgroups in the total of all families all rose: the share of families with young heads rose from 5 to over 6.5 percent of all families; that of families with heads aged 65 and over, from 12 to 14 percent; and that of families with female heads aged 25 to 64, from 7 to almost 8 percent (column 7, lines 1 and 5, 6 and 10, 11 and 15). For the total of the three subgroups, the combined share rose from about 24.2 to 28.5 percent (column 7, lines 16 and 20), a substantial rise over a relatively short period. The preliminary data for 1969 indicate that the rise continued for one of the groups distinguished here; in 1969 the proportion of families with young heads was 6.9 percent, a rise from 6.6 in 1968; but that of families with old heads declined slightly, to 13.8 percent (from 14.0 percent in 1968; no data were given for families with female heads).[4]

Perhaps partly because of the rise in the proportions of families with head aged 65 and over and with female heads, partly because of a decline in the labor force participation rates among the old family heads (indicated in table 1, line 15), there was also a marked rise in the proportions, in the total of all families, of those with heads not in the labor force—from about 13.5 percent in 1947–51 to 19 percent in 1968 (column 7, lines 21 and 25). With only one million members of the Armed Forces included in this subgroup in 1968 (see S-II, p. 4), and not all of them heads of families, and over 9.5 million of all heads not members of the labor force (see S-II, table 23, p. 59), it is doubtful that any increase in the Armed Forces component contributed much to this rise in the share of families with heads not in the labor force.

The increase in the proportions of families with quite young and relatively old heads, all other conditions being equal, should have made for a *decline* in the average number of persons per family— since these two family subgroups are characterized by a lower than average size of family (see table 1, line 9). But table 2 shows that the average number of persons per family rose, at least through 1962–64; and while declining slightly thereafter, was still above the 1947–52 average in 1968 (see column 7, lines 26–30). Apparently the other conditions did not remain equal; and the

---

4. See U.S. Bureau of the Census, *Current Population Reports, Series P-60, no. 70* (Washington: July 1970), table 1, p. 3.

higher birth rate that marked the period, reaching a peak in the late 1950s, must have contributed to a slight rise in the average size of the family unit.

We can now turn to the movements, even more significant for our purposes, in the shares of the selected family subgroups *within* the ordinal divisions. And here there is a marked set of trends similar in all three subgroups: the proportions of these subgroups, of the families with young heads, or old heads, or female heads (aged 25–64, but presumably also female heads of all ages), *within the lower* ordinal divisions rose, and rose much more than their proportions in the total of all families; whereas the shares within the upper ordinal divisions either declined, or rose much less than they did in the total of all families. Thus, the shares of families with young heads within the lowest fifth rose from 6.2 percent in 1947–52 to 10.4 percent in 1968, a rise of some seven-tenths—while it rose from 5.1 to 6.6 percent of all families, a rise of less than a third. And similar comparisons can be made for the shares of families with old or female heads.

With families with young, old, and female heads conspicuously drifting downward, over the period, within the family income distribution, i.e., toward the lower ordinal divisions, the average income per family within these three subgroups, while below the average for all families throughout the period, naturally declined in proportion to that average. Column 7, lines 1–5, 6–10, and 11–15, reveals that the relative income per family, relative to per family income for all families, declined: for families with young heads, from about 73 percent in 1947–52 to about 66 percent in 1968; for families with old heads, from 75 percent at the earlier date to 64 percent in 1968; and for families with female heads, from 69 percent in 1947–52 to 57 percent in 1968. For the three groups combined, the per family income relative dropped from 73 percent in 1947–52 to 63 percent in 1968 (lines 16 and 20, column 7).

The downward drift within the income distribution of the families with heads aged 65 and over, and with female heads, presumably contributed heavily to a similar set of trends in families with the head not in the labor force (columns 1–6, lines 21–25). The rise in the share of this group was particularly striking within the two lower fifths (columns 1–2), compared with their significant decline within the top 80 to 95 and the top 5 percent (columns 5–6). And correspondingly the income relative for this group dropped from 66 percent in 1947–51 to 58 percent in 1968 (column 7, lines 21 and 25).

We noted that the average number of persons per family failed to decline over the period—despite the rise in the shares of families with very young and very old heads. But even here the downward drift of these two family subgroups meant that, after a while, the average size of the family in the low ordinal divisions tended to drop, whereas the average size of the family in the higher ordinal divisions tended to rise. This difference in trends in family size among ordinal divisions, which emerges after 1955–58, can be observed in columns 1–2 for the lower ordinal divisions, and columns 4–6 for the higher divisions (lines 26–27, compared with lines 29–30). This difference results in a widening of the disparity in size of family among the ordinal divisions, shown in column 7 —the over-all measure of disparity rising from 0.16 in 1955–58 to 0.27 in 1968.

Lines 31–32 of the table show that differences among the four family subgroups distinguished by age and sex of head in their shares within ordinal divisions contributed heavily to differences in average size of family between the lower and upper ordinal divisions. Both in 1947–52 and in 1968, the estimate reflecting interfamily subgroup differences in both family size and shares within the several fifths accounts for between one-half and seven-tenths of the total ranges of differences in family size among the ordinal divisions in the family distribution (0.38 points out of 0.81 in 1947–52 and 0.65 points out of 0.91 in 1968. Compare the difference between columns 6 and 1 in line 31 with that between the same columns in line 26; and likewise for the differences between the same columns in lines 32 and 30). This effect of differences among the four family subgroups in their shares and family size is particularly conspicuous in the movement from the lower to the middle fifths. Even of greater interest is the fact that the downward drift of the three selected family subgroups contributed markedly to the widening divergence among the ordinal divisions with respect to average family size; of the 0.110 points of rise in the average deviation in the total distribution between 1947–52 and 1968 (see column 8, lines 26 and 30), the shifting weight of the three family subgroups contributed 0.076 points (see column 8, lines 31–32), or about seven-tenths.

(b) EXPLANATORY SUGGESTIONS. Why did the proportions of families with young, old, and female heads rise, and why did their income relative to that of all families decline? No tested answers can be provided within the limits of this paper; but some exploration, with the help of data easily at hand, would be of interest, if only to permit us to glimpse the more general implications of the effects of these trends upon inequality within the total family distribution as usually measured.

The rise in the proportion of families with heads 65 years of age and over, and partly also of those with young heads, appears to have been associated with similar trends in the proportions of these age groups in the country's adult male population. Thus, the proportion of males aged 65 and over within the total population of males aged 20 and over (we exclude the population under 20, since we need comparability with heads of families) rose from slightly under 12 percent in 1950 to about 14 percent in 1960, and then tended to remain at this level to 1968; similar proportions for females were slightly less than 13 percent in 1950, 16 percent in 1960, and 17 percent in 1968.[5] Table 2 shows that the proportion of families with heads aged 65 and over was 12 percent in 1947–52, 13.6 percent in 1959–61, and 14 percent in 1968. The trend in these shares in table 2 is thus a reflection of the rise in the proportion of groups 65 and over within the total adult population, particularly male—and this rise in turn must have been associated with the decline in the birth rates in the earlier decades, and the extension of life associated with declines of death rates at advanced ages at rates possibly greater than the declines in the younger adult ages.

There is a rough parallel also between the proportion of families with heads aged below 25 and the proportion of males 20–24 in the total of all adult males (i.e., all males over 20). The latter proportion was about 11.5 percent in 1950, declined somewhat by 1960—about 10 percent, and then rose again to 12.5 percent in 1968. The percentage shares of this subgroup among all families

---

5. These rates are from sources already noted, i.e., *Historical Statistics of the United States, Continuation of Historical Statistics,* and the *Statistical Abstract of the United States, 1969*—all cited in earlier footnotes and in the notes to the tables. Only new sources will be indicated in the discussion in this subsection.

in table 2 moved from 5.1 in 1947–52 to 5.4 in 1959–61, and 6.6 percent in 1968. Here the rise in the proportion of young family heads is more consistent, and relatively more substantial, than that in the share of all males aged 20–24 among all male adults. The implication is that there must have been a rise in the marriage rate and in separate family formation—and some corroboration is provided by the indication that the median age of the groom at first marriage declined from over 23 years in the early 1950s to below 23 in the late 1950s and the middle (but not late) 1960s.

The trend in the proportion of families with female heads aged 25–64, shown in table 2, can *not* be explained by movements in the proportion of all females of these ages within the total of all adult females. The statistics here refer to the incidence of broken or otherwise affected family units deprived of the male head by death, desertion, or divorce. And the rise in the share of such units, in this case estimated on the basis of ratios for 1968, from 7 percent in the early 1950s to 8 percent in the late 1960s, must reflect a greater incidence of divorce or other types of separation. Part of the explanation may lie in the greater weight of urban population in the later years, considering that urban families show greater incidence of female headship (see table 1, lines 12–13); and there is enough evidence of a higher level of divorce rates to suggest why the share of families with female heads should have risen.

When we ask why there should have been a downward drift of these three family subgroups within the ordinal divisions of the total family distribution, why the average income of these subgroups relative to that of all families should have declined, the answer is not easy to find in the available demographic data. And in considering this decline in relative income it must be recognized that, over the period covered, the sample data showed a substantial rise in per family and per person money income in constant prices. Table 3 below shows that per family money income in 1964 dollars increased from 4.9 thousand in 1947–52 to 8.6 in 1968, or some 75 percent over the period. Thus, even though income per family of the three subgroups did not grow as much over the period, it still grew some 61 percent for the group with heads aged below 25, and some 51 percent for the groups with heads aged 65 and over and with female heads—all rather substantial growth rates; and they would be about the same on a per person basis.

The lower growth rate of per family or per person income in the three family subgroups may be due to a variety of demographic and economic variables. The subgroup with older heads may have been characterized by a gradual rise in the average age over 65—suggested by the fact that within total male population over 65, the proportion aged 65–74 declined from 70 percent in 1950 to 64 percent in 1968, and that aged 75 and over rose from 30 to 36 percent.[6] And insofar as pensions and other fixed types of income formed an increased proportion of the incomes of heads aged 65 and over, rising inflation might have kept down the growth of their real income. There may also have been increasing difficulty in retaining one's participation in the labor force, with continuous shift from self-employment to employee status within the active labor force.

The trend in the case of families with young heads may have been due to an increase in relative importance of occupations with a wider life cycle range of earnings—in which the younger entrants would be receiving incomes much lower than the occupational lifetime average. If this be true of groups such as professional workers or salaried managers and executives, the greater concentration of young entrants in these occupations might, despite their generally higher compensation levels, make for a lag in the growth of per family income for these entrants behind the average. Sources S-I and S-II show that the proportions of professional workers and of salaried managers in the total (including heads not in the labor force but excluding unemployed) rose from about 11 percent in 1948–52 to over 20 in 1968. And some contribution to the trend might have been made by young family heads who were still in training, even if in advanced stages, with some but rather limited income.

For the families with female heads one would have to consider the possibility that the proportion of Negro heads in this particular group increased over the period—with a very substantial shift of the Negro population to the cities, where the incidence of female headship is so much greater than in the countryside. Such a pos-

---

6. The data for 1950 are from Henry D. Sheldon, *The Older Population of the United States,* a volume in the census monograph series, Social Science Research Council and Bureau of the Census (New York: 1958), table A-2, p. 139. The 1968 data are from the *Statistical Abstract, 1969,* table 8, p. 10.

sible rise in the proportion of Negroes among all female heads aged 25–64 would retard the growth rate of income per family for that subgroup—which could also be affected by fixed income components (such as pensions or relief payments) that do not respond adequately to rises in consumer prices.

The suggestions above are clearly *ad hoc,* and could be pursued further with greater effort to assemble and probe into the relevant data. But within the limits of this paper, we can only suggest the variety of demographic and economic variables that would be involved in attempts at explaining the downward drift in the relative income position of the three selected family subgroups; and identify some of the obvious variables because they may be typical of other developed countries in similar stages of their economic growth and social development.

3. Effects on the Income Distribution

The trends illustrated and noted in the preceding section have clearly contributed to wider inequality within the distribution of money income among families. The rise in the proportions of families with young heads, old heads, and female heads, would have contributed to widened inequality even if the income per family, within each of these three subgroups or for the three combined, relative to average family income of all families, would have remained the same. But the relative income for each of these subgroups, and for the three combined, declined rather than remained constant—which contributed further to widening income inequality.

The question to be asked now is whether the contribution of the three selected family subgroups to wider inequality has resulted in wider inequality in the money income distribution among all families; and what happens when from the money income distribution among all families, we subtract these special family subgroups, whose income could be expected to be lower than average—given the characteristics of the head. A tentative answer is provided by the calculations summarized in table 3.

Panel A of this table (lines 1–5) shows the income shares of the ordinal divisions distinguished in the sources, with slight adjustments of the shares in 1968 for greater comparability with earlier years. The impression is of relative stability of the distribution for

TABLE 3

Percentage Shares of Income Received by Ordinal Groups; Distributions of
Families by Money Income, Original and Omitting the Three Family
Subgroups, or Allowing for Differing Size of Family among Ordinal
Groups, 1947−1968

	Ordinal Groups						Average Income per Family, $ 1964 (000's)
	Lowest Fifth (1)	Second Fifth (2)	Middle Fifth (3)	Fourth Fifth (4)	Top 80 to 95% (5)	Top 5% (6)	(7)
A. Shares and Averages in the Original Distribution							
1. 1947−52	4.8	12.1	17.2	23.4	25.3	17.2	4.93
2a. 1953−58	4.8	12.3	17.8	23.8	25.1	16.2	5.83
2b. 1955−58	5.0	12.4	17.9	23.6	24.9	16.2	6.02
3. 1959−61	4.9	11.9	17.6	23.5	25.3	16.8	6.69
4. 1962−64	5.1	12.1	17.5	23.8	25.6	15.9	7.21
5. 1968	5.6	12.3	17.7	23.6	26.3	14.5	8.63
B. Shares and Averages, Distribution excluding Families with Young, Old, and Female Heads (Column 7 shows relative of income per family in the adjusted distribution to that in lines 1−5)							
6. 1947−52	5.8	12.9	17.5	23.0	24.8	16.0	1.08
7. 1953−58	6.1	13.5	18.1	23.1	25.0	14.2	1.09
8. 1959−61	6.3	13.2	17.8	23.1	24.4	15.2	1.12
9. 1962−64	6.6	13.2	18.1	23.2	24.7	14.2	1.12
10. 1968	7.3	13.6	17.9	23.5	24.9	12.8	1.15
C. Shares and Averages, Distribution Adjusted for Differences in Average Size of Family among Ordinal Groups (Column 7 shows average income per person, thousands, in 1964 $)							
11. 1947−52	5.4	13.1	17.6	24.0	24.6	15.3	1.37
12. 1955−58	5.9	13.1	17.8	23.4	24.8	15.0	1.62
13. 1959−61	6.0	12.7	17.5	23.2	24.9	15.7	1.80
14. 1962−64	6.3	13.0	17.5	23.2	25.0	15.0	1.91
15. 1968	7.1	13.6	18.1	23.1	24.8	13.3	2.37

(Continued)

(Table 3 continued)

	Periods						% Change, Col. 1–6
	1947– 1952 (1)	1953– 1958 (2)	1955– 1958 (3)	1959– 1961 (4)	1962– 1964 (5)	1968 (6)	(7)
D. Aggregative Measures of Inequality							
16. Average Gini ratio, distributions in lines 1–5	0.373	0.360	0.355	0.370	0.359	nc	nc
17. Sum of deviations, lines 1–5	51.8	50.2	49.4	51.2	50.6	48.8	−5.8
18. Sum of deviations, lines 6–10	47.6	44.6	nc	45.4	44.4	42.4	−11.3
19. Sum of deviations, lines 11–15	47.8	na	46.4	47.6	46.4	40.4	−15.5
E. Range: Ratio of Shares of Top Fifth to that of Lowest Fifth							
20. Distributions in lines 1–5	8.86	8.60	8.22	8.59	8.06	7.29	−17.7
21. Distributions in lines 6–10	7.03	6.42	nc	6.29	5.89	5.17	−26.5
22. Distributions in lines 11–15	7.02	na	6.75	6.77	6.35	5.37	−23.5

nc—not calculated
na—not available

Notes

Lines 1–4, columns 1–6: Calculated from S-I, table 25, pp. 182–87. This table shows annual shares of the five fifths and of the top 5 percent groups; and the entries here are arithmetic means of these shares for the periods shown in the stub. The share of the top 80–95 percent group was calculated from those of the top fifth and the top 5 percent

Lines 1–4, column 7: Arithmetic mean income per family in current prices is shown annually in the table cited for lines 1–4 above. Reduction to 1964 prices was by the index shown in S-I, p. 33 (consumer price index). The averages for the periods are logarithmic means.

Line 5: Derived from S-II, table 8, p. 22 (shares in income of ordinal divisions) and table A, p. 1 (which shows income in current and 1968 dollars for 1947, permitting us to shift the price base to 1964). Since some revisions were made in the sampling procedure between 1966 and 1968, there was slight incomparability in the percentage shares

(Notes continued on the following page)

(Table 3 notes continued)
of income of identical ordinal divisions. An overlap, given for 1966, permitted the slight adjustments in the 1968 income shares needed to make them comparable to those in earlier years.

Lines 6–10, columns 1–6: The underlying calculations assume that within each ordinal division, average income per family of the three subgroups is the same as that for the rest of the division. This assumption is corroborated when we compare the arithmetic mean income relative, derived from multiplying the shares in columns 1–6, lines 16–20 of table 2 by the per family income relative indicated in columns 1–6, lines 1–5 of the present table, with the average income relative directly calculated (in column 7, lines 16–20 of table 2). The two sets of relatives for the successive periods are: 0.736 and 0.726; 0.695 and 0.686; 0.668 and 0.655; 0.666 and 0.660; 0.639 and 0.629. The assumption over-estimates the shares of the three omitted subgroups, but so slightly that the error is negligible.

Given the above assumption, we subtract the omitted subgroups, both their number and their income, from the total number and income of each ordinal division; recumulate the arrays of shares in number and of shares in income remaining; and interpolate a new set of ordinal partition lines (based on logarithms of the cumulated new percentage shares in numbers and in income).

Lines 6–10, column 7: From columns 7 and 8, lines 16–20 of table 2.

Lines 11–15, columns 1–6: Lines 26–30, columns 1–7 of table 2 show average number of persons per family, within each ordinal division and for the total distribution. Multiplying by the percentage shares of the ordinal divisions within the total of families gives us the proportion of all *persons* (in families) in the lowest fifth all families, in the second fifth, and so on. Given these percentage shares in total of persons, and the percentage shares in total of income (both limited to families), the latter shown in lines 1–5, columns 1–6 of this table, we can recumulate the percentage shares in numbers and in income, and interpolate new partition values (again based on logarithms of the cumulated percentage shares in persons and in income).

Lines 11–15, column 7: Calculated from the average income per family, column 7, lines 1–5 of this table; and average number of persons per family, column 7, lines 26–30 of table 2.

Line 16: The Gini ratios are given annually in S-I, table 25, pp. 182–87. The entries are arithmetic means (logarithmic means would be almost the same).

Lines 17–19, columns 1–6: Sums of deviations of percentage shares in income from the percentage shares in numbers, signs disregarded—obtained from lines 1–5, 6–10, and 11–15, respectively.

Lines 20–22, columns 1–6: Ratio of the income shares of the top fifth to that of the lowest fifth—calculated from lines 1–5, 6–10, and 11–15, respectively.

the 1950s; the shares in 1959–61 are about the same as they were in 1947–52. Thus, as per family income grew by over a third, relative inequality remained about the same. It was only in the 1960s that inequality narrowed somewhat, with the share of the lowest fifth rising to over 5.5 percent, and that of the top 5 percent division dropping from 16.8 to 14.5 percent. But these movements toward greater equality were minor.

Panel B shows the effect of the exclusion of the three family subgroups, and of the resulting recalculation of the shares of similar ordinal divisions in the distribution. The details of the procedure are described in the notes to the table and need not be repeated here—except to indicate that the procedure is approximate, and that a more thorough recalculation might have had a somewhat greater, but not much greater effect. The panel reveals, first, that the per family income of the new distribution (column 7, lines 5–10) is, expectedly, above that of the original, wider distribution, by a percentage that rises steadily from 8 in the earliest period to 15 in 1968. Second, the general level of the shares of the lowest fifth, and to a lesser extent of the second fifth, are raised perceptibly, while those of the 80–95 percent, and particularly the top 5 percent group, are lowered—thus narrowing inequality significantly. Third, and most important, the adjusted distribution in lines 6–10 shows a steady contraction of inequality—in that the share of the lowest fifth now rises steadily from 5.8 to 7.3 percent; that of the second fifth less steadily from 12.9 to 13.6 percent; while that of the top 5 percent drops from 16.0 to 12.8 percent (lines 6 and 10, columns 1, 2, and 6). In short, the comparison of the two panels reveals that while the income distribution among all families in panel A is relatively stable, with only slight movement toward greater equality in the 1960s, the distribution in panel B, among families with male heads aged 25–64 (what might be called "standard" family units), showed a sustained movement of some magnitude toward greater equality through almost the whole period.

Largely as a result of the trends in the proportion and relative distribution of the three family subgroups distinguished, there were movements in the differences in number of persons per family among the ordinal divisions. The adjustment, in panel C, allows only for the changing differences in *average* number of persons per family among the six ordinal divisions. It does *not* represent conversion of the original distribution among families to an approximation of a distribution among persons. In such a conversion, each of the size groups of families within each income class (if not each individual family) would have to be reduced to a per person basis, and then the resulting cells recumulated and new partition lines drawn. Depending upon the assumptions used, the conversion might result in a different range of income inequalities, if not in different time trends. The adjustment in panel C is far more limited, being only for differences among wide ordinal divisions in average size of family, differences largely associated with the shares and family size of the four family subgroups distinguished. In short, the adjustment is for family size largely as *affected* by and *associated* with families with distinctive age and sex characteristics of head.

Given the nature of the adjustment, it is not surprising that the differences between panel C and panel A are similar to those between panels B and A. Here also, the adjustment narrows perceptibly the range between income shares of the lower and upper fifths, and reveals a sustained narrowing of inequality over the period.

Panels D and E provide crude measures of inequality. Panel D concentrates on the sum of differences, signs disregarded, between percentage shares in numbers and in income, of the six ordinal divisions distinguished. This measure is closely connected with the Gini ratio, the latter being based on the differences between *cumulated* percentage shares in numbers and income, whereas the sum of deviations used here is the sum of differences of *uncumulated* percentage shares (the two arrays being the same); and the similarity between the movements of entries in lines 16 and 17 reveals this close association. The average deviation shows, as might have been expected from panels A–C, a much more substantial reduction of inequality in the adjusted than in the original distributions. And the reduction is not minor: with full equality, the average deviation would be 0; a reduction of over a tenth or a seventh toward 0 is a substantial step toward the goal of complete equality, if it be considered a warranted goal.

Panel E provides a measure of the range—which has narrowed relatively more than the average deviation from equality. And here again the reduction of inequality was significantly greater in panels B and C than in panel A.

4. Summary and Implications

The findings here can be summarized in four brief paragraphs.

First, the family units with young, old, and female heads, which in 1968 accounted for 28.5 percent of all families, are concentrated in the lower income brackets; and particularly dominate the lowest fifth, of which they formed two-thirds in that year. The lowest quintile, to the extent of two-thirds, is thus comprised of young, old, and "broken" families.[7]

Second, over the period since the late 1940s, the proportion of these three family subgroups rose—the combined share rising from 24.2 to 28.5 percent; and, more important, these groups drifted downward within the total distribution, their per family income relative to average income of all families declining over the period. Thus, the share of these three subgroups within the lowest fifth was below 50 percent in 1947–52, not two-thirds, as in 1968; and the combined per family income of the three groups relative to that of all families declined from 0.73 to 0.63.

Third, if we exclude these three subgroups, and limit the family distribution to those with male heads aged 25–64 (what might be called "standard" units), the new income distribution shows an appreciably narrower inequality; and it is particularly interesting that this new distribution reveals a more consistent and larger narrowing of inequality over the period. Whereas in the original distribution inequality remained about the same during the 1950s and declined slightly in the 1960s, it narrowed more and more consistently through most of the period in the adjusted distribution.

Fourth, a somewhat similar result is found if we recognize that the young and old family head units are characterized by much smaller families than the average; and contribute greatly to differences in average size of family among the wide ordinal divisions in the total family distribution. An adjustment for these differences in *average* size of family would also yield an income distribution with a more sustained and larger movement toward equality over the period.

While the discussion above dealt with a rather limited component and aspect of the family income distribution, age and sex characteristics of the head, the findings suggest broader implications—in the sense that there is a rather wide variety of demographic and noneconomic aspects of family structure that may affect the family income distribution; and also in the sense that the

---

7. A similar finding was stated in my earlier paper, published in 1962 and based on the series through 1959 (see "Income Distribution and Changes in Consumption," in Hoke S. Simpson, ed., *The Changing American Population* (New York: Institute of Life Insurance, 1962), pp. 21–58, particularly pp. 33–41.

effects on the *meaning* of income inequality may be far-reaching. This paper concludes with brief comments on these possible wider implications.

To begin with, trends in proportions such as were illustrated in table 2, viz., the rises in the shares of family units with young, old, and female heads, are likely to be found in other developed countries—in which the movements of birth, death, and marriage rates, and increasing urbanization with progressively easier divorce and separation, may have had similar effects. By the same token, differences in the proportions of these three family subgroups may be expected between the developed, urbanized economies, with their nuclear families, on the one hand, and the less developed, agricultural, more traditional economies that may still retain many of their larger, extended families, on the other hand. Also, at any given period (say over the last two decades), the trends in the proportion and relative income position of special family subgroups such as those distinguished here may have moved in the less developed countries in ways different from the trends in the developed countries. Thus, the adjusted income distributions in the former might move differently from those in the latter, even if the unadjusted distributions in the two groups of countries were changing in a similar fashion.

Furthermore, other demographic aspects of family structure, besides those emphasized here, may have considerable effect on the income distribution among families. Two illustrations may suffice.

The first relates to number of children under 18, or below whatever age is treated as one signifying readiness for active participation in the labor force. While we observed that the families with heads aged 65 and over are, expectedly, characterized by a very low proportion of units with children under 18, the differences in number of young children among all other families must still be quite wide, and affect the income position of families, particularly when reduced to a per person basis. Variation in this characteristic of family structure is clearly dependent upon the general level of birth rates, and the extent to which the transition from high to low birth rates has resulted in major differentials in the birth rate among the various economic and social groups within the population.

The second illustration is directly connected with the first. The rates of natural increase may differ substantially between lower-

and upper-income families, particularly in the developed countries, because birth rates differ substantially and the higher birth rate among the lower-income groups more than compensates for any excess in the death rates compared with the upper-income groups. Thus the next generation of descendants of the lower-income groups accounts for a larger share of total population, and probably of family units, than these lower-income groups did earlier. What is the effect on the ordinal shares in the distributions for the two successive generations? And what is the consequence or the absence of such effects in less developed countries, in which such differences in rate of natural increase, associated negatively with income level, may not prevail, or be of smaller amplitude?

Finally, one may ask what is the nature of income inequality contributed by the present and lower income of family units with young or old heads. One could argue that from the standpoints of productivity, equity, and welfare, the incomes of these units, on a per person basis, should be lower than those in the standard family units. After all, young family heads are in their training period, may look forward to much higher returns that would compensate them later, and no equity or welfare considerations warrant claiming for them a per person return as high as that which they themselves will secure later—so long as the current returns are minimally adequate otherwise. Old family heads, largely in their retirement period, do not contribute sufficiently to earn an income equal to that of prime members of the labor force; nor do they need such income for purposes of further investment, either for improving their efficiency or for retirement, or for utilizing the variety of new products—given the limited time prospects of the older family heads, and their lesser receptivity to new products than among the younger family units. It is thus permissible to argue that the income inequality contributed by the lower incomes of the young and old head units represents no contribution to unwarranted earnings differentials. If so, the demographic trends that raise the proportions of the family units with these young and old heads, or even those that make for a decline in their standing within the income distribution, contribute to a widening of income inequality that has none of the analytical meanings often attributed to wider inequality. And a similar argument may be made for all demographic and other noneconomic differences which may affect the income distribution, and in fact, represent life cycle and other near-biological differences that have a "warranted" reflection in income differentials and inequalities. The very meaning of income inequality in the customary distributions, and of trends in such inequality, is obscure unless the income effects of these demographic and other noneconomic, institutional, differences, and of their movements, are recognized.

Income-Related Differences in Natural Increase: Bearing on Growth and Distribution of Income

1. Differences in Natural Increase among Income Classes

The operating hypothesis here is as follows. If among the population in its reproductive ages (say women 18 to mid-40's and their husbands), groups are distinguished by long term levels of family income (allowing for family size), the rate of natural increase will be found higher among the low-income than among the upper-income groups. This hypothesis appears to hold for many developed countries during the long transition, in the course of industrialization and economic growth, from high to low birth and death rates. The basic shift began at the upper-income levels, and spread only gradually downward. The same hypothesis may have become relevant to many less developed countries, as they recently entered the phase of urbanization and modernization. Subordinate hypotheses would specify the negative association between income and fertility; and while admitting that the death rate is also associated negatively with income, would recognize that the income-related mortality differentials are, and were, much narrower than the fertility differentials—thus assuring a negative association between income and the rate of natural increase.

A slightly different version of this paper appeared in Paul A. David and Melvin W. Reder, eds., *Nations and Households in Economic Growth: Essays in Honor of Moses Abramovitz,* (New York and London: Academic Press, 1974), pp. 127–146.

These statements may sound familiar, and are apparently amply confirmed by the findings in the demographic literature on the subject.[1] Yet the evidence to support the main hypothesis, as formulated with precise relevance to the implications for growth and distribution of income, is difficult to come by. Long-term family income levels would have to be established for population groups at ages when most of the reproduction takes place—in so far as effects on fertility are concerned; and the income levels would have to be undisturbed by annual fluctuations, and with proper allowance for the phase of the long lifetime cycle of earnings and income (so that low incomes of physicians in their late 20's or early 30's are not mistaken for their long-term income levels). Furthermore, family income would have to be related to size of family. Data that would yield such information are quite different from the commonly available sample data on family income, for a given year, and shown for family units of differing size (e.g., the data used in tables 1 and 2). While observations on fertility would have to be concentrated on the major reproduction ages (i.e., roughly from 18 to the mid-30s for the wife), data on mortality would be needed for the long span over which a given generation in its prime reproductive ages is replaced by its direct descendants entering their income earning and family formation careers; and such mortality data would have to be given with different death rates (or life tables) for the several long-term income levels. A full test of the quantitative dimensions of the main hypothesis here is probably impossible with the present data, and would certainly be out of place here.

---

1. See, for example, the discussion of differences in fertility by economic status in United Nations, *The Determinants and Consequences of Population Trends* (New York: 1953), pp. 86–87, which begins with the sentence: "That the poor have more children than the rich is a well established fact"— and then proceeds to summarize the findings, with proper qualifications. Other sources that summarize the evidence are the three papers (by Gwendolyn Z. Johnson, Clyde V. Kiser, and Richard and Nancy Ruggles on differential fertility in the European countries and in the United States, in Ansley J. Coale, ed., *Demographic and Economic Change in Developed Countries,* for the Universities-NBER Conference by Princeton University Press, 1960 (pp. 36–72, 77–113, and 155–208); United Nations, *Population Bulletin no. 7, 1963* (with special reference to conditions and trends of fertility in the world (New York: 1965), particularly chapters VIII and IX, pp. 122–51; and the "Background Paper on Fertility," prepared by George W. Roberts on behalf of the United Nations, for the 1965 World Population Conference in Belgrade (mimeo).

TABLE 1

Children under 5 and Children Ever Born, per 1,000 Married Women,
by Age of Woman and 1959 Family Money Income,
United States, March 1960

	Number of wives (000's) (1)	Median Family Money Income ($) (2)	Children per 1,000 Wives Family Income Classes (in 000's $)					
			Less than 2 (3)	2 to 3.99 (4)	4.0 to 6.99 (5)	7.0 to 9.99 (6)	10.0 & over (7)	Total (8)
A. Children under 5								
Wives Aged 20—24								
1. White	3,028	5,158	1,300	1,306	1,260	887	819	1,124
2. Nonwhite	292	3,265	1,674	1,596	1,408	1,000	1,000	1,511
3. Total	3,321	4,983	1,397	1,346	1,267	891	825	1,218
Wives Aged 25—29								
4. White	3,967	6,012	1,342	1,325	1,304	1,113	1,030	1,237
5. Nonwhite	414	3,851	1,595	1,445	1,264	924	915	1,339
6. Total	4,381	5,855	1,417	1,349	1,301	1,105	1,028	1,247
Wives Aged 30—34								
7. White	4,585	6,504	932	867	845	760	771	817
8. Nonwhite	459	4,102	1,261	1,060	872	707	646	966
9. Total	5,044	6,330	1,031	908	847	758	767	830
Wives Aged 35—39								
10. White	4,880	6,880	582	538	504	418	410	468
11. Nonwhite	451	4,337	870	690	589	441	383	633
12. Total	5,331	6,698	667	568	511	419	409	482
Wives Aged 40—44								
13. White	4,382	7,223	270	249	223	178	158	200
14. Nonwhite	388	4,205	462	345	280	220	192	320
15. Total	4,771	5,868	321	267	228	180	158	209
Wives Aged 45—49								
16. White	3,972	7,095	63	62	52	42	38	48
17. Nonwhite	343	3,864	137	139	106	83	74	118
18. Total	4,315	6,836	82	80	56	43	39	53

(Continued)

(Table 1 continued)

	Number of wives (000's) (1)	Median Family Money Income ($) (2)	Children per 1,000 Wives Family Income Classes (in 000's $)					
			Less than 2 (3)	2 to 3.99 (4)	4.0 to 6.99 (5)	7.0 to 9.99 (6)	10.0 & over (7)	Total (8)

B. Number of Children Ever Born

Wives
Aged 35–39

19. White	4,880	6,880	3,316	3,053	2,737	2,515	2,440	2,672
20. Nonwhite	451	4,337	4,432	3,537	3,081	2,527	2,340	4,059
21. Total	5,331	6,698	3,625	3,148	2,765	2,516	2,448	2,727

Wives
Aged 45–49

22. White	3,972	7,095	2,935	2,729	2,364	2,228	2,244	2,383
23. Nonwhite	343	3,864	3,579	3,023	2,637	2,573	2,757	2,969
24. Total	4,315	6,836	3,091	2,779	2,385	2,260	2,257	2,430

Notes

Lines 1–18: Taken or calculated from U.S. Bureau of the Census, *U.S. Census of Population: 1960. Subject Reports. Women by Children under 5 Years Old*, Final Report PC (2)-3C, tables 56 and 57 (Washington: 1968), pp. 114–117. The median income was calculated from the more detailed income distribution given in the source.

Lines 19–24, columns 3–8: Taken or calculated from U.S. Bureau of the Census, *U.S. Census of Population: 1960. Subject Reports, Women by Number of Children Ever Born*. Final Report PC (2)-3A (Washington: 1964), table 38, pp. 187–198.

Yet it is possible to accept the hypothesis as plausible, not only because of the direct evidence on the negative correlation between income (although annual) and fertility, and hence implicitly the rate of natural increase, but also because of much more numerous findings on differential fertility (and natural increase) by degree of rurality (rural vs. urban, and small cities vs. large cities), by occupation (manual unskilled vs. white collar professional), and by industry of attachment (agriculture and mining vs. manufacturing and services)—all of which are fairly closely and negatively correlated with implicit income differentials.[2] Under the circumstances we can assume that the hypothesis is sufficiently

2. Discussion of these differentials can be found in the references cited in footnote 1. See also Peter M. Blau and Otis Dudley Duncan, *The American Occupational Structure* (New York: John Wiley, 1967), particularly chapter 11, "Differential Fertility and Occupational Mobility," pp. 361–400.

plausible to warrant exploration of its implications, and use the available data only to illustrate and convey the sense of the magnitudes involved.

The data selected for this illustrative presentation relate to the United States, a country for which relevant statistics are available, and one that, despite the high level of economic development, still shows substantial income-related differentials in fertility (and implicitly in rates of natural increase).[3] All the data relate to 1960, the last census year for which a wide coverage of the detailed statistics on fertility by income class is available and one that comes close to a high level of the post–World War II birth rate in this country. Even so, tables 1 and 2 omit a variety of possible and otherwise interesting detail.

The summary measures in table 1 suggest several findings.

1. The ratio of children under 5 to married women, which reflects fertility over the last quinquennium reduced by death rates over that period, is consistently, at every age level of the wife, higher at the low family income levels than at the high (lines 1–18). The cumulative effects of this are confirmed by the ratios of children ever born (not reduced by deaths) to wives aged 35–39 and 45–49 in lines 19–24.

2. This negative association between family income and fertility (and implicitly rate of natural increase) is more conspicuous for the nonwhites, with their higher general level of fertility and lower median income levels, than for the whites. With the rise in income levels, fertility for the nonwhites declines much more sharply than for the whites; and for some high-income levels, the rates for the two groups become about the same, or that for nonwhites is lower (lines 4–5, columns 5–7; lines 7–8, columns 6–7; lines 10–11, column 7; lines 19–20, columns 6–7).

3. Comparing the cumulative ratios of children ever born in

---

3. It would have been of interest to use data on rates of natural increase, or at least fertility, by family income classes for a less developed country. But no such data are available. The evidence would have to be derived from sample data on family income for families of differing size, a task complicated by the importance of the extended family in some less developed countries (so that large size does not necessarily mean large numbers of children). Such exploration was not feasible here. The whole field of economic determinants of differential rates of natural increase within the less developed countries requires systematic study yet to be undertaken.

lines 19–21 with those in lines 22–24, we find that with the over-all birth rates in 1945–59 dominating lines 19–21 higher than those in 1935–49 dominating lines 22–24, the spread in birth rates between the lower- and upper-income groups, absolute and *relative,* is also wider in lines 19–21. Thus, for whites the range between the top and lowest income groups (columns 7 and 3) is 26.4 percent of the higher fertility ratios in line 19 and 23.5 percent in line 22; for the nonwhites, the range (in percent of the top fertility level) is 47.2 percent in line 20 and 23.0 percent in line 23; for total population the two ranges are 32.4 percent in line 21 and 27.0 percent in line 24. Apparently, when birth rates are kept down by adverse circumstances, the reduction is proportionately greater at the high fertility, low-income levels, than at the upper-income, low fertility levels; and the relative income-related differences in fertility are narrower.

4. Although the point is not covered in table 1, one may add that the ratios, either of children under 5 or of children ever born, to wives at different age levels, reveal the same consistent negative association with family income, when we distinguish urban and rural groups, or subgroups among the nonfarm population by degree of urbanization.

While the summary measures in table 1 illustrate the prevalence of the negative association whose implications are explored below, they tend to understate, by a substantial margin, the differences in rate of natural increase associated with long-term family income per person (or per consuming unit). There are several sources of such understatement. First, the grouping in table 1 is based on income for the current year. High secular incomes, associated with low fertility and rate of natural increase, if reduced for the year by a transient factor, would therefore be grouped with low incomes and tend to reduce the birth rates or rates of natural increase shown; and the same effect would be produced by low long-term incomes raised temporarily to high levels during the single year. Second, the income classification makes no allowance for low life-cycle phases of long-term high incomes (e.g., for the early years already cited of medical practitioners or lawyers); yet clearly the birth rate and natural increase patterns of these groups are set by their high lifetime incomes. Third, even assuming mortality rates somewhat higher for the low- than for the high-income groups, the effect of differences in fertility on those in rate of natural increase tend to be greatly magnified with the subtraction of attrition by mortality. Thus, assume that the entries in line 19 refer to the income levels of a cohort all through the childbearing period, and relate to the cohort at the end of the period when the parental generation has practically moved out of the labor force and out of full-time earning. If so, the 2,000 husbands and wives in line 19, column 7, would have produced 2,440 children; and allowing for an attrition of 10 percent, would yield 2,196 survivors, a net rise of 9.8 percent. The 2,000 husbands and wives in line 19, column 3, would have produced 3,316 children; and allowing for an attrition of 20 percent, would yield 2,653 survivors, or a rate of natural increase of 32.6 percent.[4] Finally, the family income used for the classification in table 1 is *not* adjusted for the number of persons or consuming units in the family. Yet the low-income family that tends to produce more children in the early years of the production period increases in size, as compared with the upper-income family with its smaller number of children born somewhat later; and even if the two families start, in our analysis, with husband and wife, by the time the wife is in her late 20s or early 30s, the low-income family will be larger than the high-income family; yet it is the former that will continue to have more children. A reclassification of families

---

4. The illustration is clearly crude and exaggerated. The survival rate to the age of say seventy (from the age of thirty) is from 94.4 percent of the original cohort to 53.8 for white males, and from 90.3 to 39.9 for nonwhite males, an attrition rate of about 43 percent for white males and 56 percent for nonwhite males (see U.S. National Center for Health Statistics, *United States Life Tables: 1959–61* [Washington: December 1964], tables 5 and 8, pp. 16–17 and 22–23). If we use these as proxies for the top and bottom income levels in line 19, and also allow for an attrition of children ever born of 7.6 percent for the top income group and 14.3 percent for the lowest income group (corresponding to survival rates from age zero to age forty for white and nonwhite males, respectively), the survivors would be $(2,000 \times 0.44) + (3,316 \times 0.857) = 3,722$ for line 19, column 3, and $(2,000 \times 0.57) + (2,440 \times 0.924) = 3,395$ for line 19, column 7. Even here the rate of natural increase, for the low-income group, of 86 percent, is distinctly higher than that for the high-income group, 70 percent. But the major relevant difference is in the *second* of the two brackets in the two equations above—in the number of descendants who at the end of the period account for all of the working force (with the parental generation seventy years of age or older). And it is the rise in the economically active members of the population, in the second generation relative to the first, that is important. It was potentially 2,000 each in the illustration for the first generation; it grew to 2,842 and 2,255 respectively, a rise of 42 percent for the low-income group and about 13 percent for the high-income group.

TABLE 2
Distribution of Families by Number of Related Children under 18, by Number of Persons, and by Average Family Money Income (1959), Urban and Rural Nonfarm, United States, March 1960

	(1)	(2)	(3)	(4)	(5)	(6)	(7)
			A. Urban Families				
1. No. of children in family	0	1	2	3	4	5 and more	Total
2. No. of families (000's) by groups in line 1	11,845	5,512	5,052	2,869	1,290	1,052	27,620
3. No. of persons in family	2	3	4	5	6	7 and more	Total
4. No. of families (000's) by groups in line 3	9,546	6,176	5,525	3,352	1,620	1,361	27,620
5. Estimated no. of adults, groups in line 1 (000's)	30,043	11,024	10,104	5,738	2,580	2,104	61,193
6. Estimated no. of children, groups in line 1 (000's)	0	5,512	10,104	8,607	5,160	6,312	35,695
7. Estimated no. of adults per family, groups in line 1	2.54	2.0	2.0	2.0	2.0	2.0	
8. Estimated persons per family, groups in line 1	2.54	3.0	4.0	5.0	6.0	8.0	
9. Estimated consuming units per family, groups in line 1	2.54	2.5	3.0	3.5	4.0	5.0	

(Continued)

(Table 2 continued)

	(1)	(2)	(3)	(4)	(5)	(6)	(7)
A. Urban Families (continued)							
10. Arithmetic mean income per family, groups in line 1($)	6,438	6,524	6,770	6,722	6,356	6,015	6,525
11. Family income per person, groups in line 1 ($)	2,535	2,175	1,688	1,344	1,053	752	A-2,090 C-1,435
12. Family income per consuming unit, groups in line 1 ($)	2,535	2,610	2,257	1,921	1,589	1,203	A-2,377 C-2,004
B. Rural Nonfarm Families							
13. No. of children in family	0	1	2	3	4	5 and more	Total
14. No. of families (000's) by groups in line 13	4,658	2,686	2,847	1,873	848	730	13,642
15. No. of persons in family	2	3	4	5	6	7 and more	Total
16. No. of families (000's) by groups in line 15	3,827	2,811	3,008	2,046	1,022	928	13,642
17. Estimated no. of adults, groups in line 13 (000's)	12,166	5,372	5,694	3,746	1,696	1,460	30,134
18. Estimated no. of children, groups in line 13 (000's)	0	2,686	5,694	5,619	3,392	4,380	21,771

(Continued)

(Table 2 continued)

	(1)	(2)	(3)	(4)	(5)	(6)	(7)
B. Rural Nonfarm Families (Continued)							
19. Estimated no. of adults per family, groups in line 13	2.61	2.0	2.0	2.0	2.0	2.0	
20. Estimated persons per family, groups in line 13	2.61	3.0	4.0	5.0	6.0	8.0	
21. Estimated consuming units per family, groups in line 13	2.61	2.5	3.0	3.5	4.0	6.0	
22. Arithmetic mean income per family, groups in line 13 ($)	5,491	5,895	6,424	6,541	6,200	5,370	5,943
23. Family income per person, groups in line 13 ($)	2,104	1,965	1,606	1,090	1,033	671	A-1,729 C-1,240
24. Family income per consuming unit, groups in line 13 ($)	2,104	2,358	2,141	1,869	1,550	1,074	A-2,049 C-1,791

Notes

The underlying data are from U.S. Bureau of the Census, *Trends in the Income of Families and Persons in the United States: 1947 to 1960*, Technical Paper no. 8 (Washington: 1963), table 4 (for persons per family), pp. 100–113, and table 5 (for related children per family), pp. 114–129. Lines 1–4, 10, 13–16, and 22, are directly taken, or calculated from this basic source.

Lines 5–6 and 17–18: The number of adults is calculated on the assumption that the excess of families with 0 children over families with 2 persons is allocable among families with 3, 4, etc. persons in accordance with the shortage of families with 1 child relative

(Notes continued on the following page)

(Table 2 notes continued)
to families with 3 persons, of families with 2 children relative to families with 4 persons, and so on—recognizing that the average number of children per family in the group with 5 and more is roughly 6; and that the average number of persons per family in the group with 7 or more is roughly 8 (these averages for the open-end classes are derived from the more detailed data from the same source for more recent years, specifically 1968 through 1970). This assumption leaves just 2 adults per family unit in all groups of families with children, and shifts all excess of adults into the group with 0 children. Given the assumption (and the means for the open-end classes), the derivation of the totals in lines 5–6 and 17–18, and of the averages in lines 7–8 and 19–20, is automatic.

Lines 9 and 21: Calculated on the assumption that a child under 18 is equivalent to .5 consuming unit, that for an adult being 1.0. This is a rough approximation, and probably understates the consuming unit equivalent per child.

Lines 11–12 and 23–24, column 7: The entries here are weighted arithmetic means, using the income per person or per consuming unit and the numbers in lines 5–6 and 17–18 as weights—A standing for adults (weights in lines 5 and 17) and C standing for children (weights in lines 6 and 18).

by per person or per consuming unit income would shift many large, multi-children families to the lower income levels, and many small, no-children families (including unmarried adults, not covered in table 1) to higher income levels, than they are now in table 1. The contrast between a greater number of children per wife in the lower income brackets than in the higher income brackets would thus be substantially accentuated.

This latter comment is of importance because it points to the fact that a greater proportion of children than of adults is in families at low income levels; and this implication bears on the assumptions that we can make concerning growth in per capita product of the descendants of low- and high-income groups. Table 2 is included here partly because it illustrates the association between number of children and income per person or per consuming unit in the family, and partly because it separates nonfarm families, for whom *money* income is by far the dominant type of income.

This table exploits the availability of classification of families by money income and number of related children under 18; and, combining this information with that on family by the number of persons, presents an estimate of the numbers of adults and of children, *within* each of the number-of-children groups among families. The details of the calculation are described in the notes to the table: the important point, worth mentioning here, is that the calculation overestimates the number of adults in column 1, the 0 children group, and underestimates them in the other columns—thus *understating* the differences in real income per unit between families with large numbers of children and those with small numbers or no children.

The major finding of the table is in lines 10–12 for urban families and lines 22–24 for rural nonfarm families. These lines reveal that while arithmetic mean income per family rises from the 0 children families to the families with 2 or 3 children (lines 10 and 22), and then declines but moderately for families with more than 3 children, the reduction to a per person or per consuming unit (with a somewhat exaggerated reduction of a child under 18 to one-half of a consuming unit) shows a sharp decline in family income with increase in the number of children. Thus income per unit for a family with 5 or more children is between a third and a half of the per unit income for families with no children or only one child.

It follows that a large proportion of children is in families with rather low per unit income, a much larger proportion than among adults. The two sets of arithmetic mean incomes in column 7, lines 11–12 and 23–24, are intended to summarize this difference in average economic status of children as compared with adults. On a per person basis, the average family income of the universe of children is about 30 percent lower than the average family income of the universe of adults (lines 11 and 23, column 7); on a per consuming unit basis, the shortfall for children averages about a seventh. But the distributions are more important than the summary arithmetic means: a substantial proportion of children is in families whose per person or per consuming unit income is much below the average for the relevant universe, whether it be all urban or all rural families.

The statistical evidence of the type summarized in tables 1 and 2, particularly in table 2, could be extended to other years in this country; and perhaps to other developed countries. But their value is necessarily only illustrative; and we can rest with the presumption that the negative association between the rates of natural increase and levels of family income per relevant unit is persistent and significant—even if the income differences represent differences in rurality, occupation, industry attachment, and the like;

that this association will be found, with differing and changing amplitudes, in both economically developed and in the less developed countries, in current years and probably in the future. We can now turn to exploring the implications, the possible bearing on growth and distribution of income.

2. Implications for Growth and Distribution of Income

In considering the effects of the higher rates of natural increase among lower-income groups on growth and distribution of income, we deal with notional quantities and illustrative examples. Indeed, in view of the lack of data specifically relevant to the properly formulated variables in the negative association, any substantive research would have to focus for a long while on samples of limited scope and of too narrow a base to yield broad findings. The purpose here is mainly to suggest the directions in which possibly significant implications lie, to raise the questions rather than to provide the answers.

Table 3 begins with a set of realistic figures relating to an initial distribution of income among quintiles (lines 1–3)—realistic in that such shares are found in the statistically recorded distributions of income among families, although usually for annual income. (Indeed, distributions in several less developed countries show even wider inequalities.) It then introduces various differentials in rate of natural increase among given income groups (cases 1–3); and with the help of one major assumption calculates the effect of these differentials on total and per unit income at the end of the period of increase in numbers. The major assumption is that over the period, the per unit income grows at the *same percentage rate* for the groups and their descendants in the several initial quintiles. Thus, the assumption specifies that the original relative inequalities in per unit income among the quintiles remain unchanged with the increased numbers of surviving units and their descendants.

The significance of this assumption, which is retained throughout this illustrative exercise, is discussed below; and will become clearer as we note the various effects that the calculations in table 3 suggest. They may be listed briefly:

(i) If the rate of growth of per unit income is assumed to be g,

TABLE 3

Effect on Growth of Income per Unit of Differentials
in Rate of Increase of the Different Income Groups
(With a Given Inequality in Size-Distribution of Income)

| | Quintiles | | | | | |
	First (1)	Second (2)	Middle (3)	Fourth (4)	Top (5)	Total (6)
Initial Shares						
1. Number	20	20	20	20	20	100
2. Total income	4	8	16	24	48	100
3. Income per unit	0.2	0.4	0.8	1.2	2.4	1.0
Case 1						
4. Assumed % increase in numbers	100	75	50	25	0	
5. Terminal numbers	40	35	30	25	20	150
6. % shares, line 5	26.7	23.3	20.0	16.7	13.3	100.0
7. Assumed terminal income per unit:						
a. line 3 × 2.0	0.4	0.8	1.6	2.4	4.8	
b. line 3 × 1.5	0.3	0.6	1.2	1.8	3.6	
c. line 3 × 1.25	0.25	0.5	1.0	1.5	3.0	
d. line 3 × 1.0	0.2	0.4	0.8	1.2	2.4	
8. Total terminal income, line 6 times:						
a. line 7a	10.68	18.64	32.00	40.08	63.84	165.24
b. line 7b	8.01	13.98	24.00	30.06	47.88	123.93
c. line 7c	6.675	11.65	20.0	25.05	39.90	103.275
d. line 7d	5.34	9.32	16.00	20.04	31.92	82.62
9. First component of shortfall (change in share in numbers)	6.7	3.3	0	-3.3	-6.7	
10. Second component of shortfall (deviations in per unit income):						
a. line 7a	-1.6	-1.2	-0.4	0.4	2.8	
b. line 7b	-1.2	-0.9	-0.3	0.3	2.1	
c. line 7c	-1.0	-0.75	-0.25	0.25	1.75	
d. line 7d	-0.8	-0.6	-0.2	0.2	1.4	

(Continued)

(Table 3 continued)

	First (1)	Second (2)	Middle (3)	Fourth (4)	Top (5)	Total (6)
			Quintiles			
			Case 1 (Continued)			
11. Total shortfall (line 9 times lines 10a−10d)						
a. for line 8a	−10.72	−3.96	0	−1.32	−18.76	−34.76
b. for line 8b	−8.04	−2.97	0	−0.99	−14.07	−26.07
c. for line 8c	−6.70	−2.475	0	−0.825	−11.725	−21.725
d. for line 8d	−5.36	−1.98	0	−0.66	−9.38	−17.38
			Case 2			
12. Assumed % increase in numbers	50	37.5	25	12.5	0	
13. Terminal numbers	30	27.5	25.0	22.5	20	125.0
14. %, line 13	24.0	22.0	20.0	18.0	16.0	100.0
15a. Total terminal income, line 14 × line 7a	9.6	17.6	32.0	43.2	76.8	179.2
16a. Sources of shortfall of total in line 15a from 200	(4.0) × (−1.6) = −6.4	(2.0) × (−1.2) = −2.4	(0) × (−0.4) = 0	(−2.0) × (0.4) = −0.8	(−4.0) × (2.8) = −11.2	−20.8
			Case 3			
17. Assumed % increase in numbers	70	60	50	40	30	
18. Terminal numbers	34.0	32.0	30.0	28.0	26.0	150.0
19. %, line 18	22.7	21.3	20.0	18.7	17.3	100.00
20a. Total terminal income, line 17 × line 7a	9.08	17.04	32.00	44.88	83.04	186.04
21a. Sources of shortfall of total in line 20a from 200	(2.7) × (−1.6) = −4.32	(1.3) × (−1.2) = −1.56	(0) × (−0.4) = 0	(−1.3) × (0.4) = −0.52	(−2.7) × (2.8) = −7.56	−13.96

the inverse association between initial income level and the rate of increase in numbers, yields an *aggregate* per unit growth that falls short of *g*. The source of this shortfall is the rise in the share of the survivors and descendants of the lower-income brackets, which means an increase in relative weight in the terminal distribution of groups with per unit income below the expected country-wide average (i.e., initial income times $1 + g$).

(ii) The proportional shortfall is the greater, the larger *g,* the assumed growth rate of per unit income (compare lines a–d, under line 11, column 6). With *g* assumed to be 100, 50, 25 percent, the shortfall is 34.8, 26.1, and 21.7 percentage points respectively. But the effect in reducing total rate of growth *per unit* is the more striking, the lower the assumed *g*. Thus, the 100 percent growth rate of income per unit is reduced, in the aggregate, to 65 percent, i.e., to two-thirds; the 50 percent growth rate is reduced to 24 percent, i.e., to less than half; and the 25 percent growth rate was cut to 3.3 percent, i.e., almost completely offset (all of this for case 1, see lines 8a–8c, column 6).

(iii) This shortfall in the aggregate growth rate per unit is partly a function of the magnitude of the differences assumed in the rate of natural increase (i.e., of numbers) among the initial quintiles. It is the *absolute* differences among the rates of increase in numbers, rather than the relative differences in these rates, that are important. Thus, in case 2, the *relative* disparities in rate of increase in numbers among the quintiles are the same as in case 1, with that for the first quintile being double of the increase rate in total population; that for the second quintile being one and a half times of the aggregate rate of population increase; and so on (compare lines 4 and 12). But in case 1 the aggregate rate of population incrase is 50 percent, double that of case 2, and the *absolute* differences in rates of increase among the quintiles are double those of case 2. In consequence, for the same *g,* of 100 percent, the shortfall in case 2 of 21 percentage points is only somewhat over half that for case 1, of 34.8 percentage points. And the reduction in the shortfall is further marked in case 3, in which the rate of increase in numbers among quintiles differs much less than in case 1, both on an absolute and relative basis.

(iv) It is clear that with the rate of increase in per unit income being the same for all initial quintiles, the negative association between rate of increase in numbers and initial income level *must* result in an aggregate rate of growth of income per unit short of *g*. If it is desired that the aggregate growth rate in per unit income reach *g*, either the growth rate (the same) assigned to each initial quintile must be above *g*, or the assumption of equality of growth rates of income among the initial quintiles must be abandoned.

If it is abandoned, the modification, involving raising growth rates for some quintiles more than for others, will necessarily change the size-distribution of income from that assumed originally. If it is the growth rates of the lower quintiles that are to be raised, thus making for lesser inequality, it is important to note that the shortfall represents a large magnitude relative to the shares of the lowest two quintiles as derived before the modification. Thus, in case 1a, the total income of the lower two quintiles, the only ones that show large deviations below the countrywide average, was 10.68 + 18.64 or 29.32 (line 8a, columns 1 and 2); whereas the shortfall that had to be offset amounted to 34.76. Even for case 3a, the shortfall to be offset was 13.96, compared with the total income of the lower two quintiles of 26.12 (line 20a, columns 1 and 2). Adding the shortfall, for the purpose of reaching *g*, to the income for the lower two quintiles would raise the growth rates of their per unit income strikingly, compared with the growth rates initially assumed and retained for the higher quintiles.

Before we discuss the significance of the assumptions and the relevance of the implications suggested in table 3, it would be well to round out the illustration and consider the effect of variations in the range of income inequality among the initial quintiles —given a fixed set of differentials in rates of increase of numbers among low- and high-income levels. The relevant illustrations are in table 4.

(v) The extent of initial income inequality is clearly of effect on the magnitude of the shortfall, once we assume a given differential in rates of increase in numbers negatively associated with income levels, and the same growth rate in per unit income for all initial income levels. The greater the initial income inequality, the greater the shortfall. Thus, cases 2 and 3, which begin with income inequality somewhat narrower than that in case 1, show more moderate shortfalls than the latter.

(vi) The major effect is associated with *total* deviations of quintile shares from equality, rather than with the *range* between the

TABLE 4

Effect on Growth of Income per Unit of Differing Initial Inequalities
in the Size Distribution of Income (With Given Differentials
in Rate of Increase of Numbers Among the Several Income Groups)

	First (1)	Second (2)	Middle (3)	Fourth (4)	Top (5)	Total (6)
			Quintiles			

	First (1)	Second (2)	Middle (3)	Fourth (4)	Top (5)	Total (6)
Assumed Differences in Rate of Increase of Numbers						
1. Initial shares in numbers	20	20	20	20	20	100
2. Assumed % increase	100	75	50	25	0	
3. Terminal numbers	40	35	30	25	20	150
4. %, line 3	26.7	23.3	20.0	16.7	13.3	100.0
Case 1						
5. Initial shares in income	4	8	16	24	48	100
6. Initial income per unit	0.2	0.4	0.8	1.2	2.4	1.0
(here proceed with lines 7–11 of case 1 of table 3, which is identical with case 1 here)						
Case 2						
7. Initial shares in income	7	9	12	30	42	
8. Initial income per unit	0.35	0.45	0.60	1.50	2.10	1.00
9a. Assumed terminal income per unit (line 8 times 2)	0.7	0.9	1.2	3.0	4.2	
10a. Total terminal income (line 9a times line 4)	18.69	20.97	24.00	50.10	55.86	169.62
11a. Sources of short-fall in line 10a from 200	6.7 × (−1.3)= −8.71	3.3 × (−1.1)= −3.63	0 × (−0.8)= 0	−3.3 × (1.0)= −3.30	−6.7 × (2.2)= −14.74	−30.38

(Continued)

(Table 4 continued)

	First (1)	Second (2)	Middle (3)	Fourth (4)	Top (5)	Total (6)
			Quintiles			
			Case 3			
12. Initial shares in income	11	15	18	23	33	100
13. Initial income per unit	0.55	0.75	0.90	1.15	1.65	1.00
14a. Assumed terminal income per unit (line 13 times 2)	1.10	1.50	1.80	2.30	3.30	
15a. Total terminal income (line 14a times line 4)	29.37	34.95	36.00	38.41	43.89	182.62
16a. Sources of short-fall in line 15a from 200	6.7 × (−0.9)= −6.03	3.3 × (−0.5)= −1.65	0 × (−0.2)= 0	−3.3 × (0.3)= −0.99	−6.7 × (1.3)= −8.71	−17.38

top and bottom. Thus, in case 2, line 7, initial inequality is characterized by a range of 6.0, half that of case 1, line 5. Yet the reduction in the shortfall, from 34.8 to 30.4, is relatively minor (the sum of deviations from equality for cases 1 and 2 is the same, at 64.0). It is only in case 3, where the sum of deviations from equality, in line 12, is halved, that the reduction in the shortfall (to 17.4) becomes significant, the latter being half of that in case 1. The reason, of course, is that second component in the product forming the shortfall (lines 11a and 16a) is a direct reflection of the deviation of the quintile share from equality.

Given that the shortfall is a function of initial income inequality, of the assumed differentials in rate of increase in numbers, and is likely to be most reductive of aggregative rate of increase in per unit income when the assumed rate of growth in per unit income is moderate, what is the realism of the basic assumption and what is the meaning of the implied shortfall? a. Is it realistic to assume the same rate of increase of per unit income for the low and the high ordinal groups in the initial size distribution of income? b. What is the significance of the shortfall of the actual aggregate growth rate of per unit income, relative to some imaginary aggregate growth rate that would be attained with no natural increase differentials negatively associated with income?

a. Beginning with the first question, let us consider it over a fairly long period, so that we shall be dealing largely with the per unit income of the descendants, second generation, compared with the per unit income of the parents, the first generation, within the initial quintiles. Let us also view the units here as workers rather than as families or persons, implying that the rate of natural increase of workers is also inversely related to the incomes of workers. Are there grounds for assuming that the increases in per worker income or product are a function of the initial level, so that relative or percentage increases tend to be similar among the various per worker income groups?

Examining this question with reference to long-term income levels, not those affected by transient changes or by a phase in a long life span of incomes (for which the question can be answered more easily), one may note factors that would yield different answers. On the one hand, the low-income levels (and the high fertility and natural increase rates) are associated with attachment to traditional sectors (such as agriculture, handicrafts, etc.), which provide diminishing opportunities for employment and force the members and descendants of a low-income quintile to migrate to other sectors and areas—toward modern industry and urban communities. This prevalance of migration toward greater employment and higher income opportunities among the members and descendants of the lower-income quintiles would, all other conditions being equal, make for a *higher* rate of growth of per worker income and product than would be true of the upper quintiles, which are already attached to the more urbanized and advanced sectors of the economy and for whose members and descendants the possibilities of such upward migration may be more restricted. On the other hand, growth in per worker product partly depends on the investment made in the human being, in the way of education, formal and informal, and in the way of raising his capacity to face increasingly complicated problems of adequate participation in the economy and society. Here the low-income level of the parents in the lower quintiles and the associated low educational levels would make for a much lower per capita investment in the descendants, in absolute and even in relative terms (relative to income of parents) than would be true of higher quintiles. (One should bear in mind particularly the contribution of the parental household to informal training and education of descendants.) To the extent that this is so, the growth in per worker incomes among the lower quintiles may be at a lower percentage rate than among the upper quintiles and their descendants.

The two groups of factors just noted, closely associated with the differences in rate of natural increase among the lower- and higher-income brackets, may be qualified by other factors—among them government intervention to assist by providing real services in the way of education and health, largely to the low-income groups; and tendencies toward monopolization and restriction of high-level economic opportunities, combined with economic discrimination against some groups within the population. The relative weights of the two major and the subordinate factors, making for narrowing and widening inequality in the distribution of income, have probably changed in successive phases of economic growth in the presently developed countries; and may differ widely in the several less developed countries. To attempt a general appraisal, and thus to test the realism of assuming unchanging relative inequality, would require much more organized knowledge than is presently available.

We used the assumption as a simplifying step; but this is little more than an excuse, and should not be interpreted so as to neglect the major problems that lurk behind the negative association whose implications we are considering. For given the association and the higher rates of increase in numbers among the low-income groups, the ameliorative mechanisms—be they migration to better employment and economic opportunities, or provision of government assistance to offset the negative effects of low income on investment in children, or others—carry costs of their own, and may not be sufficiently effective to avoid even long-term shortfalls and widening of income inequalities. In the process of internal migration that accompanied economic growth, the migrant, from the high fertility families, had to go through a process of adjustment and assimilation that kept him for a long while at the lower-income levels. And in recent decades the sharp accentuation of income-related differences in rates of natural increase in the less developed countries, due to a rapid decline in death rates probably more marked among the low-income than among the high-income groups, must have contributed to the accelerated internal migration, increased unemployment and underemployment, and apparently a widening of inequality in the size distribution of income.

The purpose of these comments is to stress that if reduction or limitation of relative income inequality is an important desideratum—so long as it does not seriously curb the growth rate of total income per capita—the negative association between rate of natural increase and income levels represents a continuous threat and problem; and that we need to know much more about how this problem was resolved in the past growth of presently developed countries, and the magnitudes that it is assuming in many less developed countries today. Our use of the same growth rates in per unit income of the several ordinal groups in the initial size distribution of income is a simplification which, in disregarding the persistent threat of widening inequality, may be on the optimistic side and should be replaced by more realistic assumptions as soon as more specific knowledge accumulates on this aspect of economic growth.[5]

b. Given the result that a negative correlation between rates of natural increase and initial income levels, combined with an identical growth rate of per unit income in the several quintiles, will necessarily yield an aggregate growth rate per capita or per worker

---

5. The Blau-Duncan study, referred to in footnote 2, appears to suggest, for the experience of the United States, a less pessimistic picture. The members of the labor force of lower social origin (i.e., with lower-level occupations, and presumably lower income levels, of parents) show greater upward mobility than sons of parents of higher occupational and presumably higher income levels (see footnote 1, p. 402); and the discussion in chapter 11 does not show close negative association between differential fertility and upward occupational mobility. But there is a question as to whether these results would be confirmed for a more sensitive variable, like per unit family income; for differential movements on the income scale, relative to the changing absolute per unit income; and particularly for the less developed countries, in which the impact of differences in rates of natural increase (given higher population growth rates) and lower growth rates in per capita income (as compared with the developed countries) may be so much greater. At any rate, there is no basis for arguing that a long-term income level, if low, automatically guarantees a higher rate of increase in per unit income than an initial middle- or high-income level (stochastic and phase elements having been removed by definition): there is nothing that would prevent an initially low secular income level from rising not more (or less) than the rest, and thus remaining relatively as low or lower than at the start.

short of that assumed for the initial income groups, what is the significance of the shortfall? Should we be concerned about it, as if it were a loss of some possible real attainment; or is it just an arithmetic artifact, without real significance? This question may seem particularly appropriate, because in a recent paper I argued that for many types of analysis an aggregate rate of growth of income per capita should be derived by weighting by numbers the percentage growth rates of per capita income of the various income groups within the population (which procedure would, in the illustrations in tables 3 and 4 remove any shortfall).[6]

The answer to the question depends upon whether we can assume significant constraints to the rate of growth of per unit income —for say a given growth rate of total population (or total labor force). If we can argue that for an over-all growth rate in numbers over the period of, say, 50 percent, the top level of *attainable* growth in income per unit is, say, 50 percent—and that it is roughly the same for per unit income in the lower and in the upper quintiles—then the shortfall resulting from the negative association under discussion is significant. For it means that, *without* this negative association, the country, while still achieving a 50 percent rise in income per unit for each quintile and its descendants, could also attain a growth rate of total income per unit of 50 percent—and not a rate reduced by a shortfall—and thus attain a growth of total income of 125 percent, not the significantly lower figure attainable under conditions in which the second generation, stemming from the low-income levels, would be proportionately more numerous. And regardless of any distributional considerations that attainment of higher aggregate per unit and total income is significant.

It does seem more realistic to assume fairly close constraints on the percentage growth rates of per unit income, given an assumed rate of increase in total numbers, than to argue for absence of such constraints. After all, the investments in improvement of quality of labor must be limited to a moderate proportion of initial income or product; and proportional gains from migration to the more productive sectors are restricted by limitations on the

---

6. See "Problems in Comparing Recent Growth Rates for Developed and Less Developed Countries," *Economic Development and Cultural Change,* vol. 20, no. 2, January 1972, 185–209, particularly in the present connection, pp. 197 and 199.

volume of migration and by the ties between the post- and pre-migration income levels. And, with some straining, we may accept the notion that the limits on the percentage growth rate of per unit income or product are roughly the same for the several initial quintiles and their descendants. If so, it would seem that the negative association between rates of natural increase and initial income spells real losses in yielding a growth rate of total and per unit income that falls significantly short of that attainable without such negative association.

And yet this conclusion must be seriously qualified. For doing away with the negative association between rates of natural increase and initial income levels means, implicitly and particularly under the conditions of the same aggregate rate of increase in numbers, a more equal size distribution of income per consuming unit than would exist with the negative association; and this may reduce the flow of savings for investment in material capital. This might, in turn, reduce the feasible rate of growth in per unit income below those attainable otherwise. Hence, what would be gained by removing the shortfall between the actual aggregate growth in per unit income and one otherwise feasible would be lost because of the possible reduction in the limits of the feasible. We are thus back to the old problem of choice between the returns from the more equal size-distribution of income in the way of greater productivity rise among the lower-income group due to greater investment in human beings, and the returns from a more unequal size-distribution of income in the way of greater contributions to savings and material capital formation.

3. Summary

This paper began with the recognition of a feature of demographic growth, widely observed in both developed and less developed countries—the marked differences between the higher rate of natural increase in the lower-income groups and the lower rates in the upper-income groups. In attempting to explore the implications of this association, abstracting from differences or changes in the aggregate rate of natural increase, we proceeded to illustrate changes in an initial cohort of income groups (quintiles) as they were transformed into the next generation groups, of different *relative* size. While the discussion was in terms of a single cohort, it could be applied to a succession of cohorts—yielding a succession of generations of descendants. The results would be either a repetition or a cumulation, depending upon whether the initial series was of identical cohorts just moving in time, or a series that reflected cumulative changes of earlier differences in rates of natural increase among the several ordinal groups within the income distribution.

The negative association between rates of natural increase and initial secular income levels clearly poses a major problem, if wider inequality in the size-distribution of income is to be avoided—since lower-income levels of parents mean proportionately lower investment in quality of the descendants and hence possibly lower growth rates in the per capita income of the lower-income groups and their descendants. The magnitude of the problem and of the necessary compensating offsets, is clearly a function of the differential spread in the rates of natural increase and of the initial differences in income levels of parents. If no offsets are provided, all other conditions being equal, the negative association between rates of natural increase and initial income levels would result both in widening of income inequality and in probably keeping down the growth rate of aggregate income per unit (per person or per worker). "Conditions being equal" involves the same aggregate growth rate in population or labor force; the "probably" refers to the likely negative balance of the opportunity losses in higher human quality at the lower-income end over the possible gain from greater savings at the lower fertility, upper-income end.

This conclusion, particularly with respect to widening income inequality, was not explored here and was only stressed as a possible qualification on the realism of the basic assumption used in the illustrative analysis, viz., that the growth rate in per unit income product is the same for the several ordinal groups in the initial income distribution (i.e., quintiles or deciles), while their numbers would be increasing at different rates.

Given this assumption, which assures rough constancy in *relative* inequality in the income distribution, we considered the influence of the negative association between natural increase and income on growth of aggregate product or income per unit (person or worker). The illustrative analysis shows that the combination of an assumed growth rate in per unit income, the same for all ordinal groups, with the greater growth in numbers among the lower-income brackets, yields a growth rate in *total* income per unit that is *lower* than the basic growth rate assumed for per unit income within each ordinal group. This shortfall is relatively greater, the larger the differential in rates of natural increase, the wider the income inequality among the original ordinal groups, and the lower the assumed growth rate identical for all ordinal groups.

It proved difficult to establish the significance of this shortfall unequivocally. Even if we assume realistic limits to percentage growth of per unit income or product, and roughly equal limits for the several ordinal groups in the initial income distribution, it is not clear that, for a given growth rate of total population or labor force, reduction in the negative association between rate of natural increase and initial income level would raise the growth of total income per unit (by reducing the shortfall). For the implied reduction in the association would also imply a less unequal income distribution, which in the process of movement from the parental cohort to that of descendants might mean a lesser *relative* volume of savings and hence of investment in material capital. To arrive at determinate conclusions, we need empirical evidence on the weights of various factors or offsets, which tend to narrow or widen income inequality, and which, in so doing, may affect investment in human relative to investment in material capital.

Given the substantial differences in rates of natural increase negatively correlated with income, the implications for growth of income per capita or per worker, and for the size-distribution of income in the process of growth, must clearly be important. But since the operating factors are of conflicting effect, it is not possible to derive firm conclusions as to these implications, without empirical findings on the magnitude of these factors in different phases of economic growth and at different levels of economic development. There is obvious need for such empirical findings, both for the developed and the less developed countries; and only few of the available data on size distribution of income and on demographic patterns are effectively relevant to this need.